THE PRINCIPLES OF

ARCHITECTURE
STYLE, STRUCTURE AND DESIGN

THE PRINCIPLES OF
ARCHITECTURE
STYLE, STRUCTURE AND DESIGN

EDITOR
MICHAEL FOSTER

PHAIDON

Consultant editor
Michael Foster

Contributors
John Adams
Bryan Avery
James Dartford
Michael Driver
Leon Easter
Adrian Gale
John McKean
Clive Plumb
John Winter

A QUILL BOOK

Published by Phaidon Press Limited
Littlegate House
St Ebbe's Street
Oxford
First Published in the U K 1983
© Copyright 1982 Quill Publishing Limited
ISBN: 0 7148 2299 X

First Published in the USA 1982
by Excalibur Books

Distributed in Australia by ABP/Methuen Pty Limited, Sydney, NSW

This book was designed and produced by
Quill Publishing Limited
32 Kingly Court
London W1

Art director Nigel Osborne
Production director James Marks
Editorial director Jeremy Harwood
Senior editor Liz Wilhide
Assistant editor Joanna Rait
Designer Paul Cooper
Art Assistants Annie Collenette Janel Minors
Illustrators Steve Braund Ray Brown Geoffrey Denney
Picture researchers Veneta Bullen Hetty Startup

Filmset in Great Britain by Presentia Arts, Horsham, Sussex
Origination by Hong Kong Graphic Arts Limited, Hong Kong
Printed in Hong Kong by Leefung-Asco Printers Limited

Quill would like to extend special thanks to Richard Bertioli;
the Brick Development Association; Jeremy Dickson;
Terry Farrell Partnership; Foster Associates; Shirley Hind at
the Architectural Press; John Hunter and Peter
Richards; Essex County Council; The Tooley
and Foster Partnership.

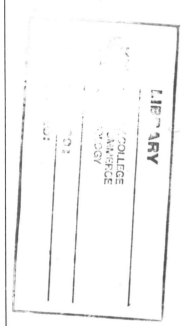

Contents

Introduction

A building, as an object that defines and encloses space, reflects the society of its time more than any other art-form. The meaning of any building is transmitted as much by the materials in which it is built as by the function it is designed to perform. The vast majority of buildings consist of external walls surrounding an interior space and covered by a roof to provide shelter. Their basic shape directly relates to the materials chosen to form that enclosure. It is the relationship between the architect's attitude to the process of design and the materials in which that design is executed with which this book is concerned.

Throughout the history of architecture, there has always been correspondence between the architect's attitude to space and the choice of materials used to define and articulate it. Abstract design parameters such as context, time, function and style must be matched to more obvious considerations, such as the availability and suitability of materials, climate and economy.

The lifespan of a building, particularly since industrialization in the nineteenth century, is often much longer than the use for which it was originally designed. Many adaptations are frequently made over periods of time which do not necessarily devalue the architect's original intention, but which are inevitably still related to the form of the building, the materials in which it is constructed and its context.

Above The Barcelona
Pavilion, designed by Mies
van der Rohe in 1923,
demonstrates the
architect's desire to achieve
a purity of form by
eliminating decoration and
treating the interior and the
exterior of the building in
the same way. With a frame
of steel, the glass was
intended only as a weather
barrier, giving the
impression that the space
was not actually enclosed.
Above left Alsop, Finch
and Lyall's model for
Riverside Studios
illustrates a post-
modernist view. They
reacted against the purely
functional design
techniques and
emphasized the enclosure
of space with decoration,
including stepped ends to
the buildings and many
changes of direction and
size.
Left Gaudi's late
nineteenth-century
apartment building in
Barcelona is plastic in form,
and intricately decorated,
illustrating an
Expressionist view.

The Art of Design

Architecture is essentially the art of reconciliation. It involves resolving specific and
general demands of its users within a
projected image of three-dimensional
form. The design of a building is a creative,
rather than a calculable process but, unlike
other art-forms, it is concerned with a
positive search for solutions. There can be
no solution without a problem, no problem
without constraints, and no constraints
without a need. Either a need is automati-
cally met at the outset and there is no
problem, or the need is not met because of
certain obstacles. Finding out how to overcome these obstacles is the design problem.

Every design consists of an effort to
reconcile a form and its context. It is the
context, in association with the architect's
stock of experience, that prompts the first
ideas. The process develops as the architect
uses both personal and general experience
to analyze the extent of the problem. These
two types of experience are very different:
personal experience is predominantly
direct and subjective, while general
experience consists of a variety of indirect
material gathered through impersonal
sources. The information is like a huge
collection of jigsaw pieces; out of this
random collection the architect begins to
assemble a completely new picture in three
dimensions. The "pieces" represent pre-
liminary considerations – including the
purpose of the building, its site, the client's
resources, and possible materials. The initial steps forward will be hesitant and
open-ended, analyzing possibilities and
detecting alternative relationships, and
gradually moving towards creating a new
order. The design process must be cyclic,
for each new relationship that is exposed
will affect and be affected by the others. As
the cycle develops, the architect will tend
to opt for solutions which further his
original intention, and to make choices
which best overcome the obstacles which
constitute the original problem.

Every building inevitably reflects the
force or weakness of the original concept. If
the pattern of relationships between all the
parts of the design seem complete and
self-sufficient, and yet there is only a
tenuous link with his original intention, the
finished building will be so far removed
from what was anticipated that it will be
incomprehensible to its users. On the other
hand, if the solution does not extend very
far beyond basic requirements, it will be
too obvious and predictable. To be successful a design must encourage new and
unexpected uses as well as having its roots
in the original proposal. The tension between these two aspects is what endows a
building with a meaning beyond the level
which is a mere sum of its parts.

Material and form
1. The elegant, sweeping curve of the Royal Crescent in Bath is perfectly expressed in Bath stone. Recent restoration work changed the colour of the stone from a dirty black to a subtle grey, with the material of the Georgian terrace showing clearly.
2. The light-well in the centre of the Bradbury apartment building in Los Angeles is structured in metal and glass in the Victorian tradition.
3. The glass walls of the Palm House in the Royal Botanic Gardens at Kew create a spectacular and extravagant conservatory.
4. Nervi's structurally efficient and economical Palazzetto dello Sport, designed in the 1950s, shows an impressive integration of glass and concrete.
5. The elaborate pseudo-Gothic style of St Pancras Station, London, could only have been achieved in brick. Much of the decoration is inherent in the brickwork; the size of the detail often matches the actual size of bricks.
6. Elaboration of another distinctive style marks the Byzantine churches in Russia. Their magnificent roofs and onion-shaped domes were shaped in intricately carved timber pieces.
7. The bold and simple-looking lines of Sydney's Opera House belie the complexity of the concrete construction, which is both innovative and imaginative.

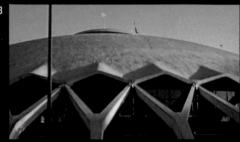

Materials and Form

Bound up with the complex process of design must be a consideration of the materials which are suitable for a particular purpose. An initial choice will inevitably be related to three basic factors – availability, physical properties and cost. In a preindustrial society, the availability of natural materials, such as the stone cut from a quarry, or bricks baked with local mud, was of primary importance in determining the style and scale of any building. However, since the nineteenth century many other factors, such as technique, structure, geography and appropriateness have made such a simple choice impossible.

How available a material is, closely relates to cost: the further it needs to be transported, the more expensive it becomes and the less "available". With the growth of mass transportation, particularly in the nineteenth and twentieth centuries, materials could be moved from one side of the world to the other, but while the actual cost

Above and left *Chartres Cathedral*, France (1194–1260). Chartres, built on the site of a Romanesque church, was completed fairly quickly – within 40 years. It possessed a holy relic – a remnant of the Virgin's robe – and was able to raise money for building through contributions and pilgrimages. By this period, the master mason was acknowledged as designer, although the architectural process was very different from what it is today. It is unknown how masons came by their considerable engineering skills, but there must have been some trial and error. Using fixed proportions, the church was constructed bay by bay, from the choir on, the whole being related to a ground plan, but without accurate drawings. Chartres provides a framework for magnificent stained glass and stone sculpture – a "living Bible" for illiterate townsfolk. The two towers were built three centuries apart. French cathedrals were important centres of town life, built in stone to last.

Right *Commercial Union Building*, London (1969, Gollins, Melvin and Ward). This is one of two new commercial towers built on a site in the City of London formerly occupied by the old Shell building. Modern architectural practice is governed by a complex of constraints: the requirements of planning departments, fire regulations, client's needs and above all, budget, must all be met. Working to the architect's design are many consultant experts – structural engineers, services engineers and other sub-contracted specialists. For reasons of economy and to provide maximum floor space, the building was built as a suspended structure: a concrete services core was surrounded by a lightweight steel structure suspended from two cantilevered steel truss sections. The steelwork was erected in 24 weeks.

of doing so may be prohibitive, it may also be entirely inappropriate to remove a natural material from its geographical region. The expense of materials such as marble is partly to do with the real costs involved in its quarrying and transport, but it is also to do with market costs relating to demand and rarity value. The availability of a material, therefore, oscillates as a result of conflicting trading forces, not because the material varies in scarcity.

Techniques

In spite of these contradictions, the use of materials which are indigenous to certain parts of the globe remains relevant. This is partly to do with the material itself, but is also to do with established techniques, both for processing and assembly. North America, for example, has the largest deposits of ore in the world, and their existence led to the manufacture of cast-iron, and subsequently steel, during the last century. Today, steel continues to be used in large quantities in the American building industry for the same resource reasons, but also because a tradition for its use has built up over many generations, encouraging more sophisticated techniques and making it more and more economical to use the material, in both capital and construction terms.

The same building types may be built in different materials, depending on their geographical location. In the case of modern high-rise buildings, it is generally more economical to construct the structural frame in steel in North America and in reinforced concrete in Europe. Both systems in fact use both materials – the steel frame is cased in concrete to comply with fire regulations; the concrete frame is reinforced with steel rods to hold it together – but the available techniques and skills to carry out these different operations mean that the decision to build in a particular material does not rest on considerations purely to do with the material itself.

In a similar way, the availability of certain timbers in different areas has meant that different techniques for their application have developed. Oak was plentiful in medieval England, and its natural hardness and weathering qualities led to its use for frame construction, with different materials such as wattle and daub used to fill in between the frame. From these materials arose a style of building indigenous to the region. Where there are large natural resources of softwoods, such as in Scandinavia, traditional cladding techniques continue. In Britain today, where there is a lack of large natural resources of timber, but areas of clay soil instead, a tradition exists for the manufacture and use of bricks.

Another aspect of material resources and the craft skills for their application, is the whole question of labour. Prior to the

Above Geographical considerations play a large part in the materials and form of building. In Mediterranean countries, whitewashed exteriors and small window openings help to keep interiors cool.
Right The sloping roof of this Swedish church is designed to allow heavy falls of snow to slide off safely. The timber construction is a natural choice considering the timber resources of the area.

Industrial Revolution, the cost of labour was minimal and labour-intensive building methods flourished; even now the costs of building in the Third World are dictated more by materials than by labour. But in developed countries the costs of labour are often high, giving an entirely different emphasis to the construction industry. It is a paradox that in spite of expensive material costs and shortages of world resources, it is often more economical to completely replace existing materials than to repair or recycle them, since the large amount of labour required for repair makes costs excessive.

Structure

The physical properties of different materials are also crucial. Masonry construction, piling heavy blocks of stone or brick on top of each other, makes a solid wall construction which encloses space and is also self-supporting. The medieval master-builders, although pushing such techniques to the limits of the material by forming arches and vaults and by buttressing the original walls to prevent buckling, were restricted in their attempt to form larger spaces by the sheer weight of construction.

On the other hand, the structural qualities of steel and timber have encouraged the development of frame systems in which the primary structure is made up of a skeleton of columns and beams, often made off site in a factory, which can then be clad in an entirely different weathering and insulating skin, made of either solid or transparent material. The potential of this

type of construction for connecting spaces and for achieving a closer relationship between the inside and the outside of a building clearly contrasts with the limitations of solid wall techniques. It is therefore hardly surprising that the type of buildings designed for twentieth-century needs have little precedent, either in function, form or constructional method.

Concrete is a material made by mixing a number of ingredients — cement, sand, stone aggregate and water — to make a slurry which can be poured into shaped moulds before it sets hard. It is consequently appropriate for both frame and solid wall structures, either made on site or prefabricated. Apart from being capable of spanning large distances when combined with steel reinforcement, its most significant quality for twentieth-century architecture is its plasticity. Freed from the rectilinear constraints of building in some form of solid block, the architect has been able to make organic compositions of free-flowing and asymmetrical shapes.

Geography

As well as considering the choice of materials in relation to a particular building type, the geological conditions of the ground on which the building will stand are important, particularly as far as weight and height are concerned. The rock base of New York City made the early skyscrapers realistic propositions, although the relatively crude methods for their construction relied on mass and weight for stability. The likelihood of earthquakes in Los Angeles or the clay soil conditions in London both dictate different attitudes to construction, which in turn influence the form and style of their architecture.

Climatic conditions dictate different constraints. In the tropics, the need for shade and natural ventilation, together with the problems of intervening rainy seasons, has led to a traditional architecture of large over-hanging roofs, with little weather-proofing on the walls beneath. On the other

Above The extreme pitched roof of this half-timbered German house (1526) accomodates the rainy north European climate. Efficient drainage and guttering is essential in countries which experience a lot of rainfall; flat roofs are rarely satisfactory.
Above right The overhanging roofs of the Summer Palace, Peking, mean that the walls are never in direct sunlight and the interiors can be kept cool. However, Chinese architecture, like other vernacular traditions, cannot simply be seen as a functional response to climate, but is the product of more complex cultural ideas.

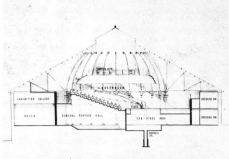

Above and left The nineteenth century saw the architects' role usurped by engineers, who understood the requirements of the new industrial age. The Roundhouse, London, was originally a railway turning house for engines, a functional shed; decoration is fully integrated with structure.
Below Modern urban renewal schemes and housing programmes have meant that architects are increasingly employed or commissioned by government agencies for large-scale projects, such as this proposed shop and office development in Hammersmith, London, by Foster Associates.

Bottom Certain architects have always been concerned not only with satisfying the practical requirements of their clients, but also with expressing aesthetic or intellectual notions. This fire station in New Haven, Connecticut by Robert Venturi is a simple functional building, which at the same time illustrates the architect's interest in signs and symbols. The "peeled" facade and lettering visually take the building around the corner, but are also a witty comment on the importance of decoration. A leading theorist, Venturi coined the phrase "decorated sheds".

hand, the conditions in northern Europe, where there is relatively light, but continual, rainfall, without great extremes of temperature, call for entirely different techniques of weathering and insulation.

Relevance

The more abstract demands of appropriateness and style cannot be ignored when choosing materials. Certain materials have become endowed with particular meanings through their continued use. Many institutional buildings are clad in stone even now, linking back to the great Renaissance palaces and to ancient Greece; in the same way, the scale and natural warmth of brick has made its use synonymous with domestic architecture. New materials also produce interesting contradictions. Often their first use will be as a substitute for existing materials; if used in a "raw" state, they are likely to be hidden from view.

Unlike in pure engineering, where the success of a design depends on a material being exploited to the full, architecture cannot rely on pure objectivity. The overlapping complexities of function, environmental quality, and social and cultural context must all be taken into account. Today it is possible to separate the structure from the outside skin, which in turn can be isolated from the inside walls. This can lead to changes of style within the same building: the materials, colours and forms of the permanent structure can make one sort of pattern, while the applied decorations can make another.

The Role of the Architect

Little would have been known about the role of the architect before the Middle Ages had it not been for a relatively unknown Roman architect and engineer living in the first century B.C. Vitruvius' *Ten Books on Architecture* survived every other contemporary work of the Greek and Roman Empires, and have remained a highly influential source in the development of Western architecture. These books contain a wealth of information, sometimes contradictory but nevertheless very detailed, giving an unprecendented insight into Classical building disciplines. Vitruvius describes the principles of symmetry, harmony and proportion, the design of temples, the construction of theatres and information on their siting, foundations and acoustics, the desirability of different materials, the education of the architect and many other relevant topics.

Approximately 50 copies of this work survived through the Middle Ages, although the master-builders of that period seemed to rely on them only for geometric and structural formulas. Not until Italian artists and philosophers in the fourteenth and fifthteenth centuries began to analyze Greek and Roman ruins and compare their findings with Vitruvius' theories, was continuity in the development of Western architecture reestablished.

The specialist demands made on today's architect, who has to undergo a minimum of

Left *Chiswick House*, Chiswick (1727, William Kent). When Lord Burlington commisioned the building of a house at Chiswick, he sent his architect to Italy to study the classical villas of Palladio: the "Italian" style was enjoying a great vogue in England during the seventeenth century. Chiswick House is accordingly a version of Palladio's Villa Capra in Vicenza, which had been built nearly two centuries earlier, in 1552. The high domed hall, portico, entrance stairs and "podium" are elements derived from the rediscovered classical forms of the Italian Renaissance, but where this style is well suited to the Mediterranean climate, it is less successful in England. The role of the patron at this time was crucial in all artistic spheres.

five years' formal training, are very close to Vitruvius' aspirations. <u>Vitruvius said that architects should have imagination, an understanding of both theoretical and practical aspects of construction, should be versed in letters, drawing, the use of geometrical instruments, optics, arithmetic, history, philosophy, music, medicine, law and astronomy.</u>

Greek architecture was the expression of a balanced community, in which the essential religious and civic institutions remained the stable ingredient. The architect was responsible for both the design and supervision of buildings in Ancient Greece and was recognized as essential in the development of that society. By Roman times the role of the architect had changed to that of technician and military engineer rather than artist.

Throughout history, the essential relationship of trust and understanding between patron, designer and builder has been critical to the realization of any building project, and in the Middle Ages it was more often the patron who was credited with the creation of a building. The great master-builders were by no means considered second-rate, but the idea of the artist as a designer did not exist. The building of the great medieval cathedrals and castles often took place over several generations, with successive master-builders adapting and adding to the building as it progressed rather than working to a preconceived design. In spite of their considerable technical skills, much of the work relied on trial-and-error, with each team learning from experience to push the techniques of their materials to new limits.

In Renaissance Italy, the importance of architectural literature as a means of transmitting ideas lost since Classical times was reestablished and the architect was again elevated to the role of artist. The existence of architectural theory provided the literate amateur with a new awareness of building design which had previously been exclusive to the craft guilds, and the subsequent combination of the academic patron working closely with the practical surveyor or engineer was the basis for the later establishment of a profession.

The importance of patronage to architecture at any time in history should not be underestimated. Without the interest of such enlightened patrons as the Earl of Arundel, with whom Inigo Jones (1573-1652) visited Italy in 1613-1614, English Renaissance architecture would not have been established in the mainstream of European culture. Originally a masque designer to the Court of James I, it was only by studying actual buildings in Italy that Inigo Jones was able to understand fully the work of Sebastiano Serlio and Andrea Palladio (1508-80), previously only known from writings and plates. Jones returned to

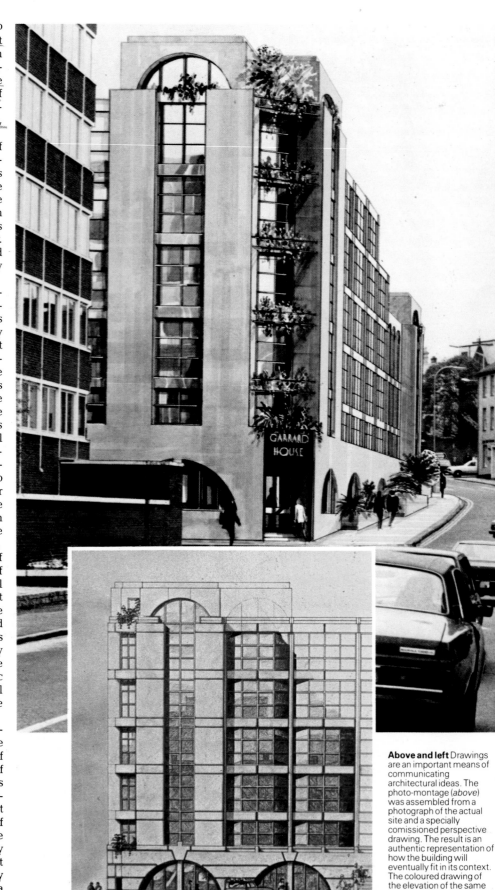

Above and left Drawings are an important means of communicating architectural ideas. The photo-montage (*above*) was assembled from a photograph of the actual site and a specially comissioned perspective drawing. The result is an authentic representation of how the building will eventually fit in its context. The coloured drawing of the elevation of the same building (*left*) helps both architect and client visualize the building.

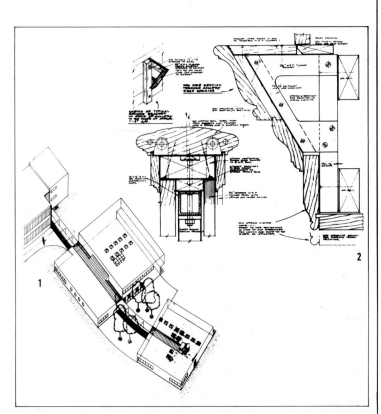

Right Axonometric drawings (*1*) – bird's eye views – are architectural projections which give an indication of the mass and three-dimensional form of buildings. Working drawings, such as this detail of a balustrade (*2*), are drawings from which builders or sub-contractors work. They include written notes specifying materials and constructional methods.

Below and below left The coloured elevation and site plan are part of a design for a housing scheme by an architectural student. The project was to design a mixed housing development for an actual site. The development had to include bungalows for the elderly, single-person flats, and two-, three- and four-bedroom houses.

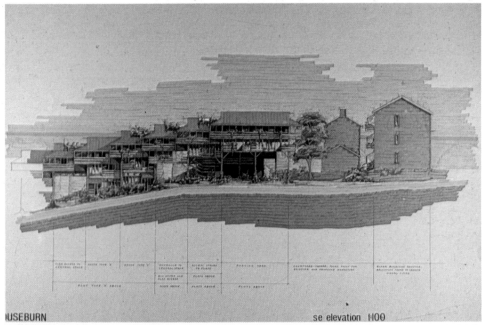

USEBURN   se elevation 1:100

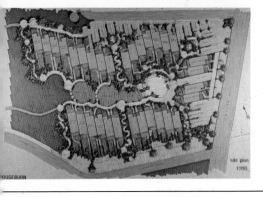

England in 1615, became Surveyor to the King, and established himself as the first English architect in the sense that we understand the term today.

Relative stability in society and a slow growth rate in the population over the next 200 years meant that architects remained primarily involved with royal, civic and institutional buildings and with urban planning. Many of the domestic Regency and Georgian terraces built within such town plans were executed from elaborate pattern books, without the direct involve-

ment of architects.

In parallel with such formal developments, the techniques and forms of rural buildings have always been handed down from one generation to the next. In vernacular architecture, an architecture without architects, the role of the individual is never predominant, and a tradition of building related to social organization and availability of materials continuously evolves within its own limits.

It was not until the Industrial Revolution at the beginning of the nineteenth century

that this social stability was rocked, and then it was the unlikely combination of the developer and the engineer, rather than the architect, who rose to prominence. The need for larger span buildings to satisfy the demands of industrialization, and the capability of such materials as cast-iron to make them possible, led to an architecture uninhibited by formal stylistic constraints. The Roundhouse, built in Chalk Farm, London in 1864, and now converted to a theatre, is a building originally designed to house railway engines. It is a fine example of form unconsciously reflecting function, not dependent on any applied decoration for expression.

Hand in hand with the demands for factories were pressures to accommodate the men and women flooding to the cities to work in industry. Unhappily a proliferation of jerry-built back-to-back housing followed, unguided by any constraints other than commercial greed. Many of our industrial cities are still suffering from the effects of this building explosion.

A personal rather than a social concern on the part of the growing middle classes at the destruction of the city prompted the reappearance of the architect as artist. Vested in the neo-Gothic stylistic revival of the nineteenth century was a belief in the truth, purity and simplicity of the society to

Above Well-designed buildings originally intended for one purpose are capable of being adapted for other uses as needs arise. This New York loft conversion creates spacious living accomodation in what was a nineteenth-century industrial building. Buildings often have a longer life than the functions for which they were originally constructed.
Right This building was a speculative warehouse development in the early 1970s which remained empty until it was adapted for use as design workshops for Middlesex Polytechnic. The architects, Rock Townsend, retained the industrial character of the building but added fittings and a colourful "high-tech" image.

which Gothic architecture originally belonged. This desire to return to what was understood to be the innate traditions of English architecture was also reflected in William Morris' Arts and Crafts Movement. An interest in individual, small-scale and handmade works was a direct challenge to the accelerating process of mass industrialization.

Although the Industrial Revolution in the United States picked up momentum rather later than in Europe, a similar pattern of architectural development preceded it. Colonial style was predominantly employed for public architecture, while everyday domestic building was a marriage between immigrants' knowledge of the traditional forms of their mother country, and the materials, in this case mainly timber, locally available to them.

In the early part of this century, the architect as a formally trained individual emerged. More and more complicated environmental and constructional problems, and a rapidly expanding birth rate, promoted trends towards specialization in all sectors of society. Once a privileged position had been established, the architect, as with other professionals, began to throw up barriers to maintain status. It is only now that those barriers are beginning to come down again. The "dis-

tancing" of the designer from the actual craft business of building originally developed to protect clients from professional and bias. In reality, this separation has probably been partly to blame for the fact that the environmental needs of society have not always been well served. In Britain, the public's rejection of much of the inappropriate mainstream architecture of the 1950s and 1960s in favour of so-called "neo-vernacular" in the 1970s, highlights the sometimes elitist and misdirected state of the profession. This over-simplified view is, nevertheless, unfair to the architect in many respects. Society demands that architects should coordinate so many diverse technical disciplines, including structural details, heating, air-conditioning, lighting and acoustics, that they inevitably are jacks of all trades but masters of none.

The architect must primarily be creative, for without a concept which is carried rigorously through all stages of its development, no completed building will be meaningful in its context nor appropriate to its function. Although everyone acts as his own architect constantly experiencing buildings, lasting architecture will only spring from a condition where the essential relationship between patron, architect and builder is allowed to flourish.

Above London nineteenth-century warehouses were built to exploit the river traffic, but are now redundant as industrial processes change. This warehouse on the Thames at Wapping has been converted to a sports centre. The high cost of new building and the movement to conserve and restore old buildings has given rise to an increasing number of schemes for restoration, rehabilitaiton and conversion.

Stone

The art of building in stone has evolved as a result of stone satisfying two basic human needs – the secular and the sacred. The first included the day-to-day need for shelter from weather, protection from enemies and communications, and more latterly storage and industry. From this set of requirements have emerged some of the greatest engineering structures, such as forts, bridges, viaducts, dams and lighthouses. The second need is concerned with higher ideals relating to the rituals of celebration, commemoration and worship and the sacred realms of gods, kings and myths.

Each need has affected the development of the other. Sacred buildings have illuminated man's intellect and ingenuity; need, the availability of stone, an understanding of geometry and an accomplished technology have all united to bestow an architectural legacy matched by no other manmade form on earth. With sacred buildings, it is the figurative and emblematic character of stone, together with its actual capacity to withstand immense loads, that have served for so long. The secular structures express the simpler, more honest elements of stone. Bridges, forts and warehouses have a recognizable and attractive functional honesty.

Geological characteristics have clearly influenced the expression of religions, legends and myths. It is no coincidence that the spiritual centres of succeeding civilizations have always been found near a readily available outcrop of rock. There has always been a close relationship between the geological pattern and makeup of a particular region, its prevailing climate and the architecture of that culture.

Most continents have a wide variety of rock deposits. The main characteristics of stone that have led to its widespread use are its availability, its durability and its intrinsic compressive strength. The ability of stone to withstand very great loads has made it suitable for large-scale structures. As a material which, unlike timber or steel, is totally inert, its behaviour under stress and load is predictable.

The Material

Stone is the oldest building material known to man. The origins of stone date back to a period nearly 4,000 million years ago. Recorded history is a mere 6,000 years old, so the use of stone by mankind in the ancient structures of Egypt and Greece represents a mere fraction of its life as an inorganic substance.

Over these millions of years, the continually evolving structure of the Earth's crust has produced a wide variety of mineral outcrops. None of these deposits are identical. This great variety of rock, sometimes found in intense proximity as in Britain, has

Above *Aqueduct at Segovia* (Roman, A.D.10). The design of aqueducts and bridges is normally considered the province of engineers. However, these types of structures have profoundly affected architectural design. The curved arch, usually associated with the architect-engineers of the Roman Empire, was able to span greater distances than the lintel and column methods of Greek construction. Here, the arches are supported on simple piers and the overall impression is one of function rather than decoration.

Right *Chartres Cathedral* (1194–1260) Reconstructed on the site of an earlier Romanesque church, Chartres has a vault which rises to a massive 120 feet (40m). It is supported by flying buttresses on three arches, one above the other. The two lower arches are attached to radiating balusters which look like the spokes of a wheel.

Left This small cottage in Cornwall, England is made from the stones quarried nearby. There is no need to transport construction materials to the site; as the granite is readily available, its proximity is exploited to the full. Vernacular traditions typically make use of local skills and materials.

Above *Falling Water*, Bear Run, Pennsylvania, USA. (Frank Lloyd Wright, 1935–7). Wright designed this house for Edgar J. Kaufman. Its form reflects the nature of the surrounding area. In plan and in elevation, the building is seen to extend out into the wooded site in a series of bold rectilinear planes on different levels. The bedrock of the waterfall running through the house is beautifully echoed in terraces of reinforced concrete which cantilever out from the heart of the house, constructed of local stone.

resulted in widely differing specimens, ranging from dense crystalline formations capable of taking a very high polish, to deeply faulted and fissured varieties whose course and variegated mineral structure exposes its own strata.

The turmoil in the developing history of the Earth's crust has left three broad families of rock. Within each are extreme varieties of mineral makeup, texture and colour. The first group, the oldest and the most consistent in character, is igneous, rock formed from the cooling mass of magma, the melting fluid of rock. Within this category are to be found the principal building materials of granite, porphyry, gabbro and serpentinite. The next group is sedimentary rock, formed from ancient deposits accumulated on waterbeds, such as lakes, rivers and seas, and subjected to great pressure which has compacted and cemented the deposits together. Within this group can be found the sandstones, limestones and travertines. Finally, the last and youngest group is metamorphic rock. These tortured rock formations, which include slates and marble, are formed from existing igneous or sedimentary deposits which have been subjected to intense stress, heat or the effect of chemicals.

Due to its crystalline formation, stone is only able to withstand limited forces when used in a mode of tension. For this reason,

traditional building development has exploited the material in compression. As with grain in timber, the crystalline formation of most rock has a distinct structure known as the "bed", a name which, as it suggests, describes the relative axis, direction or position of the stone as it originated in the ground, slowly solidifying and hardening over a period of millions of years. With the exception of sedimentary stones which are riven or split much as logs, it has been conventional practice to detail stonework so that individual pieces are exposed with the bed lying in the same direction as it did when the stone was in the ground. No two blocks of stone are alike, a quality of the material which stonemasons have always respected and exploited.

Drilling, blasting, splitting and wedging are all well-tried methods of extraction. Since the beginning of the twentieth century, more efficient production has been achieved in some quarries by the use of continuous wire sawing. Loops of wire up to several hundred yards long are threaded over pulleys from a central motor, descend into the quarry, are threaded around the stone to be cut, and are then pulled back up again to the source of power. More recently, various methods of heat-processing, such as thermal lances and flame-finishing, have become common practice.

Constraints in transportation due to both

the weight and size of the material do not always seem to have been a problem. However, there is considerable uncertainty as to how the massive stones of Stonehenge (3000 B.C.) were transported from one original source high in the Prescelly Mountains in west Wales. Water has traditionally played a major part in transportation. The water systems of the Nile have contributed greatly to the facility with which stone has been moved up and down the Nile Valley.

Building Techniques

In the simplest form of stone building, stones lying on the ground were gathered up and piled one on top of the other in a decreasing silhouette to form cones, cairns and walls. Although the methods by which these massive blocks of stone were quarried and transported is largely a mystery, much speculation also surrounds their extraction from the rock. Equal speculation surrounds the method by which the stones were raised into the vertical position and how the horizontal members were then positioned on top. The most credible theory is that earth banks were built up and then hollowed out, so that the vertical members could be lowered into the pits formed in this way. Once the vertical members were positioned, the horizontal members would be rolled and dragged up the false earth

Above This photograph illustrates an age-old process of quarrying stone manually, with the aid of a pulley system.
Right The wire-cutting process is similar in action to sawing. Blocks of stone are quarried using lengths of wire looped between pulleys, under the stone to be cut, and tensioned on a motor shreeve.

Left The regularity of the quarrying process assists the eventual transportation of stone blocks.
Below left Holes drilled in the stone prior to splitting it, leave vertical grooves in the blocks.
Below Difficulties in the transportation of this weighty material limit the size of blocks, here stockpiled before being picked up.

The variety of stone
1. The nobility of the Parthenon is unmistakeable. Built at the top of a hill overlooking Athens, between 447 and 432 B.C., it was intended as the finest temple in Greece. It was wider and longer than any other temple of the time, built out of marble, as no other Doric temple had been before, and richly endowed with sculpture. The precision of the masonry is demonstrated by the almost imperceptible dry joints. Each marble block was individually worked to key in with the next; each an essential part of the whole.
2. A detail from an Ionic capital, this shows stone's incomparable ability to accomodate minute carving or sculpturing in curves and in geometric patterns and for it to withstand errosion.
3. No two blocks of stone are alike; each has its own individual figuring. This block contains the intricate imprints of fossils.
4. The glowing sandstone of this Indian pillar both supports and decorates the Muslim interior.
5. In the Corinthian order, carefully sculptured acanthus leaves emulate the precise shape of the leaves in nature.
6. Granite's stern aspect was used by the Inca people of Peru to build city and fortress walls. The dry joints fit together exactly.
7. In attitudes representing situations in Biblical stories, stone figures were used to embellish Renaissance cathedrals, in this case St. Mark's, Venice.

1

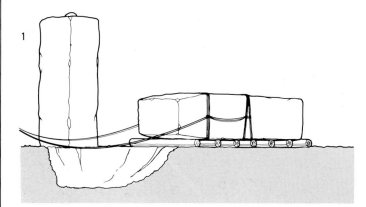

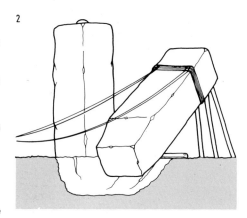

Building Stonehenge The mammoth task of raising the sarsens at Stonehenge and then dressing them with lintels demanded considerable organizational and engineering skills. Most of the stone came from local sites about 24 miles (40 km) away, though some was transported from Prescelly in Wales – a staggering distance of 132 miles (220 km).

1. The first step was to dig a foundation pit. One side of the pit was cut in the form of a ramp, so the sarsen could be slid down it to be raised against the facing vertical. This vertical was strengthened with stakes as a precaution against crushing the chalk wall. The sarsen was then hauled to the edge of the pit on log rollers.

2. Once the sarsen had reached the pit, it was levered upwards until it overbalanced to slide into the pit.

3. The sarsen was then hoisted into its final vertical position. An elaborate framework of timber scaffolding, levers and struts were used, backed up by the muscle power of labourers hauling on ropes.

4. A similar timber scaffolding was used to raise the lintel into position.

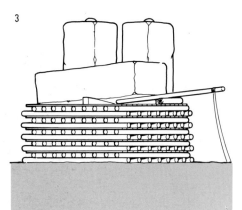

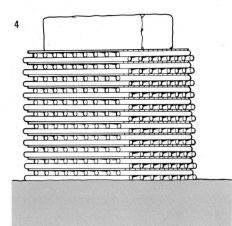

Above Stonehenge in Wiltshire, England is one of the most impressive architectural achievements of prehistoric man. Designed on a massive scale, its construction is extremely sophisticated, being a very early example of columnar and trabeated stone building. Other architectural features include the deliberate tapering of the lintels and the bulging of the standing stones, while, as originally conceived, the curve of the lintels circling the outside ring also added to the aesthetic effect. The rough-hewn nature of the stone itself conveys a sense of mystery; according to some theories, this may well be a deliberate effect planned by the builders as part of Stonehenge's religious significance.

embankment to take their place on top of their partners.

Within this family of early structures are the megalithic, Neolithic gallery graves – long narrow chambers – of 3000-1800 B.C. found in France, some of the first examples of stone arcading enclosing interior space to be found in Europe. It is interesting to compare these structures, and that of Stonehenge, with those being built in Egypt at the same time. At the other extreme, craftsmen have worked the rock-face in situ, as the Petra in southern Jordan in A.D. 120.

The great majority of stone structures have been built from pieces of stone designed to be bedded together to form a continuous fabric – an early form of prefabrication. By working and tooling the profile, the particular stone is either designed to be read as a homogeneous surface, such as the fluid, continuous structures of late Gothic arcades, or as a series of separate vertical and horizontal components, such as the framed construction of the Parthenon, or the block-on-block formation of the Florentine palazzos of the fifteenth century. In arcades, the nearly horizontal

force of the roof is visually reconciled as being integral and continuous with the vertical shafts. It is with arcaded structures of succeeding cultures that this chapter is primarily concerned.

The main stream of architectural development in stone has been based upon organized systems of assembly. Examples such as those mentioned previously have relied upon premeditated projection of the structure, which has determined the size and proportion of each piece of stone before it has been won from the raw rock. The examples to be examined here rely largely on repetitive components arranged to form a continuous arcaded enclosure. This method of construction originated in a "post-and-lintel", or columnar-and-trabeated, arrangement of horizontal and vertical components. The horizontal members carried the roof loads which were supported in turn by the vertical members.

As experience of the nature of the material grew, so did an understanding of the engineering principles of what has become known as the science of statics and dynamics. The advantages of building in stone by establishing hierarchies of space also emerged, resulting from the complex, three-dimensional geometry which is appropriate for the exploitation of stone in compression. This understanding reached two great apogees in the history of stone building: the ancient, Classical Greek temples of the fifth century B.C., and the Gothic cathedrals of northern Europe, built between the tenth and fourteenth centuries. It was in this latter period that horizontal roof members and vertical col-

umn members became tooled, worked and profiled into a continuous, almost plastic, composition of ribs and shafts. At the same time, despite the fluency, a clear representation of the structural anatomy can easily be understood. All subsequent architectural developments have been in the shadow of these two important ages of architectural refinement.

It is possible to trace an increasing sophistication and awareness, as stone became refined and lightened in a conscious attempt to "dematerialize" stonework, a process that resulted in the high Gothic of northern Europe. Stone technology evolved from being the structure itself in 300 B.C. and in the tenth to fifteenth centuries, to being overtaken in the nineteenth century by cast-iron, steel and later concrete as the economic base material. Nowadays, it is frequently used as a respectable veneer in institutional public building or organizations anxious to project a picture of well-established importance; stone today carries a derivative significance. Round this question ranges an argument about the honest expression of the use of materials in modern building. The use of stone only as a representational material is not new. Brick and stucco have been painted to emulate stone's authority. The embellishments added to a number of major housing terraces in London during the early nineteenth century, such as the Adam terraces, were formed in stucco and painted. The mouldings, brackets, entablatures and cornices have their origins in the Classical detailing of the stonework of antiquity and the Renaissance. Similarly,

Above and left Petra, Jordan. Petra's importance as a trading centre and its resultant prosperity combined to make the city one of the architectural jewels of the Levant. This was particularly the case in the 2nd century A.D. when Petra was the capital of Roman Arabia and many of the city's buildings are deeply influenced by Roman styles. Architecturally, Petra is particularly noted for its rock-cut temples. These, in common with buildings such as the Treasury (left) are prime examples of the in situ use of materials.

baroque embellishments of the late seventeenth century, which blurred the distintion between building and sculpture, were frequently detailed to represent stonework in their execution.

Development and Application

Early Stone Building

Once man had discovered the stability resulting from cultivation of the soil and animal husbandry, settlements required consolidation. Quest for shelter and protection required buildings of permanence. The three main centres of civilization were in the Middle East, in Egypt and Iraq and northwest Pakistan. Early enclosures were formed of mud walls and timber roofs. Where stone was available in Turkey in 3000 B.C., the mud walls were placed on stone foundations. The first indications of stone in common use appear to be the fortifications on the perimeter of these settlements. Early evidence can be seen in the ritualistic temples of Sumeria in Iraq.

The Egyptians

Although Egyptian civilization rose and subsided over a period of 3,000 years, it was comparatively early in its development that the dynastic art and technology of building in stone became consolidated. There was an intense period of early development, followed by 2,000 years of repetitious and eclectic building construction.

The Egyptians used stone in two quite different ways. Firstly, external walls and pylons were detailed to describe a single homogeneous surface upon which were inscribed figures and symbols. Like vast billboards, the calm surface of the background was then exploited by the carving that was subsequently inscribed upon it.

Secondly, the Egyptians will always be known for the construction of their temples and palaces – the first buildings to use post-and-lintel construction. This column and beam system was limited to the interior.

The character of Egyptian architecture stemmed directly from the geological and climatic circumstances of the Nile Valley. The stone was quarried directly from the banks of the Nile, adjacent to the centres of population. The details of the column reaching upwards to make a comfortable connection between the column, and the largely undecorated lintel members, were inspired by the lotus, the papyrus and the palm which were found growing beside the river.

Not fully appreciating the structural potential of stone, Egyptian builders placed columns at relatively close centres to avoid long-span lintel stones at roof level. The columns themselves were also relatively squat in proportion. The pillared

(hypostyle) hall at Karnak (1500 B.C.), gives the impression that the galleries were literally quarried from solid rock.

Although the Pyramids remained the highest buildings in the world for 5,000 years and required methodical ingenuity in construction, by comparison with the temples and palaces higher up the Nile at Luxor, Karnak and Edfu, they remain monuments to engineering rather than architecture.

Classical Greek Architecture

The Egyptian palaces and temples were built for the satisfaction of priests and royalty; the public at large never penetrated these sanctuaries. Greek society, however, was totally inclusive and stone was used for structures covering uses that reflected a much wider and more open society. Literature, music, drama and sport thrived, and stone was used for the construction of stadiums, gymnasiums and theatres.

The art of architecture throughout the Western world has never been disengaged from the theory and practice concentrated upon the construction of Greek temples between 700 and 500 B.C. Buildings of apparent simplicity, the Greek temples embodied a development that unfolded over 200 years, and resulted in the highest

Above *The Great Temple of Ammon*, Karnak, Egypt (c. 1312–1301 B.C.). This temple complex was not built to a single masterplan. It owes its existence to the work of many kings, having started as a modest shrine and only slowly expanding in size and complexity over the centuries. Each individual addition, however, remains in style, so preserving Karnak's architectural integrity as an organic whole. One of the chief features of the complex are the solid stonework pylons on the exteriors and the use of very closely centred columns in the interiors.

The effect is extremely atmospheric and imposing (*above centre*). The walls, column shafts and architraves (*above right*) are elaborately decorated with coloured inscriptions and reliefs. As well as lists of kings and tributes to the gods, these decorations include a description of Thutmose III's victory at Megiddo, the earliest known account of a battle.

Right Rescue work on the temples at Philae took place after the building of the dam on Lake Nasser. Though the great buildings of the valley of the Nile were largely constructed of sandstone, a surprising amount of detail has survived. This is because of the lack of corrosive carbon dioxide in the clear desert air.

refinement of technique and proportion.

Greek temples were designed to house either a figurative or a symbolic figure, or an oracle. The composition of elements that we see on the exterior of a Greek temple is a direct reflection of the organization of the interior space in relation to the exterior loggia. This loggia or portico was devised to prepare the visitor for entry. It is thought that the long colonnades on either side running back from this loggia were also to help protect the inner cellular wall to the main hall, constructed of mud in the early temples, from the intense heat of the sun. Egyptian temples had internal columns and exterior walls; Greek temples had internal walls surrounded by columns.

Although not all historians are agreed, it is generally accepted that the vocabulary of construction used in the stone detailing of a Greek temple is a direct interpretation of the timber detailing found in primitive huts – the easily legible components of an earlier use of timber were transposed into stone. Thus, the well-known motifs in Greek Classical stone construction had their origin , as did the capitals in Egyptian architecture, in nature. The basic components of the construction were the stepped podium or stylobate (the base to the column), the column or shaft itself, the capital, and the entablature, (the horizontal member at roof level). At either end above the entablature was the triangular form of the pediment. All the timber clips, pegs and notches of the original timber construction were replicated in stonework, embellished and decorated to give the finished building a precisely detailed refinement.

These components were developed in three modes known as "the orders": Doric, Ionic and Corinthian. The principal difference between them can be seen in the capitals, although there were minor differences in the entablature as well as the fluting to the column. The simplest, most widespread and famous order was the Doric, with the cushion-like profile to the capital making a comfortable junction with the vertical shaft beneath and horizontal lintel above. The evolution and refinement of Classical Greek architecture that took place over this intense period of building activity can be examined by comparing the details of the capitals on the Basilica (c. 530 B.C.), one of the three well-preserved temples at Paestum in southern Italy, with the most famous of all Greek temples, the Parthenon (447-432 B.C.), on the Acropolis in Athens. In the earlier building, the profile of the column and capital is clearly exaggerated. These same components become slimmer, more subtle and apparently more at peace with one another, as seen in the outline at the Parthenon. It is worth noting that such was the skill of the Greek masons that in some instances base, column and capital were made of one piece

Above *The Propylaea,* Athens (437–432 B.C.). The Propylaea was designed by Mnesicles in the time of Pericles to form the imposing entrance to the Acropolis. This view is of the walls of the unfinished hall in one of the wings; the lifting bosses and beam sockets characteristic of Greek building methods are still visible, while the lifting blocks have not been cut off. The building may have been left unfinished

because of the outbreak of the Peloponnesian War. **Below** The jointing method for a Doric column involved square inserts in the centre of each block, joined with a pin. Lifting bosses to aid positioning of each block would be cut off when the building was complete.

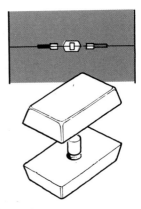

of stone. The second order, the Ionic, emanating from Asia Minor, introduced capitals with a scroll on the inner and outer faces. This endowed the column with a back, front and sides, giving it an axis for direction. The last and most complex of the orders was the Corinthian, whose capitals sprouted in an organic flourish of leaves.

The mathematical module of all these Classical compositions was the diameter of the column measured at one-third of the height from its base. The columns of the temple at Paestum were four modules high and those of the Parthenon six modules high, relative proportions that illustrate the gradual slimming down of the Doric column. In addition to the mathematical relationships resulting from the use of such a module, further delicacy was achieved by the deliberate distortion of members, both in profile and alignment.

One such adjustment was the "entasis" or bulging silhouette of the column which was designed to avoid a waisted and so weak-looking column. On a larger scale, distortion of the alignment of the podium, the columns and the pediment resulted in a posture which was perceptibly more comfortable to the eye than it would otherwise

Left *Temple of Concord*, Agrigentum, Sicily (*c*. 430 B.C.). The Doric columns of the Temple of Concord, with their careful proportions and slightly convex profiles, are typical of much Greek architecture of the Hellenic period from 650 to 323 B.C. Such temples were deliberately designed for outward effect, since worship took place in the open air outside them.

Below *The Erechtheion*, Athens (421–405 B.C.). Designed by Mnesicles, this temple is unusually irregular in plan. This was in part the result of necessity; the architect was forced to preserve several sacred spots and sanctuaries, while the site itself is awkward and falling. The column bases are firmly Ionic, while the sides are solid. The general effect, however, appears more Roman than Greek.

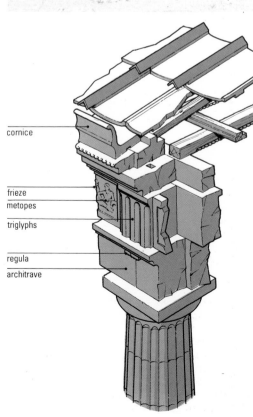

cornice

frieze
metopes

triglyphs

regula

architrave

Left The Doric entablature, or upper part, of the column. It consists of the architrave, frieze and cornice, with the supporting colonnade. The architrave is the main beam. This is two or three slabs of stone deep, the outer slab showing one vertical face. It is capped by flat projecting bands called the *taeniae*, under which run strips known as *regula*. These are positioned at intervals corresponding to the *triglyphs*, blocks with vertical channels which are part of the frieze. These alternate with gaps, or *metopes*, which are often ornamented with sculpture. The cornice is the crowning part of the entablature.

have been. These illusionary, but visually corrective, devices must have grown from years of trial-and-error, and illustrate the Greek peoples' striving for elegance and clarity rather than technological innovation. In the hesitant beginnings, the lintel headstone was kept as short as practicable and as light as possible; the columns appeared squat and drumlike. As the Greeks developed a greater understanding of the material, confidence grew and the proportions of both column and beam became slimmer and finer. The distance between columns became greater and the arcade more generous.

The majority of early Greek temples were constructed from Parian marble. This had a smooth, hard and creamy consistency, it could be tooled easily on either axis, and was capable of taking a fine polish. Later, from about 500 B.C. onwards, stone was quarried from the Pentelic Mountains, more readily accessible to Athens.

The precision with which the stones were cut and laid would be a match for us today. The faces of the stone pieces which abutted one another were dressed to be concave, facilitating the close fitting of the hairline joints on the exposed faces of the stone. In this manner, the stones were so exactly matched that they were set with dry joints — without any additional setting agent to fill the gap between the stones.

Later, the pieces of stone were mechanically coupled one to another by a metal tie of bronze, or more usually iron, which was set in dovetail pockets on either face of the stone joint. These ties would then be set in position with molten lead.

Right The three orders of Greek architecture were Doric, Ionic and Corinthian. The first two developed simultaneously in different parts of the Greek world; the Corinthian order was a later development, which greatly influenced the Romans. The Doric column (*right*) is unique in having no base. The shaft is fluted, while the capital, or crowning feature, is plain. The Ionic column (*centre*) is slimmer and more elegant. Its distinguishing feature is the *volutes* (scrolls or spirals) that decorate the capital. The capital of the Corinthian column (*left*) is bell-shaped, while the volutes are supported by eight acanthus leaves. Doric shafts are always fluted; the other two orders generally follow the same style.

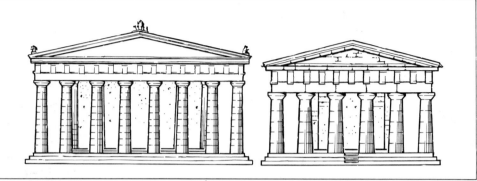

Temple development The Temple of Poseidon, Paestum (*left*) is a well-preserved example of early Hellenic architecture, though the plan is still long and the proportions rather heavy. The Parthenon, Athens (*right*) shows how style became refined. A unifyign feature of the two buildings is the even number of columns, hence the uneven number of bays.

Left Base of an Ionic column from The Erechtheion, Athens. This detail shows clearly how the column sits firmly on its base cushion. The moulded base design evolved into a standard form, known as the Attic base because it was perfected in Attica. It consists of an upper and lower torus, or moulding, divided by a scotia and fillets.

Above *The Theatre*, Epidauros, (*c.* 350 B.C.) Designed by Polycleitos, the geometric exactness of the layout is a triumph of Greek design. The use of stone for the seemingly prosaic purpose of seating, as well as flooring in the area called the orchestra, was carefuly calculated to improve the acoustics, while sight lines for the audience were as carefully planned.

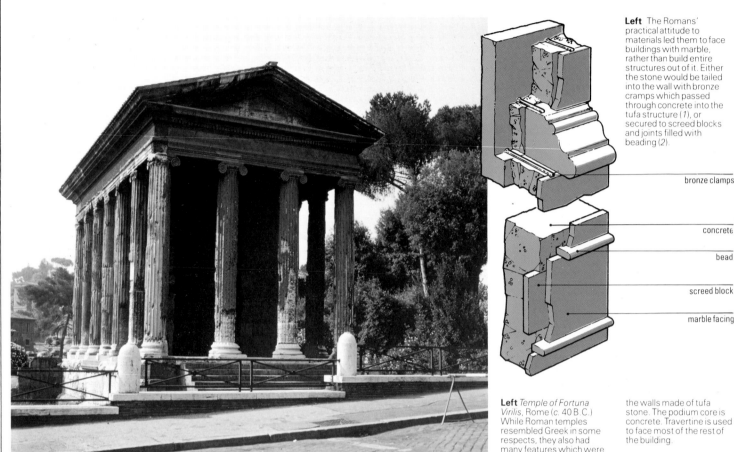

Left *Temple of Fortuna Virilis*, Rome (c. 40 B.C.) While Roman temples resembled Greek in some respects, they also had many features which were derived from Etruscan temples. Typically, this temple has a deep portico in front, similar to Etruscan style, with steps leading up. The sides are "blind", with half-columns attached to the walls made of tufa stone. The podium core is concrete. Travertine is used to face most of the rest of the building.

Roman Architecture

As stone had a wider use in the structures of the Greek civilization than in that of the Egyptians, in the same way, Roman stone buildings covered a wider range of uses than those of the Greeks. Basilicas, baths, triumphal arches and aquaducts are found with temples and open forums, all reflecting the broader Roman pattern of life.

Superficially Roman architecture was simpler in detail, and on a larger, more robust, scale than the delicate buildings of the Greeks. It is characterized by the large open structures built at the height of the Roman Empire. The Romans also gave their buildings a richer mix of detail. Although the arch was not unknown to the Greeks, it was the Romans who exploited this Etruscan invention. The circle, semicircle and half-sphere became the principal geometric figures upon which Roman architecture was based.

The Romans, as well as adopting and in some cases bowdlerizing the Greek orders, also adopted the triangular profile of the pediment, revealing the principle of structural rigidity resulting from triangulation. The base chord becomes a tension member, which, together with the angled compression members, constitutes a truss.

Roman stonework, more inventive, more alert to engineering principles, was coarser in comparison to Greek stonework. The Romans made use of dressed facings, frequently relying on concrete to provide structural integrity and rubble to provide mass. The skeleton work was made of stone, brick and tile which held the rougher sandwich infill construction together.

The Roman temple in general character is similar to the Greek, but the open porch or collonade is positioned at the front on the axis of the entrance. Steps lead up to the collonade on the front face only. The sides or flanks are blind, and the walls are modulated by half-columns or pilasters.

Byzantine Churches

Constantine moved the capital of the Roman empire from Rome to Byzantium in A.D. 324. The main building material in Constantinople, mud, was made into bricks and tiles. The techniques of construction and the geometry of space were more Eastern than Western. Earlier buildings were plundered, and the components incorporated into new structures.

Santa Sophia (532 B.C.), built by Justinian, was the first square volume space to be capped by a dome. The geometrical reconciliation of square and circle was absorbed by "pendentives", the triangular void between the arches and the underside of the circular plan. The massive and homogenous nature of the church expresses no one material more than another. The colossal piers are stone and the dome is brick. The surfaces have been covered successively with paint, marble and mosaic, not as an illumination of structure, but for religious decorative purposes.

Byzantine churches proliferated throughout Asia Minor, relying on an arrangement of clay domes supported on stone piers. The roofs of all other major spaces constructed at this time were timber, but it was in north Italy that the construction of basilicas first made use of the Roman barrel vault. In order to facilitate light entering the space spanned by the principal barrel vault, secondary vaults were introduced at right-angles to the main space, the junction between the two vaults being known as the groin vault. It was from the Gothic architectural style, particularly visible in pointed vaulting and arches, was born.

Left The Romans built cross-vaults over square apartments, long halls or corridors. The cross-vault was formed from the intersection of two semicircular vaults, equal in span. The lines of intersection are known as "groins".

Below *Basilica of Constantine*, Rome (A.D. 310–13). Also known as the Basilica of Maxentius or Basilica Nova, this building has a central nave covered by a groined vault in three sections, and anticipates the development of Byzantine architecture. Basilicas were used as law and business centres and structurally form a link between Classical and Gothic architecture.

Imperial Rome As masters of the known world, the Romans developed a particularly massive architectural style. The Temple of Romulus in the Forum Romanum (*left*) was the central point from which various emperors laid out subsequent forums as tributes to themselves; the temple of Castor and Pollux (*above left*) and the Arch of Titus (*above right*). The temple was built to a rectangular design. Its three columns have unique Corinthian capitals, the central volutes (scrolls) intertwining and a tendril rising between them and the angle volutes to carry along the abacus. The Romans were fond of such ornamental features, as the Arch of Titus shows. This, with its broad single span, was built to commemorate that emperor's capture of Jerusalem. The attached columns flanking the opening and at the outer angles are the earliest surviving examples of the fully-developed Roman composite order. A relief in the centre depicts the apotheosis of Titus, while a carved relief of the emperor in a triumphal car decorates one side of the opening. The other side depicts the spoils taken from the temple at Jerusalem. The keystones are faced with figures of Roma and Fortuna, while the attic story carries the arch's dedication. Similar monuments are to be found throughout the Roman Empire, together with more utilitarian Roman structures such as baths and aqueducts.

Gothic Architecture

Although "Gothic" derives from "Goth", a term of abuse which referred to barbarians, we understand this label to refer particularly to that lofty range of north European buildings built between the tenth and fourteenth centuries. Gothic architecture was total in the sense that the visible sinew-like shafts of stone are actually performing the role of support and are not simply a representation of that load-carrying role.

It is difficult to be precise about the moment that Romanesque developed into fully fledged Gothic. Historians also argue over whether the French or the British were first to erect a true Gothic structure. In France, Abbot Suger (1081-1151) prompted the construction of the St. Denis abbey in 1144, but in Britain, Durham Cathedral, which is strictly Romanesque showing some Gothic characteristics, was begun in 1093. France and England developed similar but not identical traditions of construction. The lofty cathedrals of northern France and the longer lower cathedrals of England together constitute a parallel development in Gothic building.

The Gothic period saw the development of inventive and innovative techniques exploiting the characteristics of stone. Stone was not simply used on a grand scale to its fullest capacity to create space; the stones were shaped, formed and profiled to produce a fabric which, by use of tracery, virtually became dematerialized.

Pointed vaulting was the key discovery of French and English Gothic architecture. Ribs and shafts, the essential components of the Gothic arcade, ran together in an almost continuous composition whose

Above *Durham Cathedral,* Durham, England (1093–1220). This interior view of Durham Cathedral gives an impression of the robust grandeur of its structure. The walls are thick, the arches rounded and a number of the massive piers boldly incised with chevron, diaper and vertical flute patterns, which emphasize their weight.
Right Developments were however, being made with the proportions at the time of its construction. Durham Cathedral was the first building in Europe to have ribbed vaults throughout, and one of the earliest to have pointed transverse arches to divide the nave into bays. The Gothic style was emerging, as can be seen in this view of Durham's nave looking east.

Right *Chartres Cathedral,* Chartres, France (1194–1220). Within the Gothic development, the use of stone became more economical and there was less and less flat masonry in the cathedrals of the time. In contrast with the view of Durham's nave, this view looking east through the nave at Chartres gives a light impression. The vaults and piers are related by thin supporting columns, and with ribbed vaulting and pointed archways, the structure flows and seems almost skeletal. Windows gained in importance as the development of the flying buttress, bearing the outward thrust of the roof, allowed for the reduction in mass of the nave wall.

Top *Henry VII's Chapel,*
Westminster Abbey,
London (1503–1519). The
chapel was built on the site
of The Lady Chapel of 1220.
The stone fan vault must
rank, with that over the
choir at Christ Church,
Oxford which was
completed in 1503, as the
most elaborate
achievements of the late
Gothic era. The pendants,
which seem to be
unsupported, are really
elongated voussoirs of
half-concealed transverse
arches, from which the
stone web is built up.
Above Westminster Abbey
was constructed next to a
Benedictine monastery, the
greater part being
sponsored by Henry III

between 1245 and 1269.
The nave, extended later, is
a fine, almost exemplary
version of Gothic vaulting. It
is 102 feet (31 m) high,
which makes it England's
tallest medieval vault The
outer wall buttresses are
constructed with octagonal
piers, between which
multisided windows light
the recesses of the side
aisles.

objectives were to make the fabric as light as possible. An old Indian proverb says, "the arch never sleeps": the arch is always pressing out as well as down. The Gothic vault originated in the intersection of two barrel vaults. It was the introduction of the rib at the intersection of the two barrel vaults which led to the development of the pointed transverse arch. The development of the pointed arch brought great advantages – first, an adjustable geometry was possible as ribbed vaults of different spans could be arranged to meet one another at their crowns; second, where the resulting descending faces were more vertical than horizontal, the weight could be carried to ground level without too great a horizontal thrust. By introducing a rib at the intersection of the two vaults, it was unnecessary to use complicated "centering" to support the vaults during construction. Once positioned, the ribs formed the bones of the structure, upon which the "voussoirs", or vaulting panels, could then be placed. A subtle difference between French and English cathedrals is that the stone courses to the voussoirs in a French vault are domical, resulting in a thrust being placed at the crown of the adjacent wall arches, whereas the English coursing is horizontal and produces no lateral thrust – a more

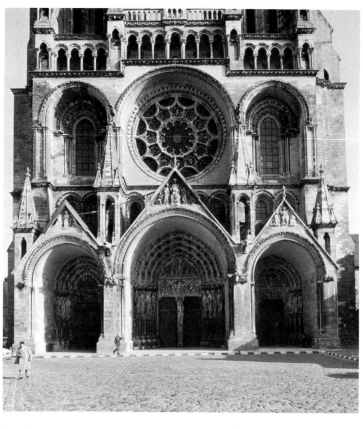

Above *Cathedral of Notre Dame*, Paris (1163–1250). Notre Dame is one of the oldest French Gothic cathedrals. The wide-spreading western facade served as a prototype for many later churches. A central wheel window of great delicacy and beauty is set above three recessed portals and tiers of statues, with an arcaded screen above it stretching in front of the roof. Slender flying buttresses along the length of the cathedral and round the east end, with chevet chapels constructed between them later, create a particularly impressive Gothic vision on the flat Isle de la Cité, above the Seine.

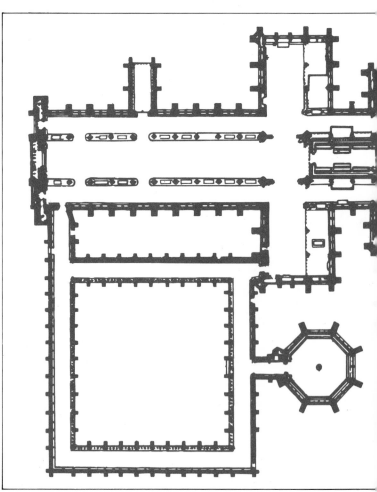

Far left *Laon Cathedral*, Laon, France (1160–1225). The west facade of Laon Cathedral is an architectural masterpiece. Three boldly projecting porches are emphasized by sculpturing and turrets and matched deeply gabled windows above, one on either side of the magnificent central rose window. The towers are adorned with figures of the so-called miraculous oxen, who carted the stone up the ramparts to the site.
Left *Bourges Cathedral*, Bourges, France (1192–1275). It is similar in plan to Notre Dame, seeming short in proportion to width. This view of the southeast exterior shows an enormous number of double flying buttresses over the aisles, with pinnacles and other decorations creating an over-impressive confusion.

Gothic cathedral plans French cathedrals, such as Bourges (*below*) tend to have whale-like plans, with a rounded east end or apse. Transepts barely project. English cathedrals, by contrast, tend to be longer and more narrow, as the plan of Salisbury shows (*left*). The transepts project quite definitely and there are sometimes double transepts. The east end is square.

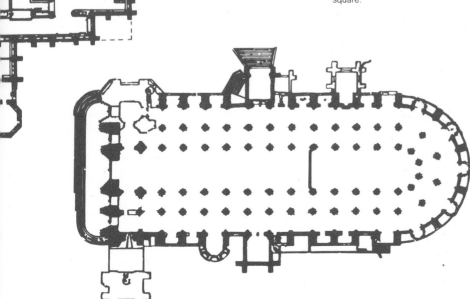

logical refinement.

The structure of Gothic cathedrals was highly tuned and no more stone was used at any one time than was believed to be absolutely necessary. A revolutionary innovation was the "flying buttress", which conducted the horizontal forces from the roof and vault outside the enclosing walls, down to ground level. In addition, the groin vault conducted the weight of the roof below at four concentrated points at the four corners of the tower, like the legs of a table. The shafts allowed the maximum amount of light to enter the interior.

As with ancient Greek temples, Gothic cathedrals were continuously refined over a period of time – in this case, 500 years. English cathedrals developed in several distinct stages from the robust and monolithic character of Romanesque beginnings, through Early English, Decorated and Perpendicular. The use of stone became increasingly economical and the fabric of enclosure more transparent, with less flat masonry. The use of ribs to break up flat plains of masonry became more intense. The patterns of ribs and panels became finer and more intricate. The fan vaulting of the Perpendicular period was a riot of geometry in which its extrovert, over-developed complexity lost the clarity and dignity of the Early English period. English Gothic construction had plan forms of greater complexity and variety compared with the whale-like plan forms of the French cathedrals.

Above *Basilica*, Vicenza, Italy (1549, Andrea Palladio). Most of the works of this influential Renaissance architect are in Vicenza. Palladio trained as a mason; his studies of ancient ruins led to his reworking of the Classical orders in new compositions which had a great effect on many other architects, notably Inigo Jones. For this medieval building (1444), Palladio designed arcades which were applied to the original Gothic structure. The arcades are built of hard stone and consist of Doric and Ionic orders which frame arches supported by twin columns. The rhythm of the major and minor arcading is a hallmark of Palladio's style.

The Renaissance

Filippo Brunelleschi (1377-1446) is said to have founded the Renaissance style of architecture. Architecture was a major part of the flourishing of the arts generally, a tide that swept northwards from Florence in the mid-fifteenth century.

The Renaissance was characterized by artists, town planners and musicians, all involved in a quest for the ideal. A search for refinement, a preoccupation with symmetry and the study of the relationships between light and dark, solid and void, and the general belief in the visual and spiritual advantages of harmony, became the bases of Renaissance architecture. Mathematical systems furnished formulas for studies in the proportion of objects. Similar analysis was used for establishing relationships between objects and buildings. This led to a greater comprehension of the phenomenon of perspective and the techniques for portraying it. The proportion of the human body also took on a renewed significance and proportional lessons were drawn from it.

The writings and lessons of Vitruvius, who was a Roman architect and engineer of the first century B.C., were reexamined. An architectural vocabulary taken from classical forms and the systems to which it referred became the basis of Renaissance inventiveness. The classical measurements and ideals were used in a new series of compositional relationships and prompted the appearance of a new professional class of builders, described as architects. The architectural furniture of the Renaissance included the classical column, the pediment, the entablature, the Roman arch and the podium, and what was to become known as the "piano nobile". This was the name for the first floor of Italian palaces where the main apartments were located.

Churches, palaces and organized open, urban spaces are the architectural works most often associated with this time. Great skill was exercised in ordering the interior of buildings, frequently using the same motifs as had been traditionally associated with the exterior. The ordering of the exterior was a separate problem, solved by taking into account abstract considerations.

Whereas Gothic architecture was a direct expression of structure, the stonework of the Renaissance developed into contrived derivations of authentic Classicism. Although stone played a part in furnishing the architecture of the Renaissance, it was

Above *Villa Capra (The Rotunda)*, Vicenza, Italy (1552, Andrea Palladio). One of the villas Palladio built in and around Vicenza, the Villa Capra had a tremendous influence on European architecture for its use of the components of the Classical orders in a new design. The building is square, with a portico on each side and a central domed hall. For reasons of economy, the villa is built in brick, rendered with stucco to emulate stone.
Left *Palazzo Capitanio*, Vicenza, Italy (1571, Andrea Palladio). The lower storey is fortified and the columns are extended to give the building unity. The *piano nobile* – the first floor of Italian palaces – contains the main social apartments. The publication of Palladio's book in 1570, *I quattro libri dell' Architettura*, had widespread influence on European architectural style.

habitually used as a dressing material and not in a strictly functional sense. It was frequently used simply as ornamental infill, such as on the main facade of Santa Maria Novella in Florence (1456-70) which was designed by Leon Battista Alberti (1404-72). Stone facings were added to walls frequently built of nothing more than rubble; exceptions were the Palazzo Riccardi (1444) by Michelozzi (1396-1472) and the Palazzo Rucellai (1466) by Alberti. In Palazzo Ricardi, the detail of stone is given exaggerated definition to illustrate the differences between the much fortified wall of the ground floor, the public floor, and the open formal rooms on the first floor or piano nobile. Although the ultimate Renaissance architect, Andrea Palladio (1508-80) used the motifs of stonework, his buildings were mainly built of stucco. As with late Gothic architecture, the designs of the Renaissance became over-developed, eventually adopting forms that were later known as Baroque.

Neo-Classic and Neo-Gothic Revivals

After the Renaissance broke up in Baroque extravaganza, architecture looked back to history for guidance. There followed a complete absence of originality, while architecture devoted itself to a reiteration of historical styles. From Greek and Gothic stone building stemmed two quite distinct types of architectural expression. It became a matter of taste as to which style was selected for a particular design. Having made the choice, architects used either style, or in some cases both styles, to design buildings expressing their own individuality.

John Nash (1752-1835), James Watt (1746-1813) and A.W.N. Pugin (1812-52) were the progenitors of the Neo-Gothic style. In the hands of Pugin, the nineteenth-century architect who worked with Sir Charles Barry (1795-1860) on the competition-winning design for the rebuilding of the Palace of Westminster, stone was actually used as a medium of construction. Pugin pursued a particularly rigorous and academic course and paid great attention to what he considered to be a proper use of the material. However with the emergence of iron, steel and concrete, stone became used less and less for the bones of the building and became simply a clothing material, a skin by which the importance of the building was expressed. With scholarly detailing, it is difficult to detect whether a building is actually constructed from stone or whether a stone skin has been applied.

Above *Glyptotek*, Munich (Leopold von Klenze, 1784–1864). Von Klenze and K.F. von Schinkel were two German architects of the late eighteenth century who used the classical language in the "antiquarian" movement, a revival of Greek style which lent importance to significant buildings of state.

Right The classical language was also used to furnish interiors, as in the Signet Library, Edinburgh. Over the centuries, the Classical orders have been used and reused to suggest authority and permanence.

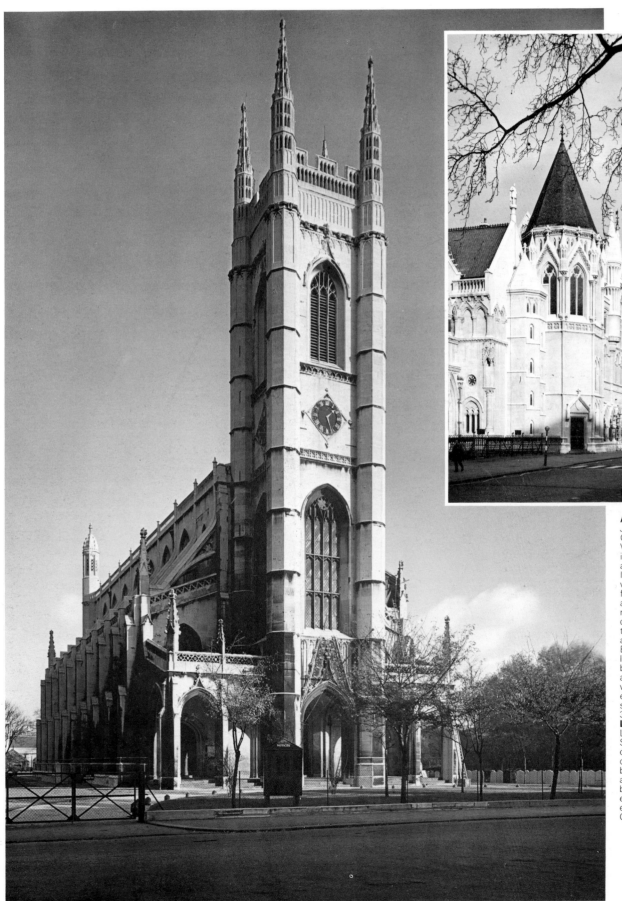

Above *Royal Courts of Justice*, London (1871–82, G.E. Street). Architects in Victorian England took inspiration from Gothic architecture, particularly its Italian form. This revival was bound up with a taste for the romantic and antiquarian, and given moral force by Pugin, who declared that Gothic was the only appropriate architecture for "Christain Englishmen". One of the last High Victorian Gothic buildings, the Courts show a romantic extravagance which belie official economies. The architect is said to have made over 3,000 drawings himself.
Left *St. Luke*, Chelsea, London (1820–4, James Savage). An early example of Gothic revivalism, this church has flying buttresses spanning the aisles. Not only churches, but town halls, colleges and even railway stations were executed in versions of the Gothic style.

Art Nouveau

The Arts and Crafts Movement in Britain towards the end of the nineteenth century was a signal to abandon the historical approach. The renewed interest in natural materials did not lead to a complete regeneration of stone buildings, but instead the use of stone became abbreviated and symbolic. Stone was used for quoins (cornerstones),lintels and keystones in compositions which were finished in cement render.

At the same time, several distinct schools of design appeared in Europe which led to an original and unexpected use of stone. This new design loosely fell under the general label of Art Nouveau, a northern European style of which the strongest strain was found in Brussels, often described as the home of Art Nouveau. In Art Nouveau building, stone was used in an almost organic way, dissolving the conventional organization of structure that lay behind. Much as in a Chippendale chair, the joints in the stonework were played down, making stone appear to flow continuously like plastic.

Antoni Gaudi (1865-1934), a totally original architect, built a number of exceptional buildings in Barcelona between 1880 and 1910. His apartment building, Casa Mila, looks like it has been moulded in wet clay, while his design for the incomplete cathedral, Segrada Familia, anticipates the Expressionists who were to emerge in Europe as a limb of the Modern Movement.

Charles Rennie Mackintosh (1868-1928) had a short active life as a practising architect. He built few buildings, but his most famous, the Glasgow School of Art (1897-1909), displays an assured originality in the detailing of stone. The main entrance facade has a large scale asymmetry in its regular bays. The stone could be read as masonry – a wall punctured with windows – or could be covering a framed structure lying behind. The sides and rear of the building have few windows, by contrast, and are more solid.

In Brussels, Josef Hoffman, the leading architect of the Sezessione Movement built a luxurious palace for the Stocklet family (1905-11) which was faced in marble. The bird's beak corners are a clear illustration of stone being used as a veneer only. Hoffman's contemporary in Vienna, Otto Wagner (1841-1918), a prolific architect who completed many public works for the city of Vienna, built the Post Office Savings Bank there in 1906. Here the use of stone as a veneer is expressed by the aluminium stud bolts that hold the stone panels in place. Vienna became the home of a new kind of expression in the use of stone. Without masquerading as structure, the stone is expressly treated as a veneer.

Left *School of Art*, Glasgow (1897–1909, Charles Rennie Mackintosh). In a restrained British version of Art Nouveau, Mackintosh's work shows a highly original fusion of the Aesthetic Movement and the Arts and Crafts Movement. His most notable building, the School of Art uses stone in two completely different ways. Granite facing on the northwest flank suggests traditional Scottish architecture and is used as a plain, functional veneer.

4 *Originality in stone*
The work of the Spanish
architect Antoni Gaudi
displays an eccentric,
fantastic use of stone that
anticipates the organic
qualities of concrete and
plastic. Gaudi was
profoundly religious,
inspired by the forces of
nature and by the Middle
Ages. Although his style
can be seen as the most
dramatic form of Art
Nouveau, its eerie and
sinuous imagery is more a
unique expression of his
artistic genius.
1. Casa Mila, Barcelona
(1905–10). Also known as
"La Pedrera", this
apartment building has a
rippling stone facade which
gives the impression of
molten lava. Inside, the plan
is irregular; no two rooms
are alike and all are
many-sided and without
right-angles. The balconies
are ironwork and spiky in
form; the windows have
rounded corners.
2. Casa Battló, Barcelona
(1905–7). The sinuous
shape of the stone
dressings on the lower part
of the building is repeated
in the curved metal
balustrades. Around the
windows are pieces of
coloured glass embedded
in the wall.
*3, 4. The Church of Segrada
Familia*, Barcelona. Gaudi
began work on this church
in 1884, but it is still
unfinished. When he
started, his style was still
eccentric Gothic, but as
building progressed, the
forms became more surreal
and unorthodox. The
stonework displays a soft
quality and is formed into
complex naturalistic
ornament. Pieces of broken
ceramic stud the tops of the
four openwork spires.
Gaudi worked on the site
himself, supervising his
builders and devising
solutions as the need
arose.

Modern Applications

Apart from a few examples, there were not many occasions when stone was used within the Modern Movement, the dominant architectural style of the 1930s. One such use was in the Italian Fascist Party headquarters in Como in 1936 by Guiseppe Terragni (1904-1942). Only on close examination does the marble veneer become legible. The severe architecture of the building has an ageless precision, a reminder that stone has been part of construction in Italy for 2,000 years.

Frank Lloyd Wright (1867-1959), Le Corbusier (1887-1965) and Mies van der Rohe (1886-1969) have all made use of stone. In 1936, Le Corbusier constructed Maison aux Mathes, a simple house using stone in orthodox uninterrupted panels.

The vertical elements of the Kaufmann house (1936) by Frank Lloyd Wright are clad in stone. In both these instances, the stone is calculated to add a rustic look, appropriate to the particular context. In 1929, Mies van der Rohe was commissioned to design the German Pavilion for the 1929 Barcelona World Fair at very short notice. The height of the building was determined by the block of onyx that the architect discovered and decided to use. The panels of highly polished onyx were treated as screens or partitions and not as structural members, which were made of steel.

The decline of the use of stone as a basic material in the twentieth century has mainly been due to economics, and partly due to a shift in human values. Over the years, there have been few substantial improvements in quarrying, transporting, working and laying; stone has remained a labour-intensive material the use of which only flourished when manpower was cheap and plentiful. At the same time, greater equality in society has meant that the authoritarian imagery of stone has less currency in modern architecture.

It is interesting to note, however, that while stone is no longer a principal building material, existing examples of stone architecture are the focus of increasing attention. Stone structures, however modest, are being preserved, renovated and reconstructed. In a changing world, stone's enduring qualities and its traditional association with higher ideals provide a welcome reassurance.

Above *Casa del Popolo*, Como, Italy (1932–6, Guiseppe Terragni). In stark contrast to the vulgar pomposity of Mussolini's Fascist architecture, this headquarters for the Italian Fascist Party displays a purity and severity of line and form which is derived from the Modern Movement. Although built of reinforced concrete, a marble veneer has been applied. The four facades are unsymmetrical and each one is different.

Above, left and below *The Stocklet House*, Brussels, Belgium (1905–11, Josef Hoffman). This opulent mansion shows a lavish use of marble as a veneer, both internally and externally. The design is asymmetrical with neat rectangular windows emphasized by bands of terracotta decoration (*below*). Unlike at the Casa del Popolo, the stone is treated to appear a veneer, not just as a functional facing to the structural material.

Timber

Right Firs, which are softwoods, occur in forests in central and eastern Asia, central and southern Europe and in North America. Other commercial softwoods include pine, cedar, cypress, larch, spruce, redwood, sequoia, hemlock and yew.
Far right This 150-year-old oak was felled in the New Forest, Hampshire, where some of the best oak ever was grown. Other commercial hardwoods include maple, alder, teak, birch, boxwood, rosewood, ebony, walnut, beech, ash, mahogany, poplar and pear. White oak is still an important structural wood.

Timber is one of the most important natural building materials. Timber is self-renewing, and trees have always exerted significant effects on people and the environment.

Timber's reputation for impermanence, compared with other materials, is not entirely justified, particularly where hardwood is concerned. In any case, this attribute has never stifled the imagination or enthusiasm of builders. It has been argued that the barbaric northern peoples developed an architectural tradition in timber which was perhaps earlier than, and just as valid as the accepted Graeco-Roman prototypes. Although timber has none of the monumental associations of materials such as stone, when pure timber structures express the intentions of the designer, function well and reflect contemporary culture, they merit the same consideration

as buildings executed in other materials. Historically, Europe has produced the best and most varied examples of timber building, and there is evidence that another phase of wood architecture is now beginning.

Since the immediate postwar years, timber has gradually become more accepted, particularly by organizations which finance building. In fact, timber has become so popular worldwide that the earth's forests are currently disappearing at the rate of 40 million acres per annum, resulting in irreversible changes to the subtle ecosystems which tree growth has supported for thousands of years.

Timber is an essential component of buildings constructed in all other materials – generally, as scaffolding or levers, or, specifically, as centering for masonry, formwork and lining for concrete, or fixings

for steelwork. Its historical role in the construction of roofs (including stone vaults and domes) is unique, while in the past it has been extensively used as piles for foundations on unstable ground.

Most everyday buildings built in other materials could be copied entirely in timber, but the opposite is certainly not true. The chief reason for this is that the fibrous nature of wood, combined with the use of shaped and pegged joints, enable it to accommodate both linear and rotational tension in structures.

The comparative lightness of timber means that it has been used in the earliest forms of mobile constructions – wagons, ships and caravans – contributing to exploration and colonization. Today, whole townships are often prefabricated, mainly in timber, in one country and shipped to another for erection.

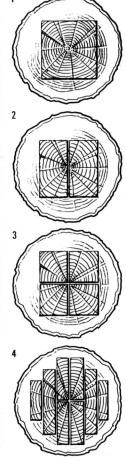

Lowgrade timber or waste (chips and sawdust, for instance) can be used to make all sorts of by-products, from insulation boards to pit-props, while the material itself has very good thermal insulation properties. Although timber is extremely combustible, its structural performance in fires is by no means as bad as is often thought. Timber does not distort like steel and, when used in large sections, surface charring tends to form fire protection.

The preparation of material and assembly of members by a carpenter (or wright) to form a building is called "carpentry", as distinct from "joinery", which is the fitting and finishing of the timber elements within the structure. It is interesting to observe that there is little in the form of written craft instruction available to us today which accurately describes the working methods of the period between the thirteenth and eighteenth centuries when the craft tradition was at its peak. Paradoxically, as the pure craft declined and became debased at the end of the seventeenth century by the acceptance of the lower-pitched Renaissance roof forms and the use of iron bolts and straps, there followed a proliferation of textbooks which, although comprehensive from a contemporary standpoint, pay no more than lip service to the craft tradition. The preface from *The Carpenter and Joiners Assistant* published in the 1800s reads:

> The Framing of Timber for structural purposes may be regarded both as a mechanical and as a liberal art. As a mechanical art, it embraces the knowledge of the various ways of executing different works, of the process of fashioning timber, of the tools which have to be used, and the manner of handling them. As a liberal art, it includes a knowledge of geometry, of the principles of mechanics, of the nature and strength of the material, and its behaviour under the strains to which it is subjected.

This grand description seems to imply dissatisfaction with the status of the carpenter and indicates an attempt to redefine his role in the context of the artistic and engineering achievements of the period. The unfortunate carpenter, for all his skill, seems to have been condemned to second place since the earliest times when, arguably, he was initiated by the stonemason into the work of church building, learning only by degrees the special qualities of the more elastic wood.

The Material

Timber from broad leaf or deciduous trees is called "hardwood", while conifers produce "softwood". Although it is true that hardwoods are generally harder than softwoods, there are exceptions to this rule.

Above *Methods of conversion* The carpenter was traditionally responsible for converting whole logs into beams as well as fitting the beams together in a frame. Different saw cuts used in timber conversion include: boxed heart (*1*), halved (*2*), quartered (*3*), and slabbed (*4*).
Left At this sawmill in Staffordshire, a metal wedge is being driven into a log so that the cut timber is held apart and the saw does not bind.

Wood, like all plant material, is cellular and the disposition of these cells produces the characteristic "grain" or pattern on the cut surfaces. Knots are a familiar feature of much timber, and are produced by the embedding of a portion of a branch.

The annular band of wood nearest the bark is called the sapwood. It is just as strong as the heartwood, or main core of the trunk, but is particularly prone to attack by insects and fungi.

The term "conversion" is used to mean the cutting up of a log into sawn timber. The method used has a bearing upon the resultant grain pattern. Traditionally, a log was converted over a sawpit by two men operating a two-handed saw. One man (the sawyer) stood on the log and pushed the saw down while the other (the "underdog") pulled and pushed from below in a continuous rain of sawdust. Today, huge machines achieve in minutes what would have taken the sawyer and his mate a week.

Seasoning is the process of drying the natural moisture out of the timber, so that it will relate properly to the humidity condition of its ultimate use without shrinking or warping. It is achieved by air-seasoning naturally in some form of open-sided structure, or by artificially drying in an oven or kiln. Modern kilns are so designed that an accurate control of moisture is achieved.

Types of Timber

The earliest use of timber for building did not depend upon fitness for purpose – more upon what came to hand as forest was cleared and rudimentary hutted encampments were constructed. The extent to which timber was adopted as a structural material relied upon availability. In the limitless pine forests of Russia, for instance, everything was built in timber and wood was used extravagantly. Further south, where hardwood trees take longer to mature, management policies have always been implemented to maintain continuity and stability. At least as far back as Anglo-Saxon times in Britain, the controlling processes of "coppicing" and wood pasture or "pollarding" are known to have been employed.

In the British Isles, oak became generally accepted as the most important timber because of its strength, resistance to decay and, possibly most importantly, its ability to be "cleft" – run from end to end in a controlled way when split with beetle and wedge, thus avoiding the laborious process of conversion over the sawpit. As tools improved, this characteristic became less important at conversion stage, but it greatly aided the forming of the complex joints of the medieval period.

The selection of trees for conversion demands a great deal of skill and experience to ensure that the resulting timber is top quality. For example, in luxuriant

Above *Westminster Hall*, hammerbeam roof (1397–99). In the medieval period, carpenters achieved a masterful understanding of both the structural and aesthetic potential of timber construction. The hammerbeam roof at Westminster Hall has arched ribs which spring from the wall to a collarpiece. This gives additional rigidity to the structure and reflects the skill of the master carpenter who built it, Hugh Herland.

Above right This seventh/eighth century merchantman ship of Nordic origin bears some similarity in appearance to the hammerbeam roofs of traditional English timber construction. While the timber roof appears light and airy, the open wooded hull of this boat provides space for cargo and room for eight oarsmen. A long steering oar was used as a rudder on the righthand side of the boat (hence the term "steerboard" or "starboard").

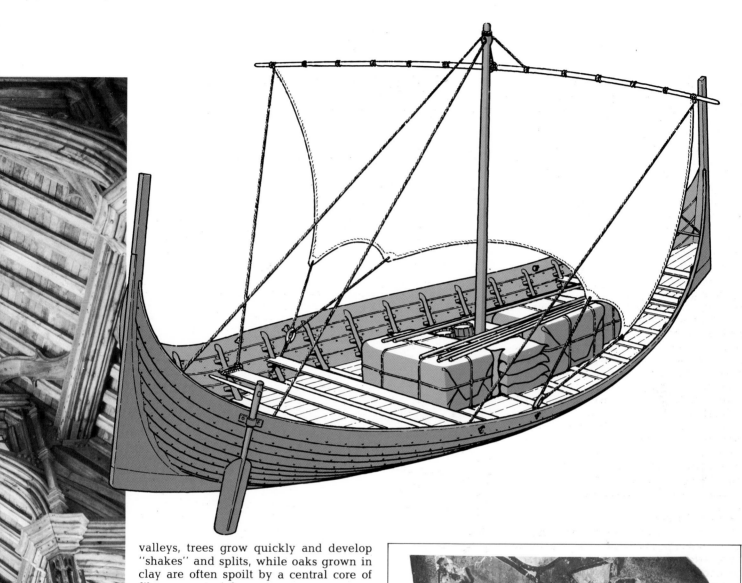

valleys, trees grow quickly and develop "shakes" and splits, while oaks grown in clay are often spoilt by a central core of fibrous material.

Other timbers used in early European building were elm (most common), sweet chestnut, ash and black poplar, while teak and cedar were common in the East. It must be remembered, however, that broad-leaved trees do not extend north-wards above a certain climatic frontier and that beyond this, pine and fir predominate. The difference in the character and length of the resultant timber has an effect on the architecture. (Compare the post-and-beam English medieval halls and church roofs in oak, with the largely softwood Norwegian mast churches). It is also reasonable to assume that many early examples of soft-wood structures have perished. The oak barley barn at Cressing, England dates from 1200, but few of the hundreds of churches known to exist in eastern Europe are more than 300 years old.

Timber was often reused in successive rebuilding of structures, and new timber of any sort would generally have been what was left after other tradesmen such as the wheelwright and cooper had had first choice. This is particularly significant since the incorporation of only one piece of poor timber in a vital place could reduce the useful life of a structure by many years.

This tomb painting from Egypt, Middle Kingdom dynasties (1991-1633 B.C.), illustrates a carpenter at work using sophisticated tools. Scholars of that period believed craftsmen to have more power than their richer patrons, because of their ability to handle materials and apply their skills productively.

Dating Timber Buildings

Before early buildings from different cultures can be compared, a system of accurately dating timber is necessary. The fact that trees grown in temperate situations, when cut through the trunk, display annual growth-rings is well known. Simply counting them is a good indication of the age of the tree. However, for all sorts of reasons, the actual growth patterns vary with each year and the conditions encountered. It follows that these growth-ring variations will occur in a different position in trees of differing ages. By taking trees of very long lifespan and overlapping them, a fairly accurate chronology can be established. (The best example is the bristlecone pine from the Californian mountains which lives some 6,000 years).

The modern atomic laboratory has provided a method of verifying this science of dendrochronology by the use of radiocarbon, or carbon 14 as it is called. By radiocarbon dating growth rings several thousand years old, crosschecks can be made which form a basis for dating all

Right *Stave Church,* Borgund, Norway (1150). Less than 10 stave churches remain and most of these have been reconstructed. Built entirely of softwood, these timber cathedrals were supported with four big posts. Openings were small, giving a dark, mystic atmosphere to the interiors and incidentally providing the temperature control necessary for the preservation of the wood. During the Lutheran movement larger holes were made to let more light in and dispense with the mystic associations. These alterations were responsible for the deterioration of many stave churches. The detail *(below)* shows the arcade running around the perimeter of the interior.

Above This sixteenth-century Japanese screen shows a carpenter at work using an adze, the traditional wood-shaping tool worldwide. Strangely, in Britain, the axe was used for this purpose.

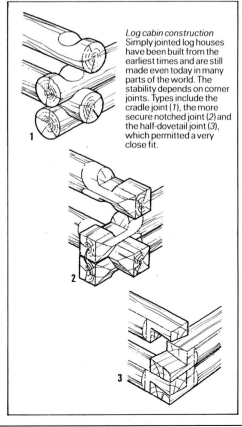

Log cabin construction Simply jointed log houses have been built from the earliest times and are still made even today in many parts of the world. The stability depends on corner joints. Types include the cradle joint (*1*), the more secure notched joint (*2*) and the half-dovetail joint (*3*), which permitted a very close fit.

surviving timber buildings. However, the amount of radiocarbon in the earth's atmosphere fluctuates. Prior to 2000 B.C. there was much more radiocarbon than there is today, so that dating of timber fragments from before then is inaccurate.

A more precise method of dating the buildings of the last thousand years is by typological evolution. Much valuable work has been done on the subject by the timber expert, Cecil Hewett, in his study of timber buildings in Essex. His research throws up a good case for dating by joints – particularly "scarf" joints, since this joint alone enables long members to be made from two or more pieces. Joints were developed and refined over long periods of time but were developed separately, and therefore attained perfection at different dates. For instance, a building found to have perfect floor joist joints may well have defective scarf joints, since scarf joints had begun to deteriorate in design long before timber floors evolved.

Prior to the recent invention of preservatives, softwood structures, such as the churches of northern Russia or Poland, may well have needed such frequent and extensive repair that for all practical purposes they must be considered to have been rebuilt.

Building Techniques

Historical Methods

It is not possible to compile a straightforward chronological list of building techniques, nor is it easy to trace the development of styles throughout the forest areas, since the methods varied with the type and availability of suitable timber. The main historical methods are as follows:

Solid timber construction This method involves building with logs set close together and is found generally in eastern Europe where the vast forests could support the extravagance. It is sometimes referred to as "blockwork" and the method has continued to the present day in Russia, Finland and the alpine areas. This "logcabin" technique involves horizontal members interlocked at corners by a variety of jointing methods. Shapes are achieved by a progressive lengthening or shortening of the logs.

Half-timber construction This is a framework of structural timber (usually hardwood) infilled with lathing or other materials. It was almost always prefabricated and assembled in sections on the ground, giving rise to the various forms of carpenter's marks found on framed structures. Historically, it attained its greatest sophistication in the northern countries of western Europe and subsequently developed in North America and Scandinavia to become the "balloon" or "platform" framing.

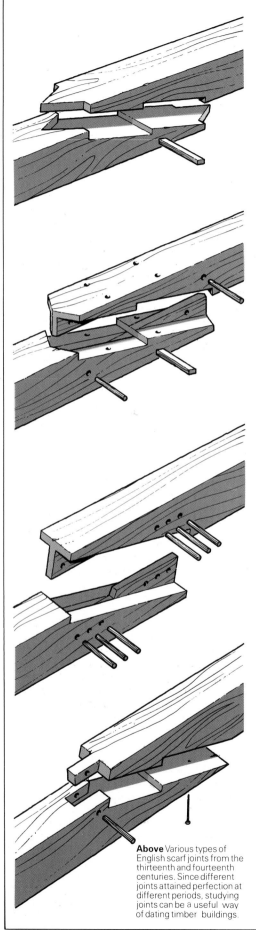

Above Various types of English scarf joints from the thirteenth and fourteenth centuries. Since different joints attained perfection at different periods, studying joints can be a useful way of dating timber buildings.

Mast or stave work is a particular style apparent in the churches of Norway, which has little evolutionary connection with solid or half-timber construction.

The post-and-beam or "trabeated" style found its best expression in China and Japan, having travelled with Buddhism from India. This method shares with mast work the principle of entirely non-load-bearing walls.

Modern Methods

Modern timber-framed structures are assembled from standardized softwood components. In turn, these rely on the careful selection of material which has been graded for stress, according to its particular use within the finished building.

The walls are framed panels formed of studs and plates. Diagonal bracing in the traditional manner is not usually employed unless it is surface-fixed within the cavity between the two panels of a composite wall; racking is more usually resisted by plywood sheathing nailed to the faces of the studs and in some cases even the effect of the plasterboard lining is taken into account in calculations. Fire prevention and noise control are achieved by isolating the main structural elements from each other where individual houses abut. In Britain, a standard section of $1\frac{1}{2}$ x 4 inches (38 x 98mm) is used for all domestic applications except floor joists – extra loads such as corners and lintel bearings are formed by doubling or tripling the studs. In Scandinavia, however, thicker members are used to contain more insulation.

Externally, the panel walls are finished either directly with vertical or horizontal boards, tile hanging or rendering; or with an independent brick skin which is tied back to the framing at intervals. The entire panel structure is usually covered by a roof system of individual trussed rafters. These are formed of very light sections, of constant thickness but varying depth, joined by metal nail-plates. The trusses are

Carpenters' marks
Because timber was cut and assembled into frames on the ground, later to be transported to a site for erection, carpenters needed a way of identifying timber members and coordinating them in the structure. Special marks – a numbering system – identified which side of a timber was the face, which way up it went and where it fitted in the frame. Marks were also a way of identifying which timber-yard the wood came from. Some carpenters' marks were a crude form of Roman numerals; others were more elaborate. They would be cut into the wood with the tools the carpenter was using at the time.

designed, cut and assembled by computer-controlled machinery.

All of the following methods rely on the evenly spread loads of cellular plans to achieve the stability and strength of the completed structure. Very little progress has been made in the design of quality mass-produced timber housing systems which permit total flexibility of internal arrangement and fenestration.

The four basic methods of contemporary timber building are as follows:

Stick construction is used mainly in North America, Scandinavia and Japan. Precut timber elements are delivered to the site and assembled. In Britain, individual builders with small sites use this method, as do self-build groups. One of the great exponents of this method is the architect Walter Segal who, over the last 20 years, has been one of the most enthusiastic protagonists of timber-framed housing. Segal has come to terms with the increasing strictures of building control and regulations and produced a series of delightfully designed houses with a Japanese flavour, which celebrate the authentic use of timber and achieve economy by simple, efficient structure and detail.

Balloon frame construction In this method, the external wall panels are fabricated in various widths, but extend to two storeys in height and are therefore erected in one operation, so that the intermediate floors are suspended from the full height studs. The size of the panels restricts flexibility and manoeuvrability.

Platform frame construction This is the predominant method of timber-frame construction in Britain. Wall panels are fabricated (usually in the factory) in storey heights and floors are then constructed on top of ground floor wall panels, acting as a permanent base for the upper wall panels.

The panels are of a size which can be easily placed into position. The flexibility of this method allows freedom of design with effective and speedy construction.

Many English new towns have recently used this method of construction for their large low-rise housing programmes. Basildon, Milton Keynes, Northampton, Peterborough, Warrington and the Midland Housing Consortium have all built schemes of this type.

Volumetric construction This method entails the fabrication of entire buildings or parts of buildings in the factory and their subsequent transportation, in a virtually finished state, to the site for erection on prepared foundations. Normal preparation includes sanitary fittings, pre-plumbing, wiring and decoration. This type of construction can ensure rapid provision of very cheap houses, but the economic necessity for rigorous standardization, together with limitations on size of units for transportation can constrict the architect a great deal.

Development and Application

The Chinese Tradition

The wood building tradition in China is as old as that anywhere in the world, but it displays a remarkable conservatism in technique and plan. Virtually all building is straightforward post-and-beam construction with non-load-bearing walls. Houses, palaces and temples from 200 B.C. to the seventeenth century were built to a similar basic plan and the hierarchical spatial arrangement was even scaled up to form the basis of city layouts.

Despite the fact that brick construction was quite advanced in China by the fourteenth century, a distinct preference for timber prevailed. This might be due to timber's comparatively high resistance to the effect of earthquakes, although it is equally likely that the choice was influenced by the ease with which the characteristic screens and carvings could be incorporated into structures. Much of the peripheral and internal subdivision of buildings took the form of timber lattices in various shapes, together with lacquerwork scenes and panels, which presumably evolved from applied coloured protection to the underlying wood.

Although the oldest surviving Chinese building dates from the T'ang Dynasty (A.D. 857), there are sufficient examples of illustrations and models of buildings on burial ceramics for us to have a clear idea of the buildings of much earlier periods. The importance of the roof is emphasized by the Chinese vocabulary. There is no word for room, but *jian* is used instead, meaning the space between roof beams. The common description of a building as, say, three *jian* or five *jian* describes its extent but gives no indication of its actual use or internal organization. In architectural terms, the overall Chinese approach to building is much more intellectually complex than the Western approach and the effect of orientation, gardens, nature and magical

Above Red, green and blue are the traditional colours used in the decoration on Chinese buildings. Here a restorer repaints motifs in the Summer Palace, near Peking.
Right This pavilion at the Summer Palace demonstrates the essential components of Chinese timber architecture, a tradition which has remained virtually unaltered for 1,000 years. Formal elaboration on a simple theme characterizes this tradition, not the development of distinct architectural styles familiar in the West.

Below In Chinese roof construction, beams decreasing in length were raised on top of one another and separated by struts. By increasing the number of pillars, the building could be made wider.

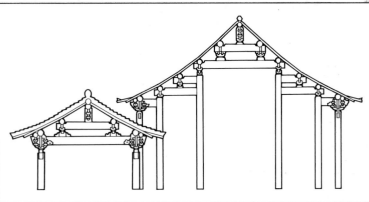

influences on siting serves to illustrate this.

The only significant outside influence on Chinese culture was Indian Buddhism. This led to a greater awareness of the idea of permanence and to the development of the pagoda and *pai-lou* (memorials) — universally recognized indigenous forms which date from the T'ang period. The earliest examples were distinguished by their delicate woodwork and pronounced roof curvature. Later examples were larger and heavier-looking. Decoration increased, but the visual and intellectual complexity never extended into the structural design, which adhered chiefly to

simple static principles for a thousand years.

Japanese Timber Building

The earliest timber dwellings in Japan were built by the Jomon people from about 8000 B.C. to 500 B.C. and had much in common with those of the Western Iron Age. The Iron Age in Japan, called the Yayoi era, came later. Although structural form continued in much the same way, the method of assembly became quite sophisticated — the use of mortice and tenon joints and "sleeper" foundations were common. Surprisingly, there was no progress in the

Above The Summer Palace complex shows the importance of the interrelationship between structural principles and nature. The Chinese approach to building relied heavily on notions of siting, the creation of gardens, both formal and informal, and the importance of magic and philosophy. The apparently random groups of buildings belie this complex, intellectual consideration.

Above *Golden Pavilion, Kinkaku-ji, Japan* (c. 1600). This garden pavilion was originally covered with gold and silver leaf and displays a mixture of styles. Japanese roofs are generally lighter and more subtle than their Chinese counterparts.

Right This tea-house at Katsura – the "Pine Lute" Pavilion – was built in the mid-Edo period and has door panels by Kano Tan-yu (1641). Determined exclusively by the tea-drinking ritual, a ceremony of artistic appreciation, tea-houses were planned around a mat module and set in pleasure gardens decorated with lanterns and landscaped trees. The combination of formal planning and integration with a natural setting had an enormous effect on many modern architects, notably Frank Lloyd Wright.

development of the trussed rafter form of roof and, as on the mainland, trabeated forms dominated.

By 600 A.D., Buddhism was well established and influenced a new approach to building. The pagoda became a firmly established form and its monumental importance was increased by the addition of a hall to house golden images. This "Golden Hall" was usually linked by roofed walkways to the other buildings in the group and was raised on a stone plinth with a rammed-earth floor.

At Horiuji, built in about A.D. 700, the overall construction is complicated but still essentially trabeated, and the effect stems from a kind of trial-and-error attitude to structural design. In this hall, the cantilever rafter was inadequate to carry the projecting upper eaves and a dragon-encircled post was introduced at each corner as a remedy. This persisted in future buildings as a characteristic feature. By A.D. 760 (towards the end of the Nara period), the system had been refined to resolve general weaknesses in stability and, although much modified, the Golden Hall at Toshodai-ji is a great improvement on earlier examples.

In the Heian period, as a result of political and religious change, temples were built away from the cities. The five-storey pagoda raised around a central column at Diago dates from the tenth century and is representative of the period. The three-

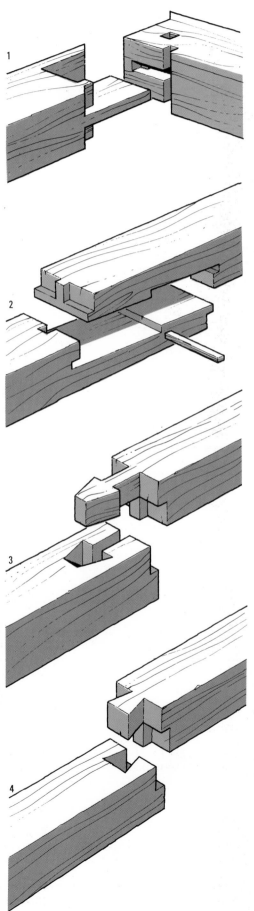

Left Joints in Japanese timber buildings are very static compared with European joints, and reflect the nature of Japanese structures. These joints, which did not have to withstand large movement or bending, were developed in the fourteenth century: arigake corner joint (*1*), kanawa-tsugi column joint (*2*), kama-tsugi joint (*3*) and ari-tsugi joint (*4*).

Above and top *Kendo Hall*, Horiuji Temple (A.D. 607). This is the oldest Buddhist temple in Japan and the oldest timber building in the world. A dragon-encircled post was introduced at each corner of the roof when it was found that the cantilever beam could not carry the projecting upper eaves. This feature persisted in later buildings, even though it was not structurally necessary.

stage timber brackets are not at all flamboyant, but dominate the external appearance in a very controlled and logical way.

The Kamakura period, from the twelfth to fourteenth centuries, saw further mainland influence in the establishment of the monuments of the Zen sect. The Engaku-ji Relic Hall is formed with heavier columns, assisted by intermediate upright members and thus achieves a considerable increase in span, while another example, the Golden Pavilion at Kinkaku-ji (c.1600) displays a peculiar mixtures of styles. At the end of this period were built the first examples of domestic buildings designed around the tea-drinking ceremony, and incorporating the "mat-module" which survives to the present day.

The tea house at Katsura epitomizes the fastidiousness of the tea-drinking ritual and its setting. The structure is perfectly coordinated with the requirements of the ritual and the plain plastered walls and natural timber columns are arranged with artistic skill. The only disappointing feature is the roof, which remains nothing more than a whimsical cover.

This peculiar amalgam of somewhat pragmatic and idealistic architecture reached its climax in the Edo period. City dwellings had simple elevations which belied the internal complexity of a plan derived entirely from the patterns of the formal rice matting, boarded floors and paper screens of the tea ritual.

Left *Pagoda*, Horiuji Temple (A.D. 607). Most pagodas are square and five storeys high. This example, thought to be the oldest still in existence, is supported by a massive central post, 100 feet (30m) high and 3 feet (1m) square at the base. Pagodas are usually supported in this way to provide some earthquake resistance. The top of this pagoda is decorated with metal rings and bells.

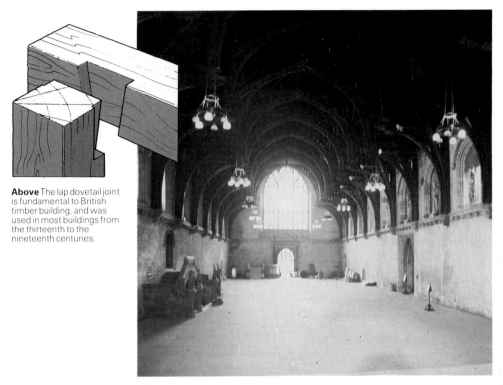

Above The lap dovetail joint is fundamental to British timber building, and was used in most buildings from the thirteenth to the nineteenth centuries.

Above *Westminster Hall* (1397-99). Like many English medieval timber constructions, the hammerbeam roof of Westminster Hall, London, was prefabricated away from the site. This roof was made at Farnham in Surrey and brought up to London on a barge. Carpenters' marks were vital at the reassembly stage.

Left This parish church at Greensted, Essex, has been dated A.D. 845. Originally a temporary building put up to house the body of St. Edmund on its way to a burial place at Bury St. Edmund's, the roof was later replaced and reconstruction carried out. The stave walls and gable ends remain of the original shrine, with corner joints of log cabin construction. It is thought that many of the logs used in the vertical staving may have come from the same 600-year-old oak.

British Timber Building

The timber building tradition in Britain can be used as a yardstick by which to measure and compare the achievements, in Western architectural terms, of other regions. This is chiefly due to the fact that the quality, antiquity, progressive development and variety of application of surviving buildings is greater in Britain than anywhere else: only in Norway are there a few complete examples which are older.

The timber building tradition in Britain was conceived during what is loosely referred to as the Anglo-Saxon period. This was a time of widespread upheaval which extended from the end of the Iron Age, through the Roman occupation (which had surprisingly little lasting influence on building) to the tenth century, by which time the splendid wooden buildings of England had few rivals in Europe and maybe even in the world.

The first real structures were circular huts with sunken floors, made of poles set in the ground and joined by a sort of ring beam to carry the rafters of a thatched roof. They exist today as archaeological remains only, (for example, Iron Age Farm, Little Woodbury) but are the forebears of the great British rafter tradition.

The increasing strife prior to the Roman invasions led to the evolution of more sophisticated building types, namely the hill fort, and "broch" or fortified tower – both dependent on timber for their construction. The Anglo-Saxon community was essentially a rural one and it was to these fortified centres that the population withdrew in times of danger. The arrival of the Romans saw the introduction of new economic and social systems, but failed to change the style of building, which remained predominantly timber after their departure.

Archaeological evidence is the only means of determining the size and form of the timber buildings of the post-Roman period, but excavations of royal sites at Yeavering and Cheddar give a fairly accurate picture of the structure of the barn-like "long houses" and aisled halls of the wealthy landowners prior to the Norman Conquest. Although the aisled halls of the late Saxons are often stated as having their origins on the European mainland, evidence suggests that the 89-foot (27 m) long aisled hall at Yeavering is a regional type. Its walls were built of squared timbers set upright in a foundation trench with no sill or sleeper beams – closely related structures are known to have existed in the Northumbrian region which date from a period when this area was controlled by the Celts. Certainly the Anglo-Saxons introduced the "ground-sill", or wall plate, to Britain and it may have been their shipwrights who first taught the native wrights how to step a mast on a keel, thus providing a sound and lasting foundation for a house. (Parallels are often drawn between the two crafts, and this is not unreasonable given the maritime traditions of the people involved.)

Only one wooden church survives from this period, and it is in a mutilated state. It is at Greensted in Essex and is distinguished by its walls of ancient timbers placed vertically side by side. These "stave-walls" are a feature of the richly decorated mast-churches of Norway.

The Norman Conquest brought the influence of Byzantium to Britain but the European tradition persisted in native timber structures. It is not generally realized that many of the motte and bailey castles of the early Normans were not the complicated stone structures usually associated with this period but often consisted of a wooden building atop a mound with a palisaded court. The carpenters' skills were still important for flooring and roofing the mighty stone keeps, which date from the time of the Crusades. There are remains of halls from the twelfth century – the Bishop's Palace at Farnham and the Bishop's Hall at Hereford are two examples – but little survives which can be ascribed to this period with any confidence.

The thirteenth century saw the last of the aisled halls, as stone succeeded timber. The carpenter was driven to apply even greater skill and ingenuity to roof the ever-increasing clear spans of cathedrals, parish churches and castle halls. The development of these magnificient roofs is well documented; more interesting is the role of the carpenter as designer and builder of complete structures. The transition in the design of large spaces from the aisled principle, through the hammerbeam variations to the base cruck, is a logical one, but studying the development of cellular structures shows the birth of a style of urban architecture whose elements have left an indelible mark on most of our old cities.

The carpenter really emerged again in the fourteenth century, when the embryonic middle class started to assert itself. Unable to afford the luxury of building in stone and hiring masons, this new class resorted to the cheaper and more readily available timber and the services of professional builders. These "yeomen", as the new class may be termed, embarked on a vast building programme which tested the village wrights to the limit of their craft. The wrights were forced to emulate the multistorey, rigid stone-built structures of the establishment. The only way this could be achieved was to develop methods of tying or "trussing" the rafters of the roof in such a way that they stiffened the stud frame wall panels, whose resistance to overturning was so much less than the stone walls of the great houses. The lap-dovetail tying joints of this period are probably the

finest of their type, and they were used at ends of buildings and at intermediate bays of 12 to 16 feet (3.5 to 5 m) depending upon the scale of the structure, where main posts occurred. At these bay points trusses were formed to tie and support pairs of larger rafters, so that longitudinal members could be carried, which in turn supported the smaller common rafters. The bay pattern was usually consistent through all floors of the building. The smaller rafters were set in pairs, joined at the top and about midway down their span, by a horizontal tying member called a collar. Longitudinally beneath this and on the centre line of the roof, ran a timber bearer which was supported on the midpoint of each tie beam by

a crown post – often carved and decorated and with a cluster of curved braces at its top to add further rigidity to the roof.

Floor joists were laid "flat-on" and it is often said that this fact, coupled with the application of the cantilever principle, led to the appearance of that most characteristic of Tudor features – the jetty. This was an essential feature of what is now called platform framing – or the framing of each storey separately and setting one on top of the other. By jettying certain parts of the building only, a great variation in elevational treatment could be obtained – for instance, the Kentish farmhouse style with its external curved braces. Elaborately carved oriel windows were introduced

Above and above right
The Barley Barn, Cressing Temple (1200). This barn survives intact, although three successive structural modifications can be identified. Study of these changes has contributed greatly to present-day knowledge of the development of medieval carpentry. The six transverse frames form a seven-bay structure, but past repairs have reduced the overall length of the original building by half a bay at each end.

beneath the overhangs, and roof-shapes were often deliberately complex.

To carry the jetty around an angle (perhaps at the corner of two streets), a diagonal beam was introduced across the corner bay and projected out over the top of a carved corner post (teazle post). This beam is known as a dragon beam. The name is thought to be a corruption of ''diagonal'', but it may also be the result of Japanese influence.

In fifteenth- and sixteenth-century Europe, as now, the tallest buildings generally were in the towns. Their similarity of form was to some extent controlled by limitation of plot size and the building constraints of the period. The ground floor

Above In southeastern England, crown post roofs were common in the medieval period. A tie beam supported a vertical post, the ''crown'' post, which in turn supported a ''collar-purlin'', thus strengthening the entire roof. Different bracing patterns were employed.

was usually partly open for use as a shop, while the merchant occupier and his family lived above. There were no models for the public buildings which this urban life demanded, so schools, assembly halls and inns took on similar form to domestic buildings. The inn, however, soon developed its own style as a direct result of the need for stabling: the double front with gated archway and internal courtyard is ubiquitous.

At the edges of towns where commercial change had made speculative development a viable proposition, rows of terrace houses appeared – sometimes a dozen or more in a row. The best examples are what would now be called "narrow-frontage" and, with a continuous jetty over the pavement, they have a simplicity of form and aesthetic discipline which is equalled only by the best practitioners today.

In the countryside, great variety is apparent in the wholly timber-framed manor houses of the sixteenth and seventeenth century. Their bay patterns were adjusted to absorb staircases and vast chimney stacks. Regrettably, this heralded the end of the craft tradition as a strong influence in design. With the familiarity of long use, joints declined in effectiveness and asymmetrical bay patterns often ceased at roof plate level, the whole structure being surmounted by an inferior roof. Whether this is due to the general decline in the state of carpentry, or whether the onset of the Renaissance is to blame, is not really clear. It is certain, however, that the brick and stone styles of the Mediterranean with their low pitched roofs, often hidden behind parapets, no longer required the same kind of carpentry – nor did they appear to offer the same kind of satisfaction for builders.

Native forms of wholly wooden buildings continued in barns, mills and sail lofts. Of these, water mills are the most striking. These buildings were essentially functional with little or no decoration, built of half-timber framing, but with larger members and closer bay patterns than houses to deal with the increased loads. Gravity was used for grain handling and the projecting hoist housing or "lucum" became the universally distinguishing feature of the superstructure.

Not until the end of the eighteenth century did the influence of a real attitude to design again become apparent in the construction of roofs. Engineering science was developing rapidly by then, and, as a result, timber roof-members were appropriately sized for their function, whether in tension or compression, and tension joints were strengthened (or wholly formed) by iron straps and shoes.

Right *Houchins Farmhouse*, Great Coggeshall, Essex. This three-storey structure, built in the seventeenth century, has a simplicity which belies the complexity of its close-timbered construction. Many of the members are elm, indicating that by this time oak had become too scarce or expensive for indiscriminate use.
Below and far right *Speke Hall* and *Little Moreton Hall*, Cheshire. These are popular examples of the ornamental studwork of the later sixteenth century, which appear somewhat vulgar compared with the restrained and orderly elevations of southeast England.

Above and left *Paycocke's House,* Essex. This simple town house shows many characteristic Tudor features: oriel windows, long-wall jettying, archway and applied decoration. It is also a good example of late fifteenth-century close studding. The detail (*left*) shows some of the decorative features around the archway.

North American Timber Building

In the seventeenth century, the last vestiges of the pure carpentry tradition were carried to America by the English colonists, where its regeneration was stimulated by contact with the skills of the many other immigrant nationalities. House plans originating in eastern England dominated, but a rapid transition took place from half-timber framing to lightweight framed panels, particularly on the eastern seaboard. Comparison with European examples is made easier by the sheer size of the country and the resulting isolation of various ethnic and cultural groups – the Puritan sects in Pennsylvania preserve to this day the structural forms and community involvement in building which originated in Europe.

In the northern half of the United States, both the size and the plan of most early houses are fairly uniform, and original East Anglian framing methods persisted. However, the wattle-and-daub infilling panels were soon replaced by the more appropriate clapboard. The widespread influence of the classical Renaissance is apparent in the shaping and painting of woodwork to imitate stone on many eighteenth-century houses.

Gradually, this influence lessened. Towards the latter part of the nineteenth century, innovators like H.H. Richardson (1838-86) created their own architectural vocabulary and used it to produce the "shingle style" – a free internal design approach using the flexibility of the wooden shingle as its outward expression, as seen in the resort towns of the New England coast.

Further south, social differences were more marked, the social order ranging from company or plantation bosses to slaves. The variety of timber buildings reflects this. The large "plantation Palladian" mansions are a truely indigenous form but most smaller buildings are very similar to English or Dutch prototypes. Gradually the warmer climate influenced a different approach to general design. This led to the introduction of more open plans employing screens and verandahs to link inside and outside spaces.

Development followed the railways westward and led to the establishment of townships where no community had previously existed. Timber was the obvious choice for building in most cases and the elements of the familiar "wild west" main street became so stereotyped that standard plans were available. In some cases entire buildings could be ordered by mail.

By 1900, all constituent materials of American houses looked alike, whether the houses were made of brick, stone or wood. The vast amount of timber which was used was in the form of joinery, both externally and internally. By this time, too,

Above This "plantation Palladian" house in the southern states of America shows a typical use of timber to emulate stone construction. Inspired by the mansions of Renaissance Italy, themselves a revival of earlier classical traditions, such colonial mansions were built in the material that was to hand, and upon which the economy was based at that time.
Right and inset These two farmhouses in New England illustrate another style of North American timber building – the clean, crisp lines later becoming symbolic of the spirit of the new republic. Such timber-frame houses were generally clad in horizontal weatherboarding, known as "clapboard", often painted to increase weather-resistance. Today, the majority of Americans still live in timber houses and wood is still the cheapest building material.

communications had made the scenery and
semi-tropical climate of southern California accessible to all with the wealth or
ambition to travel. In this ideal environment, the brothers C.S. and H.M. Greene
(1868-1957 and 1870-1954) developed their
Californian bungalow style using the Ben-
galese houses of India as a starting point.
Blending architectural skill, a sound knowledge of the fine arts and superb craftsmanship they produced results such as the
Gamble house (1909) in Pasadena.

Comparisons are inevitably made between the Greenes' work and the work of
Frank Lloyd Wright (1869-1959) but the
Greenes were part of the Arts and Crafts
Movement, while Wright was exploring
ideas which would lead to the development
of the ''Prairie School'' of organic architecture. Until then, in North America, if not the
whole of Europe, architecture was based on
Greek influence. ''Organic'' architecture
had much more in common with the Orien-
tal, mainly Buddhist, influences of early
civilizations in India, Persia, China and
Japan.

In the East, material was vital to the style
of building but the style had evolved
entirely from ceremonial organization of
space and its relationship with nature.
Frank Lloyd Wright said, ''Americans, in
seeking culture, could not accept that posts
and beams could be thrown away in favour
of folding or movable planes, nor that
organic archirure could derive from the
tall grass of the mid-western prairie. So the
idea went round the world to find recognition and was then 'imported' to its own
home as a thing to be imitated every-
where.'' Imitation was often shallow and
inappropriate and generally involved wood,
so it is no wonder there is some confusion
regarding the role of timber construction in
this period.

Following the 1910 publication in Europe
of the Wasmuth Portfolio illustrating
Wright's work, in, Rudolf Schindler
(1887-1953), who at the time was studying
in Vienna, became aware of Frank Lloyd

Right *Swan House,*
Connecticut (1975-6,
Charles Moore). This small
house is an example of a
modern use of timber by a
well-known architect, who
chose the material to
rework traditional American
building forms. The
suggestion of a portico over
the door is a
''post-modern'' touch.

Left and above *The Gamble House,* Pasadena (1909, H.M. and C.S. Greene). Imitators in the sense that they adapted the best traditions of wood architecture, and part of the Arts and Crafts Movement as superb craftsmen, the Greene brothers developed a Californian bungalow style in the early twentieth century. The detail (*above*) shows iron strapping holding the timbers together – not a traditional method of joining members, but an elegant solution.

Left *Sea Ranch,* Connecticut (1966, Charles Moore). This condominium is built entirely of timber, the weatherboarding fitting well with the seaside location. This use of wood is not just evocative of earlier traditions, but also expresses a more individual form.

Wright's work. He crossed the Atlantic and worked with Wright for a number of years before establishing a practice of his own in Hollywood. Schindler used timber extensively in the design of a series of houses, derived both from the Arts and Crafts Movement and from Wright. Later, he borrowed liberally from the Mission and Spanish Colonial revivals, which were prevalent styles in the Midwest and West Coast during the 1920s. In 1928, he committed himself to a form of DeStijl, the European-based style which mainly used concrete intersecting planes and volumes rather than static spaces. Schindler used stucco-covered wood-frame construction to achieve his objectives. The relative cheapness, ease of insulation, and dry construction, together with thin rectangular volumes which could be expressed sculpturally, appealed to Schindler and allowed him to explore and invent his original domestic architecture in wood technology.

Modern Applications

With the rise of the Modern Movement, past forms, and, to a large extent, the organic process were relinquished in favour of new "hygienic" materials which promoted the machine image. Consequently, with its limited applications and links with the Arts and Crafts Movement, building in wood was relegated to use by groups interested in the "do-it-yourself" technology. When glass, concrete and steel became increasingly available, synthetics were developed and machines made the moulding of materials, other than wood, comparatively easy, the use of timber declined to furniture and fittings.

Outside the housing arena, the early part of the twentieth century saw a proliferation of large buildings to satisfy the requirements of the increasing urban populations. Town halls, theatres, cinemas, sports centres and aircraft hangars provided opportunities to experiment with new materials and inventive structures. Timber made a significant contribution here as a result of development in jointing techniques using metal connectors and glue. With metal plates, rings and bolts to join timbers, the strength of the joint increases greatly in tension and shear. Using glues and some synthetic resins, the joints can even be stronger than the timber joined, so that small pieces of timber with different characteristics can be glued together to make up continuous structural members which are much stronger than solid wood members of the same size. Glued laminated timber has been used in many types of buildings where large uninterrupted spans are required. Beams can be curved, and cambers can be built into straight beams to accommodate loading deflections. On a smaller scale, much of the experimental furniture of the late 1920s and early 1930s made use of these techniques.

The past 20 years has seen a cyclic revival of authentic timber building in Britain, following examples set by North America and Scandinavia. These regions supply a large amount of timber to world markets and, unlike Britain, have always had an uninterrupted tradition of domestic timber building. In Britain, timber-frame housing now accounts for 20 per cent of the

Left The bowstring truss is an attractive structural form which uses small sections of material to achieve long spans. First used in the early decades of this century in aerodromes, this truss is rarely seen now, as it is not readily amenable to stress analysis.

Right *Bodafors Church,* Sweden (1969, Ralph Erskine). This is an imaginative expression of timber – both inside and outside the building – by an architect who well understands the capabilities of the material.

Left *Mannheim Multihalle,*
West Germany (1975, Frei
Otto). The ultimate in
timber engineering, this
exhibition hall is spanned
with a tensioned grid
composed of very small
pieces of wood, bolted
together where the stress
is greatest. This 200 foot
(61 m) span is one of the
largest applications of
Otto's "gridshell" idea – the
mesh is light, easy to
transport and surprisingly
strong.

1

2

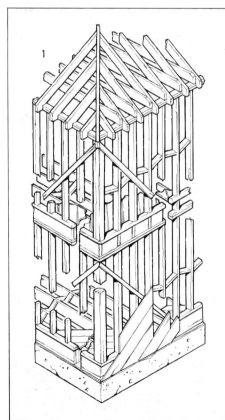

1

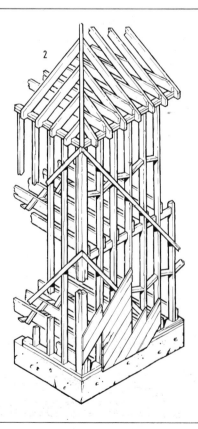

2

Methods of timber framing
Two types of timber framing arose in North America during the nineteenth century. These were balloon framing and platform framing, now the predominant timber-frame construction method in Britain.
Balloon framing (*1*) has external wall panels in various widths, fabricated to a height of two storeys. The intermediate floors are suspended from the full height studs.
In platform framing (*2*), wall panels are fabricated in storey heights and floors furnish the platform for the construction of the next storey.

3

Self-build housing In Britain, the architect Walter Segal has developed a self-build system for individual houses which uses timber in a logical and authentic manner. To do this, he had to overcome the inherent bias against timber housing in Britain, where building societies and other agencies have tended to look unfavourably on wooden construction, preferring the more "lasting" attributes of brick and mortar.

This unique system enables home owners to build their own houses cheaply and using only simple do-it-yourself carpentry tools (*2*). There is no waste of material – the timber used for temporary bracing, scaffolding and flooring is later incorporated into the structure as it goes up. An important obstacle to overcome was to get across the notion that foundations do not have to be elaborate. These houses rest on timber piles, set on concrete slabs which level the ground (*3*). This foundation system means that no specialist help is required to put the houses up and is perfectly adequate structurally. The finished houses (*1*) have their own appeal as timber buildings – the material has not been engineered as a substitute, but effectively displays its own qualities.

domestic market and is likely to increase by another 30 per cent over the next three to four years. Some of the reasons for the increase are historically based, but aptly fit the current economic circumstances. The regenerative quality of timber, allied to the low energy required to adapt timber from source, make the material economically attractive in comparison with other modern building materials. As demand for houses is always greater than supply; the building industry has sought efficient and speedy methods of dry construction which simplify and minimize site work, have good insulation qualities and can exploit the idea of factory fabrication. Wood construction fulfils these requirements and this, together with the increasing confidence that well-built modern timber structures can satisfy the acoustic, fire and other statutory criteria, means that building societies and insurance companies are finally awarding their seal of approval to the timber-framed house.

Following on from Schindler, post-modern architects such as Charles Moore and Robert Stern in the United States have used timber extensively in their domestic buildings. The use of timber, however, as it was with Schindler, is a means to an end. Timber merely assists in achieving the complex formal and stylistic content of the buildings but never asserts a rationale or discipline which is particular to the characteristics of the material. While these houses often demonstrate the flexible use of timber and contain references to the traditions of wood architecture, the "style" does not originate from a genuine use of timber construction.

A small number of European architects, such as McCormac and Jamieson, Walter Segal and Ralph Erskine, have come much closer to reestablishing a domestic wood architecture based on genuine current timber construction. This is partly due to the European preference for cellular house plans. Nothwithstanding, the current methodology of computer-designed timber components, which use minimum timber sections and jointing techniques to achieve maximum engineering and structural effect, needs to be controlled and directed by skilful designers.

Speed, efficiency and above all the quantity produced by modern timber building methods was unavailable to traditional timber house-builders. It is the difficult task of designers now to harness the advantages of those methods with the quality demonstrated by traditional wood architecture.

Right This large development of 420 houses in Basildon, Essex, is entirely timber. It demonstrates a method of building which is quick, economic, and dry to erect. This system allows flexibility of design, and at the same time comes to terms with the various performance criteria set for the walls and floors of separate buildings, which are more usually met by brick and concrete.

Above This typical timber volumetric housing unit, internally complete with all fittings and decoration, is being craned into position on prefabricated ground beams.

Left These timber volumetric housing units are shown after the addition of partial brick cladding on site. They are ready for occupation.

Brick

Brick was the first building material to be made by man. It has been used consistently since the Egyptians made bricks of sun-dried mud and straw and the Babylonians discovered the technique of making bricks by burning clay.

There are many practical and economic reasons why the use of brick should have survived: brick is a reasonably priced, standardized product made from an accessible raw material; it performs predictably; it is durable and has good insulating qualities. However, a more important reason for its continuing popularity lies in the close relationship between man and the material. There is a deep satisfaction in constructing buildings from units scaled to a man's hand. The size of the unit orders the building, making it comprehensible, and the unit itself is controlled at all stages of production and use by the skills of the brickmaker and bricklayer. Modern techniques of manufacture and construction now place less emphasis on traditional craft skills, but popular imagination has invested brick with a set of qualities derived from those human activities, and promoted its domestic appeal.

Historically, the use of brick has been influenced by the availability of raw materials. Brickwork traditions have developed in river valleys and alluvial plains which are both rich in clay deposits and lack supplies of building stone. Egypt and Mesopotamia have some of the earliest examples of brickwork; the Romans were quick to see its potential and organized production where they found the raw materials; the European development of the material was carried on in The Netherlands and north Germany around the rivers Oder and Elbe. In England, the art of brickmaking came and went with the Romans, but it revived in the Middle Ages, and since then there has been a steady growth which was accelerated by the Industrial Revolution, and the development of mass-production techniques and transport systems to deliver the products. Apart from native brick traditions in the Americas, other settlers took brickmaking skills with them. Bricks feature in many colonial buildings, although brick has never enjoyed the same widespread use in North America as timber.

Brick has also played a part in the development of building in other cultures.

Above *Eigen Haard housing estate* (1917, Michael de Klerk). The Netherlands has always had a strong tradition of brick building. This example shows the richness and versatility of brick as a material. Reference is made to traditional Dutch styles, together with an expression of more plastic qualities.

Right *Nero's Gateway,* Pompeii. The Romans used flat tile-like bricks to face structural cores. These were laid both horizontally and as voussoirs to form the characteristic round Roman arch.

Left *Hillingdon Civic Centre,* London (Robert Matthew and Johnson Marshall). The architects chose to build this large administration complex in brick to give a more human quality to an institutional development. The use of special bricks in the arches and saddleback copings, and splayed bricks on the staircase add modelling and interest. Brick has been exploited here for its variety and its domestic scale.

There is a long history of its use in India, and in China where it was used for the Great Wall. There is a growing body of opinion which thinks that the energy-starved Third World should reexamine the potential of sun-baked bricks rather than importing manufacturing techniques which use a great deal of energy in the conversion of the raw material.

The Material

A brick is strong in compression but weak in shear – hard to crush but easy to snap – hence, it is well suited to being part of a load-bearing system where the loads are compressive. Brickwork, although it is an aggregation of small units, relies on mass and the uniform transfer of load. The mass of the material is made up by bedding the bricks in mortar and bonding them together, so that loads are distributed over a larger area through a greater number of bricks. This is in direct contrast to a column-and-beam system of building, where the loads are transferred from the horizontal to the vertical.

Although brickwork as a structural material essentially takes the form of massive solid walls with no openings, it did not take builders long to discover the arch, a technique of forming openings in brick walls by using bricks themselves. It is necessary to support an arch during construction – usually on a timber framework, called centering – but once the arch is complete the centering is removed and the arch stands, always assuming that the work has been properly carried out, and there is sufficient restraint to prevent it spreading. It is a short step from the idea of the arch to the idea of the barrel vault, and builders were eventually able to pierce walls and enclose space between them using a single material. Corbelling – the technique whereby successive courses break forward of the wall face – is another way of enclosing space, especially suitable when the building plan is circular.

Although brickwork is a structural material, it is sometimes used non-structurally, as a panel in a vaulted ceiling or enclosing a steel or reinforced concrete frame building. Brickwork is well suited for this role. Not only is it attractive and durable but also it is possible to cut and shape bricks to fit into irregular spaces.

The qualities which we enjoy in brickwork are also its most serious limitations. Laying bricks is a labour-intensive operation which requires skill to carry out and experience to supervise; the raw material lacks consistency and its conversion consumes a great deal of energy; and it takes time to achieve the final result which is inevitably of variable quality.

The mass-production techniques used in

Above *The Great Wall of China* (214 B.C.). Originally an earth embankment faced with stone, the brick arches and watch towers were added later. The Wall is the only manmade feature visible from the moon.

the brick industry are inflexible, and it is difficult for the manufacturer to respond to the cyclical pattern of demand which can result when the building industry is used as an economic regulator. Although efforts are made to match supply to demand by stockpiling during a recession, it is inevitable that when building activity increases, delays caused by shortages follow.

Manufacturing Techniques

The basic principles of brickmaking have never changed. It has always been necessary to win the clay from the ground, and then for it to be prepared, shaped, dried and fired. Originally, the manufacture of bricks was carried out as near to the building site as possible – inevitably a time-consuming and labour-intensive process, whose success was governed by the quality of the raw material and the skill of the brickmaker. Developments in machinery in the mid-nineteenth century meant that production was concentrated in the brickfield, and the finished product was distributed by road,

rail or canal.

Early brickmaking followed a seasonal pattern. Once a supply of brickearth had been located, the top soil was stripped from the ground and the clay dug during autumn. The clay was left in heaps to be broken down by the action of rain and frost.

Plastic clay requires either the addition of sand or combination with a sandy clay, to counteract the tendancy towards warping and shrinkage during firing. This process was carried out in spring when the clay was puddled. It was either trodden barefoot or worked with spades. Stones were removed and any chalk broken up and mixed in. Carelessness at this stage could result in explosions during firing, and the waste of a year's effort. The clay was left to cure. Protected from the rain by canvas covers, it would be ready for forming in two months.

The form or mould was a wooden rectangle, open top and bottom, into which the clay was placed. The surplus was then struck off and the mould removed. The green (unfired) brick was then stacked for firing in either a clamp or kiln.

The clamp was a stack of bricks and fuel

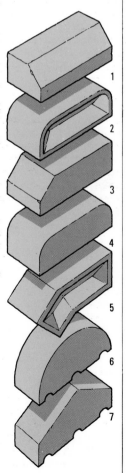

The Bricklayer's Art

The bricklayer's skill is the final factor which determines the appearance of brickwork. Apart from the basic requirements of keeping work vertical, maintaining a proper gauge and a correct bond and obtaining the proper horizontal line of each course, a good bricklayer will have developed an intuitive skill in handling the materials. There are numerous small adjustments which can be made to brickwork as the work proceeds, because few bricks are precisely the same size and there is nearly always a variation in colour or texture. The good bricklayer will accommodate the differences and the finished work will have a conviction that is easy to recognize but difficult to describe.

Traditionally the bricklayer's skills included the shaping and carving of bricks, as well as the production of gauged work. These skills are still available but they are declining, primarily because demand is low and there is lack of opportunity for practice.

A bricklayer will spend time checking the bond against the overall dimensions of the work and when he is ready to proceed he will set out the corners and build them to a maximum of 12 courses. The corners are checked for square and plumb, the level of each course being controlled by a gauge rod. When the corners are ready, the intervening bricks are laid against a line attached to steel pins. The pins are fixed at each corner into a crow joint, the line being kept tight to the top edge of the corner bricks. The bricklayer uses a trowel to pick up the mortar and lay the bed. This is one of the most important operations in bricklaying, because, unless the bed is laid solid and spread evenly to the required thickness, the work will not proceed smoothly. The cross joint is filled and the brick offered up. It should be possible to position a brick with slight pressure from the palm of the hand, leaving it within the proper gauge and the face vertical. The mortar which has oozed from the bed is removed by the trowel and the process repeated. A bricklayer will return to the work to finish the joint while the mortar is still fresh.

Bonds There are various methods of bonding, which result in different patterns in a length of brickwork. Common bonds include: stretcher bond (*1*), English bond (*2*) and Flemish bond (*3*). Where maximum strength is required, bricks must be laid frog-up.

Above *Ishtar Gate*, Babylon (605-563 B.C.). Rebuilt by Nebuchadnezzar, Babylon was one of the earliest places where brick was used as a building material. The Ishtar Gate was made of glazed blue bricks, decorated with yellow and white bulls in relief. A reference to Babylonian builders in *Genesis* states: "They used bricks for stones and bitumen for mortar"

Special bricks A huge number of bricks are available, many of them shaped to fulfil specific requirements, typically in window arches (*left*), corners or stairs. Some of the "standard" specials include: plinth stretcher (*1*), double bullnose with frog (*2*), plinth header (*3*), double bullnose (*4*), internal dogleg (*5*), half-round coping (*6*), and saddleback coping (*7*). The "frog" is the indentation in the brick which holds the mortar.

covered in wattle and daub, and earthed over. Ventilation holes were left in the covering through which the stack was ignited. The speed of burning depended on the fuel, which was timber, turf, or, exceptionally, coal, but it was not unusual for a clamp to burn for a number of weeks. The principle of the kiln was the same, the difference being that if one was to be making bricks over an extended period on a site it was worth erecting a permanent structure within which the bricks could be burnt.

The vertical pugmill was the first piece of machinery introduced into the process. Powered originally by horse-power, and then by steam, it consisted of a large wooden tub, without heads, set upright on the ground. On the vertical axis was an iron spindle carrying knives. The coarse clay was fed into the top of the barrel, and was cut and compressed by the knives until it came out through a hole in the bottom of the barrel in a smooth dough ready for the moulder.

The introduction of the Hoffman kiln in 1858, in conjunction with mechanical methods of preparing and extruding clay, brought mass-production of bricks. However, because of the different types of clay, there is still a variety of processes which are used for the preparation and formation. These are the wire-cut process for plaster clays, the stiff plastic process for colliery shales, the semi-dry process for shales with low plasticity, the soft mud process, and handmaking.

Development and Application

Early Civilizations

The essence of brick building lies in the construction of massive walls, with openings formed by arches and the space between these enclosed by vaults. Evidence of early buildings which fit this description has been found in the alluvial plains of the Tigris and Euphrates. Timber and stone were rare in Mesopotamia; the only material available in abundance was clay. The Babylonians made both sun-dried and kiln-burnt bricks. The former were generally used for the core of the walls, the latter for facing them.

The city of Babylon must have been a remarkable place. Planned on a formal grid with streets parallel to and at right-angles with the Euphrates River, the entire city was enclosed by great, thick walls. Inside the walls were terraced towers, large temples and the Palace of Nebuchadnezzar (605-563 B.C.), all built from mud bricks.

The Assyrians conquered Babylon in 1275 B.C. and the Palace of Sargon at Khorsabad (722-705 B.C.) is a good example of the way in which they accepted the

Above Arch forms from the Ziggurat of Ur-Nammu (1) and the Royal Palace at Khorsabad (2).
Right *Ziggurat of Ur-Nammu* (21st century B.C.). This monumental structure was built by the Sumerians in mud brick. The temple rose to 60 feet (20m) and has now been partly reconstructed to show the original conception of a meeting place between man and god.

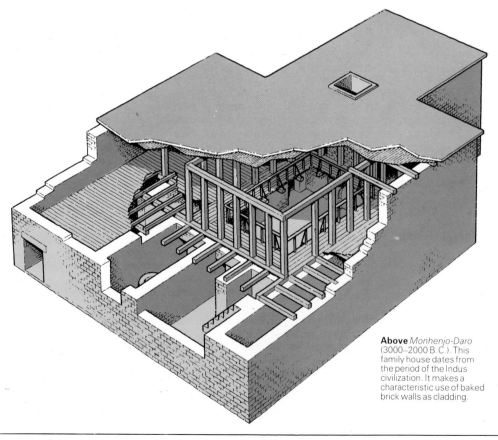

Above *Monhenjo-Daro* (3000–2000 B.C.). This family house dates from the period of the Indus civilization. It makes a characteristic use of baked brick walls as cladding.

limitations imposed by the use of a single material. The Palace was set 50 feet (15 m) above the plain on a platform of sun-dried bricks. The building, which covered nearly 25 acres (10 hectares), was planned in three sections: the Seraglio (the formal palace), the Harem (the private rooms) and the Khan (the service rooms), all of which related to a central court 2½ acres (1 hectare) in area. The massive walls, 28 feet (8.5 m) thick, and the succession of long narrow spaces grouped around open courtyards give the impression that the building was hollowed out of a huge clay pile.

Bas-reliefs have been found which suggest the Assyrians knew about the construction of domes. Sir Banister Fletcher, in *A History of Architecture*, discerns a link between Assyrian and Byzantine buildings through the work of the Sassanian Dynasty (A.D. 226-642) established near Babylon. The Palace at Sarvistan near Persepolis (A.D. 350) has a triple-arched portico, behind which is a square hall roofed by a brick-built beehive dome. The side compartments are roofed by barrel vaults reminiscent of the Assyrian palaces. The Palace at Feruz-kabad (A.D. 450) contains three domed spaces set across the plan, between the entrance hall and the main court. The problem of enclosing a square plan with a dome is that the corners of the square have to be built into the circular base of the dome. Byzantine builders were later to discover an elegant solution and the

Sassanian examples are part of the chain of development.

The Egyptians made bricks from the earliest dynasties. These were usually large sun-baked slabs laid to form the structure, which was then clad with stone or marble. The availability of stone meant that Egyptian builders could span openings with single slabs and did not have to resort to the use of arches. A distinctive feature of their buildings was the batter, or gentle slope introduced into the wall face. This was achieved by laying the bricks in concave courses and gave the walls greater stability. However, the stone column and beam were the basic components of their building vocabulary, with brickwork only used as a secondary material, so the developments begun in Babylon were unexplored.

In the same way, the Greeks, with their plentiful supplies of marble, concentrated on the refinement of a column-and-beam system. They knew about bricks but they had neither the need or the inclination to make extensive and innovative use of their knowledge.

It was left to the Romans to build in a way which combined both the trabeated style (where the beam is the main structural feature) and the solid forms of arch, vault and dome. The Romans had access to a wide range of building materials — terracotta, brick, stone and marble — but their most significant innovation in the art of

Below *Colosseum*, Rome, (A.D. 70–82). Also known as the amphitheatre of Flavius, this large arena and amphitheatre is oval-shaped. Eighty arcaded supporting walls constructed out of tufa and brick open onto tiered seating. These materials were found in the area around the Esquiline and Caelian hills where the Colosseum was built. Tufa is still exported to other cities from this part of the Roman countryside.

The Colosseum Huge piers
support three levels of
arcades which form
walkways. A combination
of materials was used: tufa
and brick for supporting
walls, lava for foundations,
pumice for vaults: all in
conjunction with *pozzolana,*
the Roman form of
concrete. Where bricks
were used to face walls,
the structural core was
concrete. Marble was used
for decoration and seating.

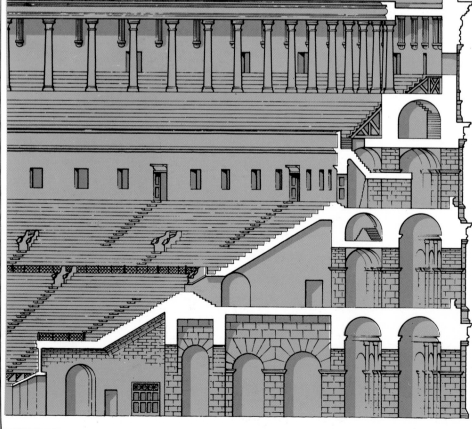

building was the development of concrete –
pozzolana – which was used extensively as
the structural core of buildings. Brick, stone
and marble were all used as facing materials, either added later or sometimes built
first to provide permanent shuttering for
the plastic concrete.

The Roman building programme was
formidable in both scope and complexity
and they learnt how to combine materials to
exploit the best qualities of each. For the
Colosseum (A.D. 70-82), lava was used for
the solid foundations, tufa and brick for the
supporting walls and lightweight pumice
stone in the vaults. The Pantheon (A.D.
120-4) also demonstrates an interesting mix
of materials. The dome is a hemisphere, the
inner surface of which is coffered in five
ranges. It has been established that the
dome was constructed from brickwork with
thick mortar laid in horizontal courses up to
the fourth range of coffers and also around
the central opening at the summit.

The Romans established brickmaking
wherever they found plentiful supplies of
clay. Their bricks look more like large tiles,
rarely more than $1\frac{1}{2}$ inches (4 cm) thick and
18 x 9 inches (46 x 23 cm) on plan. They are
well-burnt and therefore durable. This
shape grew out of the uses which they made
of the material – as bonding courses in
rubble walls, relieving arches in composite
vaults, and for voussoirs (the wedge-
shaped blocks making an arch).

In A.D. 324, Constantine moved the
capital of the Roman Empire from Rome to
Constantinople, creating the opportunity
for a fusion between the styles of east and
west, the result of which is now identified
as Byzantine. Building stone had to be
imported, but clay was plentiful, and the
Romans introduced their technique of
building permanent brick shuttering
within which was cast a concrete core. The
Eastern influence can be seen in the use of
domes to cover polygonal and square
plans. These domes were generally constructed from large flat bricks or similarly
shaped blocks of pumice. Temporary support to the structure was unnecessary
because each course could be edged out
from the one below until the form was
complete. The significant development in
the constructional system was in the use of
pendentives which facilitated the building
of domes. Arches were constructed projecting from the lines of the square plan, and
the triangular void between the arches and
the underside of the circular plan was filled
with masonry, so making an elegant transition from a square plan to a circular plan.
The triangular pendentives so formed
allowed the builders to treat the internal
face of the building as a continuous surface.
Rich mosaic designs and pictures flow from
one surface to another emphasizing the
sense of unity which a dome creates.

Santa Sophia (A.D. 532-537) demons-

Left *The Pantheon*, Rome (A.D. 120-4). The inner surface of the dome is panelled in five ranges, originally made of brickwork up to the fourth range. The coffered surface provides decoration and also reduces the weight of the dome.
Below First developed in Roman times, the barrel vault has remained a major building form. Temporary timber frame – "centering" – supported the vault, which was made of bricks filled with concrete. Brick tiles were also used to face the arch, as voussoirs.

trates the power of the central domed space. Although the building is square on plan it is given a sense of direction by the use of two semi-domes to the east and west. These are built against the arches which support the main dome so that one perceives an oval nave 225 x 107 feet (69 x 33 m) which rises to 180 feet (55 m) at the centre of the main dome. The dome is constructed from large tile-shaped bricks, 2 inches (5 cm) thick, 27 inches (68 cm) square in the lower portions and 24 inches (61 cm) square at the crown. The bricks are laid in thick mortar beds which allowed the builders to set each course on an angle to the one below, so reducing the thrust of the dome.

Early European Development

The Byzantine influence is marked in Venice and other centres, but northern Europeans tackled the problem of enclosing space in a different way. Instead of the centralized dome unifying the volume, they preferred a building with a sense of progression, and concentrated on the problem

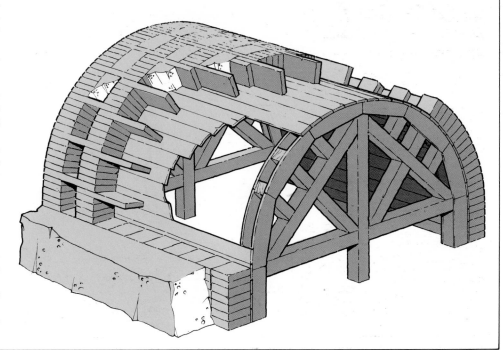

Above and right *Hagia Sophia,* Istanbul (A.D. 532-537). The external form suggests a series of different volumes, but inside a unified space is created not only by the structure but also by all-over patterning and the way that light floods into the building.

of designing roofs to span between parallel walls rather than covering spaces which were square on plan. Bricks and brickwork do not play a major role in the development of Gothic from the Romanesque in the twelfth century, although it is significant that where there were supplies of brick, it was used to reproduce the forms which history suggests were the preserve of stone. The Lombardy plain in north Italy has churches built from local brick, although this is an area in which the Roman traditions were strong. The Cathedral at Albi (1282-1390) is a fortress church built in

brick. It is a simple plan, containing one major vaulted space and an apsidal end. The brickwork walls undulate as the internal buttresses register on the external skin. Brick is well suited to this form of expression and the whole building is a powerful composition.

The most extensive use of brick was in The Netherlands and north Germany and, once more, it was the lack of building stone and the availability of clay which promoted the material. What is not clear is how or where the art of brickmaking was rediscovered in Europe. It is generally held that

brickmaking in Europe ceased with the collapse of the Roman Empire and did not start again until the middle of the thirteenth century. There were strong trading links between the towns of the Hanseatic League (a league formed by German merchants at home and abroad for the defence of their trading interests) and Venice, so it is conceivable that the brick builders of the coastal towns of The Netherlands and northern Germany could have learnt from some eastern source, or perhaps from Lombardy. Whatever the reason, the Flemish, Dutch and north German trading partners

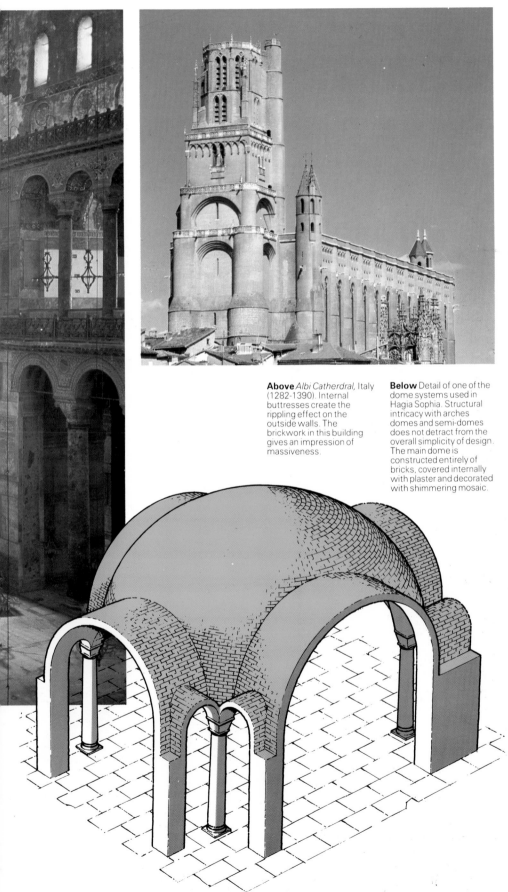

Above *Albi Catherdral,* Italy (1282-1390). Internal buttresses create the rippling effect on the outside walls. The brickwork in this building gives an impression of massiveness.

Below Detail of one of the dome systems used in Hagia Sophia. Structural intricacy with arches domes and semi-domes does not detract from the overall simplicity of design. The main dome is constructed entirely of bricks, covered internally with plaster and decorated with shimmering mosaic.

of the Hanseatic League were instrumental in nurturing and spreading the skills of brickmaker and bricklayer. Lubeck Cathedral was a north German Romanesque building which was begun in 1173 and received Gothic additions in 1335. Both stages of the building were executed in brickwork, which was even used for the window mullions and tracery. Other major brick buildings were built in the town of Lubeck, and it is certain that the work provided a stimulus for the development of brickwork building in England.

Many towns and ports in England were members of the Hanseatic League, notably York, Hull, Boston, Yarmouth, London and Bristol, so it was in the east and southeast that brickwork began to flourish. The raw material was available, the skill to exploit it arrived with immigrants from Flanders and The Netherlands during power struggles in the thirteenth and fourteenth centuries, and the desire to use it had been fostered by the northern European examples.

In the twelfth century, Roman bricks had been quarried from existing structures and incorporated in new buildings, especially around St. Albans and Colchester, but the earliest domestic brick building in England is probably Little Wenham Hall, Suffolk. It is a brick structure dating from the end of the thirteenth century, L-shaped in plan, with a tower and turret stair in the inside corner. The bricks differ in size and colour and they are used in conjunction with limestone for the dressings and windows. The bricks were burnt on the site and it is thought that the expertise was provided by Flemish brickmakers.

It was obviously sound practice, given the limitations of transport, to make bricks for a building as close to the site as possible. Many buildings were built from brick fields which were exploited for that building alone. However, in 1303, Hull established a municipal brickworks, and land at Beverley was leased for brickmaking. These two operations were obviously designed to allow Hull to compete with its Hanseatic partners. Jane Wight, in *Brick Building in England* (1972), states that Hull was England's first brick-built town. It was a fortified town laid out on a grid plan, but all that remains today is the original centrepiece of the town – the Church of Holy Trinity. Local brick was used to construct the chancel and transepts (1315-45), while the nave and upper portion of the tower were built of stone. As at Little Wenham, stone was used for the dressings and windows. Beverley Minster, in the nearby market town of Beverley, has a vault of brickwork with stone ribs, and North Bar (1409), the only survivor of Beverley's gates, is a three-storeyed brick structure with some interesting details – three blank niches on the south front and a dentilated string-course under the battlements.

Above *Oxburgh Hall,* Norfolk (1482). With the use of a single material, two different effects are created. The smooth precision of the walls contrast with the decorated entrance gate at the right – the decoration emphasizing the importance of the gateway. With brickwork, no decoration need be applied – it can simply be built in.

Right *Tattershall Castle,* Lincolnshire (1433-50). A random disposition of the window openings is possible in brick construction. The effect here is more fortified than at Oxburgh Hall.

Above The newel staircase at Oxburgh Hall shows the use of bricks carved to make shapes and as infill. Even the handrail is made of bricks.

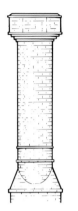

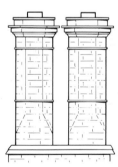
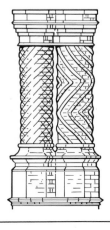

Below One of the enduring symbols of Tudor brickwork, the exuberant, decorative chimneys, express the enthusiasm and skill of their builders.

Tudor and Stuart Brickwork

Hull was unique. Elsewhere in England, during the fourteenth and fifteenth centuries, brick was used solely for important buildings, as an alternative to stone. It enjoyed the patronage of royalty, nobility and the clergy, who used it extensively in new work in the south and east of England.

The enduring image of Tudor building is the gatehouse, the symbolic gesture through which a community connects with the outside world. The major projects of the time were concerned with housing communities, whether the community was the Court, a nobleman and his retinue, or the master, fellows and scholars of a college. The plan form developed from the castle, but there was a shift of emphasis away from a building built to be defended towards one designed to serve the needs of a community. This shift was marked by the increasing use of brick, a more domestic material than stone and therefore appropriate for the new buildings.

Henry VI used brick at Greenwich and Richmond Palaces, but his most extensive use of the material was at Eton College. The College was founded in 1440 and, although the Chapel walls are stone, the rest is built from bricks which were made from clay deposits at Slough. Three million bricks were supplied to the site between 1442 and 1452. Bishop Waynflete, the first Headmaster of Eton, was also an enthusiastic builder. A Tudor bishop wielded political, as well as religious power, and there were plenty of opportunities for Waynflete to indulge his interests in education and building. He added a brick-built tower to the stone castle at Farnham and built a palace at Esher from which only the water-gate tower survives. He founded Magdalen College, Oxford in 1458, but followed local tradition and built in stone.

Three other bishops, Rotherham, Fisher and Alcock, each of whom was Bishop of Rochester at some time in his career, were instrumental in the foundation of four Cambridge colleges. Rotherham was a founder of Queens' College (1448-9), Alcock founded Jesus (1500), Fisher organized the building of Christ's (1505-11) and St. John's (1511) on behalf of the foundress, Lady Margaret de Beaufort. Brick was used in all four colleges. Although they are now obscured at Christ's, the gateways and their attached ranges are fine examples of the skill of the Tudor builders.

The brick-built gateway and courtyard form recurs at Oxburgh Castle, Norfolk (1482), a moated house with a spectacular gate tower rising 70 feet (21 m) from the moat. The tower is surrounded by polygonal turrets, between which there are crow-stepped gables and machicolations.

Tattershall Castle, Lincolnshire (1433-50) was built by Ralph Cromwell, Treasurer to Henry VI; although only the Tower House

Above *Queen's College,* Cambridge (1448-9). As a contrast to the planar quality of the brickwork in Oxburgh Hall, here the thickness of the walls is shown in the depth of the window openings.

survives, it is a powerful piece of brick building, five storeys – 110 feet (34 m) – high. The interior is finished in brick and contains four noteworthy chimney pieces made of limestone.

Caister Castle, begun in 1432 by Sir John Falstaff, still retains its remarkable lookout tower, sited at the southwest corner of the courtyard. The tower is 25 feet (8 m) in diameter and rises 90 feet (27 m) in one sheer face; the staircase turret oversails the main tower by 8 feet (2.4 m). There is a single room at each of the five levels within the tower. Caister was built from brick manufactured locally and the dressings are imported limestone.

Herstmonceaux Castle, Sussex (1441), built by Sir Roger Fiennes, seems to float within a lake rather than be surrounded by a moat. From the long-distance view one appreciates the almost elastic quality of the external wall which is one of the hallmarks of Tudor brickwork. The wall is dominant, with details such as windows secondary to the sheer mass of the brickwork.

From buildings of this period, there is plenty of evidence of intricate brick shaping and laying – the moulded handrail of

Waynflete's tower, the staircase vaults at Oxburgh Hall, the copings at Tattershall — but the crowning glory of the bricklayer's skill was in the construction of chimneys. There are many different shapes — squares, circles, spirals, hexagons and octagons — and the brickwork is covered with a variety of relief patterns. The chimneys of Hampton Court (built c. 1520 for Cardinal Wolsey) are probably the most famous examples, but celebration of the chimney was a common theme. Although some external walls were enlivened with diaper patterns formed from different coloured bricks, it was in the building of the chimneys that the bricklayers expressed their skill in exuberant patterns.

The influx of foreign artists and craftsmen to the court of Henry VIII, introducing the ideas of the Renaissance, prompted a reaction to elaborate brick detailing. The large houses built during the reigns of Elizabeth I and James I show a more restrained handling of the material. There is a change in the relationship between solid and void, as windows became larger, and the buildings take on the character of country houses rather than fortified dwellings.

Hatfield House (1607-11) is a good

Right This is a developed example of the use of gauged brickwork and polychromy. Cut bricks are used in the arches, moulded bricks at the apex of the gable and yellow and red bricks contrast effectively with the stone. **Below** *Hatfield House,* Hertfordshire (1607-11). Brick is used here to provide a continuous flat surface which contrasts with the stone framing the openings.

Above *The Dutch House,* Kew (1631). This building is the earliest example of gauged brickwork – bricks cut to fit precisely. The detail (*left*) shows one of the columns over the main entrance. The columns were built square and then the soft bricks were rubbed and chiselled into shape.

Right The stone gabling and window surrounds on this brick house in Bruges built in 1716 represent a development away from all-brick detailing. It is more logical to have these features in stone – they are easier and less time-consuming to form and weather better.

example of this change of emphasis. The openings are framed in stone and the brickwork serves merely to provide a continuous plane surface, against which the drama of the openings is contrasted. The quoins (angles at the corners) are formed in stone, which emphasizes the planar quality of the brickwork; instead of there being a continuous undulating surface able to accommodate turrets and towers, the brickwork is treated as a series of panels which meet with precision and control.

If Hatfield House anticipates the severely classical treatment of the Banqueting House (Inigo Jones, 1619-21), there was also a secondary line of development in brick construction which culminated in the wealth of late Stuart and early Georgian houses. Since Tudor times, the highest skills of the brickmaker and bricklayer had been exercised in the production of moulded and carved brickwork. These skills were reinforced by the arrival of immigrants from Flanders and The Netherlands, who introduced the technique of gauged brickwork. This involved making very soft bricks which could be cut with a saw and then rubbed to a precise, gauged shape. Since it was possible to achieve a high degree of accuracy, gauged brickwork required very fine joints. The earliest example of gauged brickwork is at the Dutch House, Kew (1631). The wall is dissolved in a series of finely moulded and carved details, surmounted with curved gables which finish in curved or triangular pediments. Although the design is robust, the building displays an enthusiasm for using brick as structure and decoration. It was this enthusiasm, together with the refinement of style, that was responsible for the fine brick buildings constructed over the next hundred years.

Georgian Brickwork

Brick served the Tudor court and the Elizabethan gentry, but in early Georgian times it became the preserve of middle class merchants and professional men. High fashion and style were the concern of those who had travelled in Italy, while a comfortable formality was the preoccupation of the emerging middle-class. Skilled craftsmanship was expected from the builders, who followed their pattern books and faithfully reproduced a wide range of details. Gauged brickwork in arches and even, in exceptional circumstances, on the whole front elevation; recessed panels with intricate patterns; raised decoration, cornices, string-courses; in situ carving and moulded brickwork – the whole range of the bricklayer's art was employed and can still be seen today forming the nucleus of many English country towns.

By 1700, brick was being used for cottages, replacing timber as the common building material. Legislation had helped

Rate houses After the Great Fire of London in 1666, the Building Act of 1667 specified four sizes of house allowed in towns: First Rate and its mews (*1*), Second (*2*), Third (*3*) and Fourth Rate (*4*) houses. The limitations on structure and height gave rise to the homogenity of Georgian London. The house types were still used up to the end of the nineteenth century.

1

2

3

4

Above and right
St. Katharine's Dock, London (1825, Telford and Hardwick). The designers of the early Industrial Revolution reacted in different ways to the challenge of building large structures. Here brick is used effectively to give a simple repetitive expression of solid and void.

the progress of brickwork. In 1605, James I issued a proclamation requiring all people to build "their fore front windows of brick or stone as ... all great and well grown woods are much spent ... so as timber for shipping waxes scarce". In 1625, and again in 1630, Charles I issued a proclamation prescribing that bricks should be a standard size (9 x 4⅜ x 2¼ inches/23 x 11 x 6 cm). The Building Act of 1667, passed in the aftermath of the Great Fire of London in 1666, laid down specifications for design, construction and location of new houses built in the city. The four house types allowed were all terrace in form and were the forerunners of the townhouses developed in the eighteenth century. The limited range of choice given to the speculative builder is one reason for the impressive consistency of Georgian London.

One of the attractions of brick is that it is a material which can be used either alone or in combination with others. The idea of using brick for the structure and stone for the dressings had been current since Tudor times. Wren had used the combination to great effect in his rebuilding of a portion at Hampton Court (1689-1702) making a sharp contrast between the red brick and the Portland stone trim. His enjoyment of this combination is well illustrated by some of the City churches designed after the Great Fire.

In the eighteenth century, however, there was a strong reaction against red brick, especially among fashionable designers. Isaac Ware writing in the *Complete Body of Architecture* (1756) disliked the contrast between red brick and stone and argued for a combination of brick and stone where

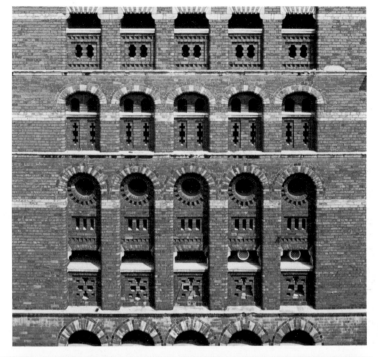

Right *The Granary,* Bristol. The ingenuity and enthusiasm of the detailing on this large brick building offer a marked contrast to the plain functional appearance of many Victorian warehouses.

there is "no violent change" between the colour of the brick and stone. The mood was then set for a ready acceptance of stucco. Rendering had already been used to simulate stone, in the best Palladian tradition, and, in 1773, Liardets cement became available.

Politicians had already taxed building by the introduction of the window tax in 1692. This was increased six times between 1746 and 1808, and was not repealed until 1851. Brick also suffered from taxation. The tax was introduced in 1784 and increased in 1794 and 1803, remaining in force until 1850. The brick tax had the effect of stimulating the use of brick tiles (or mathematical tiles), for they were exempt from duty.

Brick tiles had been available since the early part of the eighteenth century, although limited to the southeast of England. They were used to add a brick veneer to an existing building, or to clad a timber frame to give the appearance of brickwork, improving the appearance of the property as well as increasing weather resistance. The tiles had a brick-shaped face with a tapering flange above and behind. They were fixed by nailing through the flange or by being bedded in cement, the next course sitting on top of the brick face, obscuring the flange. Demand for these tiles was considerable and several large houses were faced in them, the most notable of which was Belmont Park near Faversham (Samuel Wyatt, 1792). The pale yellow colour suggests that the tiles were made from local clay between Faversham and Sittingbourne. Brick tiles are still available today.

Although brick was used for the structure of the stucco terraces of the late eighteenth and early nineteenth centuries, these buildings are not brick buildings in conception or design, the stucco being seen as a substitute for stone.

Brick terraces were built, however, to provide cheap accommodation for the families lured to the cities by the promise of work during the Industrial Revolution. Row on row of these houses went up during this period, often built of brick transported by rail from distant brickyards.

Victorian Brickwork

The Industrial Revolution changed the nature of brick. It became a mass-produced material, universally available, with new standards of consistency in size, colour and texture. Machine production also meant that it was possible to exploit new clays, notably the Jurassic clay in the Peterborough area and the colliery shales of the Midlands and the north. The developments meant that the building industry was able to respond to the increasing demand for buildings in which the growing population could work, live and enjoy themselves.

Although brick was used across the range of building types, from terrace housing to engineering structures, other materials such as stone, cast-iron, wrought-iron and steel were used extensively. Even with hindsight, it is bewildering to chart the social, intellectual and technological changes to which the Victorians were subject. It is no surprise to find that in an attempt to order the use of the materials, and to respond to many new functional requirements, they relied on interpretations of historical precedent, with all the inevitable academic arguments about style that this type of approach entails.

We are easily able to appreciate the elegant simplicity of brickwork used in the railway viaducts, bridges and large industrial buildings such as St. Katharine's Dock (1825) by Telford and Hardwick, or the Albert Dock, Liverpool (1845) by Jesse Hartley, but we need a greater understanding of the context within which the architect was working before we can appreciate the brickwork designed by William Butterfield (1814-1900) for All Saints, Margaret Street, Westminster (1849-59) or Keble College, Oxford (1867-83).

All Saints was built for the Cambridge Camden Society to serve as a model church

Above Today an expensive form of cladding, brick tiles were used widely in the late eighteenth century and early nineteenth century as a way of avoiding brick tax.
Below and right *The Red House,* Kent (1859-60, Philip Webb). Built for William Morris, this house was named after the colour of its materials, red brick and tiles. Interior decoration by Morris heralded the Arts and Crafts Movement style.

demonstrating the new Anglican approach towards ritualistic worship. The site was small, yet by skilful planning and confident handling of the masses, Butterfield created a succession of spaces, which draw the visitor from the street, across a courtyard, and into the richly decorated interior. One of Butterfield's aims was to "give dignity to brick", and the selection of the special red brick and the contrasting black bricks, which provide the patterns on the external wall, was a deliberate attempt to stress the wall's surface. Internally, the walls are decorated with geometrical flat patterns made up from a variety of materials — brick and tiles in off-white, black and red; glazed tiles in green, yellow and grey; red and black mastic inlaid in pale stone or ter-

racotta. The floor is heavily patterned, with a series of brightly coloured tiles. All Saints is now seen as the first High Victorian building, the interest in surface and decoration coming directly from the designer A.W.N. Pugin's (1812-52) concern for truth in the honesty of construction – rather than obscuring the constructional elements, the patterns serve to emphasize them.

When Butterfield selected red brick as the major material for Keble College, Oxford, in defiance of the Oxford tradition of building in stone, he told the Warden of the college that his principle was not to follow tradition, but to "use the materials, whatever they may be, which the locality and this age supply". This determination to think for oneself was well in tune with the

revival of Anglicanism as expressed in the Oxford Movement, and the design executed at Keble was uncompromising. The traditional plan of a college is disrupted, the whole composition being dominated by the chapel, which is not only the largest building, but also the most highly decorated.

The idea that a building was symbolic of a view of life applied just as much to houses as it did to churches. Pugin despised stucco villas, preferring red brick with stone dressings and slate roofs. He designed a house for himself in Alderbury, Wiltshire (1835-6) and another in Ramsgate, the Grange (1843-4). While they contain the same elements, the mood of the two buildings is different – the former has a romantic

quality and the latter, a feeling of austerity. The simple straightforward handling of the elements and the earnestness and morality of the designs were much admired by Pugin's contemporaries. The development of the small English house owes a great deal to his lead. Butterfield, William White (1825-1900) and G.E. Street (1824-81) all designed vicarages and estate houses in the same style which was also adopted by Philip Webb (1831-1915) for The Red House, Bexleyheath (1859-60), built for William Morris. The Red House is more romantic than Pugin's work, displaying a wide variety of window sizes and types, and an apparently casual composition, which reflects the demands of the plan, rather than formal precedent. The use of brick for

Left *Keble College,* Oxford (1867-83, William Butterfield). This view of the chapel shows the highly decorative use of brick: "constructional polychromy". Butterfield's aim was to build in local materials, defying the Oxford tradition of building in stone. The patterns on the brickwork are uncompromisingly geometric, similar to his earlier church, All Saints, London (1849-59).

the external walls and for interior details emphasizes the comfortable domestic character of the Red House. The ability to design buildings which display that character, rather than the academically correct handling of a particular style, impressed Hermann Muthesius (1861-1927) when he wrote *Das Englische Haus* (1904–5). As a result of his enthusiasm, this vein of English architecture made a significant contribution to the Modern Movement.

No. 1 Palace Green, designed for Hon. George Howard by Philip Webb in 1868-70, demonstrates this determination to consider a range of precedents, and then to use them as part of a unified design owing no allegiance to a particular style. The initial design was rejected by the Commissioners of Woods and Forests but Webb claimed, quite rightly, that the building possessed character and originality, and, after a struggle, he won the day. The building shows fine handling of brickwork in the use of the rubbed brick details, arches, pilasters and recessed panels.

Richard Norman Shaw (1831-1912) and C.F.A. Voysey (1857-1941) continued the development of this design approach, which is also evident in the early work of Edwin Lutyens (1869-1944). Deanery Gardens at Sonning (1901) by Lutyens shows a keen appreciation for the restrained sculptural qualities of brickwork and the architect's interest in the execution of details. The external wall folds around the chimney, the form is echoed by the stacks, and reveals its thickness as the entrance is expressed by a series of interlocking arches.

Modern Applications

Frank Lloyd Wright's (1867-1959) early work shows how brick could be exploited in the context of the Modern Movement. The Larkin Building (1904) in Buffalo with sheer external walls of brickwork, relieved only by string courses and cornices of simple rectangular section, and an internal organization which relates the surrounding office floors to a central unifying space, is a fine example of the material used to demonstrate the new concepts. Wright's interest in brickwork lasted until the end of his career. Evidence that he appreciated both its decoration and sculptural qualities can be seen in the handling of The Morris

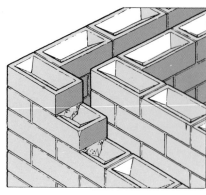

Above The cavity wall, designed in the 1920s, has two skins of brick. Today, the internal wall is often made of lightweight concrete block and insulation is put in the cavity – fibreglass batts are built in during construction or foam is injected.

Right *Valerius School,* Hilversum (1930 W. M. Dudok). Dudok's use of brick was in the context of the De Stijl Movement, an abstract style of the 1920s in Holland which influenced the Modern Movement.

Above and right *Civic Centre,* Säynätsalo, Finland (1950, Alvar Aalto). Aalto's love of bricks is demonstrated in this complex, where brick is used internally as well as externally. The detail of the steps (*above*) down from the town hall show bricks used as tiles on the floor and as a bond for the walls, contrasting effectively with the timber ceiling.

Above This detail of a staircase by Michael de Klerk shows a witty, organic use of brick. A wide range of bonds give variety to the patterning.

Below left *De Dageraad housing estate* (1918-23, Piet Kramer). Although Kramer's work was not recognized at the time, it is now receiving renewed interest. The curved forms are a good example of the plastic qualities of brickwork.

Gift Shop (1949) and the Johnson Wax Building in Racine (1949).

Brick also appeared in the work of Peter Behrens (1868-1940) for the A.E.G. Turbine Factory in Berlin in 1909. The factories were an important demonstration of the principles of design and construction as reinterpreted by the avant-garde. The High Tension Factory (1910) and the Small Motor Factory (1901) show brick used with an impressive simplicity and power. Walter Gropius (1883-1969), a pupil of Behrens, also demonstrated a keen appreciation for the qualities of brick. In the Model Factory at the Werkbund Exhibition, Cologne (1914), he designed a south elevation which contrasted the massive qualities of brickwork with the transparency of glass-enclosed staircases. In this building, brickwork expresses both a horizontal and a vertical movement, the former achieved by recessing every seventh course, the latter by allowing vertical shafts to interrupt the surface at regular intervals.

The Netherlands has always had a strong tradition of brickwork. Some remarkable buildings were designed in brick by Piet Kramer (1881-1961) and Michael de Klerk (1884-1923). Kramer's De Dageraad housing estate (1918-23) and de Klerk's Eigen Haard housing estate (1917) both have curved elements which show the plastic qualities of brickwork. The buildings were carefully designed and well built, and, although at the time they were not considered as being in the mainstream of modern architecture, they have received enthusiastic reappraisal. W.M. Dudok's

(1884-1974) work was more in tune with the aims of the Modern Movement, drawing on the inspiration of the De Stijl Movement. The simple expression of plane and mass, the contrast of solid and void, are evident in the Dr. Bavink School and the Town Hall at Hilversum (1929).

Although timber is the traditional building material of Scandinavia, the use of brick for large and important buildings is well established. The town halls of both Stockholm and Copenhagen are impressive brick buildings, but the work of the Finn, Alvar Aalto (1889-1976), demonstrates a consistency in the handling of brick without the surrender of any of the principles of the Modern Movement. Aalto's early buildings, such as the sanatorium at Paimio (1929-33) and the library at Viipuri, are finished in either exposed concrete or stucco on brick. His later work is executed in brick and his interest in the material is evident from the treatment of the courtyard walls at his summer house in Muuratsalo. There are about 50 panels in which different sizes of brick and ceramic tiles are displayed with different methods of jointing. The town hall at Säynätsalo (1950), the Pensions Bank (1953-6) and the Kulturitalo (1955-8) in Helsinki all show his skill in handling the material, which he had already demonstrated in the United States when he designed the dormitory block for M.I.T. in Cambridge, Massachusetts (1949).

Eliel and Eero Saarinen, (1873-1950 and 1910-1961), show their Scandinavian origins in their enjoyment of brickwork, the contrast between the sharp angular forms of the Lutheran Chapel in Minneapolis (1949) and the curves of the chapel at M.I.T. (1955) underlining the versatility of the material. This can also be seen in a comparison of buildings by Louis I. Kahn (1901-74) and Philip Johnson (b.1906). Kahn's brickwork at the Richard's Medical Research Building Philadelphia (1960) and the Yale University Art Gallery expresses simple rectangular forms, while the Kline Biology Laboratory (1965) and Kline Geology Laboratory in New Haven by Philip Johnson show brickwork used as a smooth skin around the reinforced concrete frame.

Scandinavian influence has been considerable in brick building. Aalto's influence is clearly discernible in two buildings at Cambridge, England, by Professor Sir Leslie Martin and Colin St John Wilson. Harvey Court (1962), built for Caius College, shows the suitability of brick for expressing large and powerful forms while the William Stone Building, Peterhouse, displays the elegance of brickwork when treated as a series of vertical planes.

The modern uses of the material, particularly the current fascination with colour and decoration, show that the only practical limitation of brickwork is set by our own ingenuity.

Above *Morris Gift Shop,* San Francisco (1949, Frank Lloyd Wright). The arched entrance to this gift shop shows how Wright was able to treat brick as a decorative as well as a structural element. One of the abiding features of Wright's architecture was this delight in the particular qualities of each material.
Right *Residential building,* Peterhouse, Cambridge, England (1965, Sir Leslile Martin and Colin St. John Wilson). Brick is used in two completely different ways in this college residential building. This view of the river front shows an open grid expressing the individual rooms; the rear of building where the services are, is more solid. The brick is treated as a series of interlocking sculptural planes, applied over a concrete frame.
Far right *Kline Science Center,* New Haven, Connecticut (1962-5, Philip Johnson and Richard Foster). In this building, brick forms a smooth skin around the reinforced concrete frame and is used for its textural qualities as surface application. The heavy columns have a monumental quality.

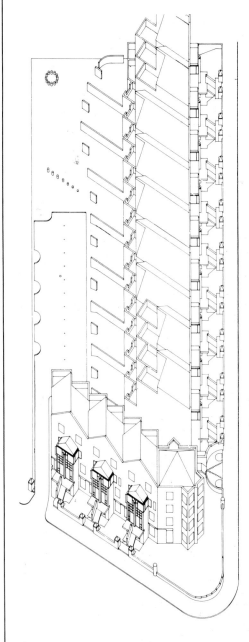

1

Left and below The axonometric (*left*) and plan (*below*) show how the angled corner site has been exploited to provide privacy in the rear and interest on the street facing side.

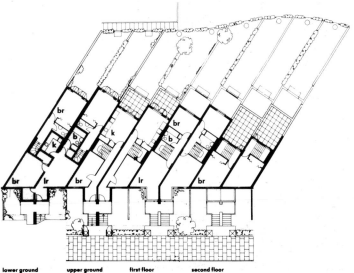

lower ground   upper ground   first floor   second floor

2

St. Mark's Road, London
(1980, Jeremy Dixon). A
concern for privacy and
individuality has
conditioned the residential
character of London: few
other major cities have less
of a tradition of apartment
living. In St. Mark's Road, a
public housing
development, both this
tradition and the particular
context of the site have been
acknowledged. Although
each unit was restricted in
size, the entire
development had to match
the surrounding Edwardian
villas in scale. The solution
was to divide each house
into several units. This
arrangement preserved the
character of the street (1).
At the rear, the angled site
gave an opportunity to
maintain privacy for the
individual gardens (2).
Colour and decoration was
reserved for the street
facade, the rear elevation
being left plain. On the
street side, colour is used
to emphasize the different
entrances. Even each flight
of stairs has a different
pattern of quarry tiles (3).
The gate posts give a
rhythm to the street and
incidentally hide garbage
bins. The use of brick in
these house fronts makes
imaginative reference to
many architectural styles,
such as Queen Anne, De
Stijl and Art Deco, but the
overall quality is one of
restrained geometric
patterning (4). The brick was
chosen to match typical
London stock. In this
example, brick has been
used to produce an
imaginative vernacular.

Iron and Steel

As building materials, iron and steel were very different from the materials that builders had used before. Earlier changes, such as the introduction of brick in late medieval England, had not implied a new architecture, as they could be used for load-bearing walls in much the same way as the stone buildings that they superseded. But iron and steel are much stronger and more expensive than older materials, and so it became logical to use them as linear members, first as tie bars, then as columns and finally as complete frames, with cheaper, more durable materials used to form the walls and to keep the weather out. The history of iron and steel in architecture is, therefore, largely the story of the framed building and how to clothe it comfortably and beautifully, while still acknowledging that powerful frame inside.

The advantages of iron and steel are that they are very strong and easy to work, but these materials also have serious drawbacks. In their most common form, they rust and decay after prolonged exposure in a damp atmosphere. Even worse, they do not behave well in a fire, for iron will shatter and steel will lose its strength. For these reasons, although steel will build a skyscraper, the material itself must be carefully covered up to protect it from the atmosphere and from fire. This has presented designers of steel buildings with something of a conundrum. For centuries,

Right and below *Eiffel Tower*, Paris (1887-9, Gustave Eiffel). Gustave Eiffel was France's greatest bridge engineer of the railway-building age, and the construction of his tower brought large-scale engineering to the heart of Paris. Only the arches linking the four bases are reminiscent of the forms of masonry construction. Regarded as "mere engineering" in the nineteenth century, artists like Antoine Pevsner and Robert Delauney later opened people's eyes to the beauty of its fine lattice structure and the spatial proportions.

Right *Centre Pompidou, Paris* (1975-7, Piano and Rogers). Ninety years after the construction of the Eiffel Tower, another dramatic structure appeared, this time the work of an English and an Italian architect. Similarly, the steel structure is lightened by the use of diagonals; triangles are more rigid than rectangles, which need heavier members to make them firm. In this building, however, the emphasis is not entirely on structure, as bold use was made, in the external design, of the mechanical services, principally air handling ducts, which are usually hidden from sight in modern urban buildings, so taking up a great deal of space and much of the budget.

the expression of a material and how it joined and supported was one of the touchstones of architecture, but it is difficult to express a material that must be covered up.

The Material

Iron is the second most common metal and the fourth most common of the elements that make up the earth. Although iron is an element, in commercial usage small quantities of other materials are always present. It is the varying amount of these other elements, principally carbon, that gives us cast-iron, wrought-iron or steel. Cast-iron is the most resistant to corrosion and the easiest to make, so its major use in building predates steel; wrought-iron is the easiest to work; steel is the strongest, but unfortunately the quickest to corrode.

The nature of steel is determined by heat treatment after it is made, and by the presence of very small quantities of other materials. These materials affect the cost and the behaviour of steel and many hundreds of different steel alloys are marketed to do different jobs: manganese steel withstands repeated knocks, tungsten steel withstands high temperatures, chromium steel does not rust, nickel steel is very tough, copper steel forms a layer of rust that adheres to the surface and so on. Mixtures of steel with elements, such as silicon,

molybdenum, vanadium, boron and others, make up the commercial range marketed by steelmakers today. Mild steel is the most frequently used for building construction, because, as its name implies, it has none of the extreme qualities of the special steels. As conditions on building sites may be less precise than in a factory, mild steel is the most useful in this application.

Steel is made from iron, and iron is made by converting ores in a furnace. These ores are found in most areas of the world, with two-thirds of the known reserves in the Americas. There is no risk of the deposits being used up in the forseeable future, but the enormous demand for iron and steel in the last 200 years has led to the exhaustion of the best ores and the industry is having to use ores of a lower and lower quality. However, technical advances in mechanical handling and in smelting, added to decreasing demand caused by world overcapacity, have led to a continuous drop in the price of steel in real terms.

Manufacturing Techniques

Iron is made from iron ore in a blast furnace, and the process is called smelting. In a modern blast furnace, hot air is blown into a mixture of ore, coke and limestone, in a continuous operation, to give a temperature of 2370°F (1300°C). It is a structure of some size and drama, about 260 feet (80 m)

high, made of steel with a fireclay lining. The products of smelting are pig iron or cast-iron, hot gases, and slag, which is either thrown away, used for ballast for railway tracks or used in cement manufacture.

Iron is more difficult to smelt than copper, and consequently the Iron Age came after the Bronze Age. The first iron used was probably meteoric iron, which needed no smelting. When the Europeans first went to the American continent they found that the Aztecs had no knowledge of smelting, but used meteoric iron which they regarded as more precious than gold.

The first smelting of iron probably took place in Asia around 2000 B.C. Its use subsequently spread to the Mediterranean countries. Iron was in general use in the classical world for making tools and weapons, but not for building.

In medieval times, the iron industry grew, and the advent of the cannon made the ironmasters crucial men in any nation. The iron was smelted by the use of charcoal, and England's forests were cleared to provide this material. In the later eighteenth century, Abraham Darby (1711-63) at Coalbrookdale began smelting with coke instead of charcoal, and, as a result, the quality of iron increased dramatically and the price dropped. Darby needed a bigger market for his iron than cannon, and turned to building and engineering structures.

During the early nineteenth century,

William Fairbairn (1789-1874) and Eaton Hodgkinson (1798-1861) applied the mathematical studies that had been undertaken in France to the iron structures underway in England and produced systems for analyzing and calculating the forces within a structure. The engineer with his slide rule began to take over from the craftsman when it came to making decisions – just in time for the construction of new bridges to take the heavy loads of the railways.

The experiments of Hodgkinson and Fairbairn revealed the limitations of cast-iron for structural work. For a while, reliance was placed on wrought-iron, and, in 1850, the Cooper Union Building in New York City was built with a structure of rolled wrought-iron beams. However, a series of bridge failures, notably the disasters at Ashtabula, Ohio (1876) and Firth of Tay, Scotland (1879), resulted in a generation of engineers who looked increasingly to steel as the better structural material.

As early as 1828, steel was used for the eye-bar cables of the 312-foot (95 m) span suspension bridge over the Danube at Vienna, but the high price of steel restricted its use during the first half of the nineteenth century principally to edged tools and similar applications; in the early 1850s, annual British production was only 60,000 tons of steel, whereas total British iron production was 2,500,000 tons.

Henry Bessemer (1813-1898), working in St. Pancras station in 1855, made malleable iron from pig iron by blowing air through a converter. This was the beginning of the steel industry. Production rose tenfold in a decade and kept on rising. By 1960, world production of steel was 350,000,000 tons annually and a sixth of this was used by the construction industry.

The air that Bessemer injected into his converter caused the carbon in the steel to combine with the oxygen in the air. Bessemer granted licences to steelworks up and down the country; however, his

Below *Iron Bridge*, Coalbrookdale (1779, Abraham Darby II). The first sizeable iron structure to be built, this bridge spans over 100 feet (30 m) across the River Severn. Coalbrookdale is in Shropshire, which was probably the only place in the world where there were the skills to cast the 70-feet (21 m) long main ribs at that time.

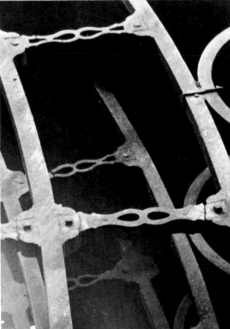

Above and left Joints between the iron members of the Iron Bridge at Coalbrookdale were made by means of wedges, dovetails and screws, which were all designed and made by Abraham Darby and his son-in-law. Bolts were not used; rivets and welding techniques were still inventions of the future.

licencees soon discovered problems. The phosphorous content made the steel brittle, and by chance Bessemer's own experiments had been made with pig iron of low phosphorous content. Bessemer suggested to his licencees that they import Swedish pig iron which was low in phosphorous, but by then no one trusted his recommendations. Despite this setback, Bessemer set up his own steelworks in Sheffield and used Cumberland iron with great success. The problem of the phosphorous in Bessemer steel was finally solved in 1879 by a London police court clerk called Thomas, a spare-time amateur metallurgist; Thomas suggested putting lime into the converter and this dealt with the phosphorous. However, by this time, the Siemens-Martin open hearth process was already challenging Bessemer's methods.

Most of the world's steel is today made by the open hearth process. Friedrick and William Siemens constructed a brick honeycomb to preheat air and pass it over a low-grade coal. This gave off a gaseous fuel which resulted in higher temperatures in the furnace. Such a furnace was used by Emile and Pierre Martin, who charged it with iron ore, steel scrap and pig iron to bring the carbon content to the required amount. The process has been continually improved, notably with the addition of control and monitoring systems and oxygen jets, but the basic process is still the same today.

Iron was traditionally used cast in moulds of oil-bound sand, but steel can be finished in many ways. Like iron, it can be cast; it can be drawn into thin wires or rolled into thin sheets which can be strengthened by corrugations. The most characteristic steel form in building is the rolled section, where steel ingots are rolled to standard profiles – I-beams, channels, tees and hollow sections. These have the advantages of being structurally efficient, easy to join and standardized, the last being important now that the calculation of dimensions is a codified procedure, enforced and checked by a government inspectorate.

The Iron Bridge at Coalbrookdale (1779) had members which were interlocked and then wedged together. This was an awkward way of joining and did not guarantee that stresses were passed from member to member, so bolting soon became the normal procedure. The introduction of rivetting gave a tighter fit than the early bolts, but modern bolts have largely eliminated that advantage. During the First World War, welding came into its own in the munitions industry, and its use spread to shipbuilding, bridgebuilding and the construction industry. It was generally found to be more expensive to weld a joint than to rivet it, but the extra cost was more than offset by the possibility of using lighter members now that they would not be weakened by holes for rivets. Although welding is now the normal method of joining structural steels, there are still problems with welding very heavy sections and with some alloy steels. As it is also more difficult to weld on a building site than to bolt, both methods continue side by side.

Development and Application of Iron

First Uses

Renaissance buildings made use of iron for tie rods across arches and for chains around domes, but it was the introduction of coke-smelted iron in England in 1747 that raised the quality and lowered the price of cast-iron so that it could be used for major building elements. Between 1770 and 1772, St. Anne's Church in Liverpool was built with cast-iron columns, and during the next half-century the material was developed first for bridges over the Severn and then for nearby factories in Shrewsbury and Derbyshire.

The first major cast-iron structure to be built was the 100-foot (30 m) span Iron Bridge at Coalbrookdale, now within the boundary of the new town of Telford. It was in October 1775 that Thomas Pritchard, a Shrewsbury architect, first suggested that the proposed bridge at Coalbrookdale be constructed of cast-iron. He was in the right part of the world for this idea to be taken up, for Abraham Darby had pioneered the use of coke for smelting at Coalbrookdale and his son was probably the only man in the world who could build the bridge, with its main ribs reaching halfway across the river and each weighing 5¾ tons. There were no precedents for the construction of this bridge. Abraham Darby and his son-in-law, Richard Reynolds, had to work everything out for themselves – bolts, rivets and welding were all in the future. They evolved techniques of joining where members were slotted one into the other and secured by iron wedges.

It is not easy to work something out from scratch, and just as the early railway engineers designed trains like a string of stage coaches, so Darby and Reynolds borrowed the arch form of a masonry bridge. Nevertheless, the bridge is beautifully constructed and stands today as an elegant reminder of the skill of the early ironmasters, and of their bravery in designing and building such a structure before it was generally known how to calculate structural materials.

The Coalbrookdale bridge might have remained an isolated example of iron bridgebuilding, but, in 1787, the 30-year-old engineer Thomas Telford (1757-1834) was appointed Surveyor of Public Works for Shropshire. The Coalbrookdale bridge fell into this parish and Telford soon aban-

Right and below *The Benyon, Marshall and Bage Mill*, Shrewsbury (1797). This is the world's first metal-framed multistorey building, and may be considered as the progenitor of all modern skyscrapers. Only the outer walls are of brick; all the internal structure is of iron so as not to burn. Columns are shaped in accordance with Charles Bage's understanding of the stresses within them and the column tops are formed to take the pulleys and drives for the original machinery. In 1803, Bage designed an extension to his mill roofed with cast iron trusses. The joints between members slide into each others and lock, like a Chinese puzzle.

doned his mason's training and enthusiastically took up cast-iron. His bridge at nearby Buildwas spanned 123 feet (40 m), yet weighed only half as much as the Coalbrookdale bridge.

Early Factories

The construction of the early cast-iron bridges coincided with the building of the first factories. The type of building constructed to house the new industries had already been set by John Lombe's silk mill built in Derby in 1718. In 1769, Richard Arkwright (1732-1792) patented his water frame, which set the British textile industry on a century of world supremacy and produced a situation where small-scale operations were no longer economic; from the time of this patent, work was increasingly concentrated and the factory, a new building type, came onto the scene. The early factories were built by Arkwright and his licencees, and they were spaced along rivers, such as the Derwent, wherever a change in water level generated enough power to turn the water wheels.

The Arkwright mills of the last 30 years of the eighteenth century followed the model of John Lombe's Derby mill, with four, five or six storeys, brick or stone outside walls and heavy timber frames. With a young and often tired workforce, oil lighting and an inflammable product in a timber-framed building, fire was more than a hazard, it was a certainty. One after another of Arkwright's mills were destroyed by fire within a year or two of completion. The entire development of the Industrial Revolution in England was held up by the lack of fireproof mills.

William Strutt (1756-1830), a millowner and son of Arkwright's partner, was the first to tackle the problem. His calico mill of 1793 in Derby was six storeys high and measured 115 x 33 feet (35 x 10 m). Columns were cast-iron, of cruciform section to give maximum strength without the casting difficulties of hollow, round columns. Timber beams spanned between these columns and between these were vaults of hollow pot construction levelled with sand and paved with bricks. The underside of the timber beam, which would otherwise have been exposed, was plastered and then covered with sheet metal for fire protection.

In 1786, Victor Louis roofed the Théâtre Français in Paris with an iron frame. In spite of revolution and war, news of this encour-aged Strutt to proceed with the development of the iron-framed mill. Although Strutt had advanced most of the way to the fireproof mill, metal-covered timber was something of a makeshift. It remained for Charles Bage, who knew William Strutt and Telford, to take one of the major steps forward in building technology, by making a building with the internal construction completely framed in metal. This flax mill, at Shrewsbury, was finished in 1797 and still exists.

The mill is a five-storey building, 180 x 39 feet (55 x 12 m), large by the standards of its time. Bage was conversant with the development of iron and the first notions of its calculation, and he shaped all the structural members to accord with his estimate of the stresses. To make the building as fire-resistant as possible, no timber was used anywhere – there were stone stairs, cast-iron window frames, vaulted floors and roof. In an 1803 extension, Bage spanned the roof with the first cast-iron trusses.

William Strutt quickly followed Bage with his own North Mill at Belper completed in 1803. This is probably the fourth metal-framed building ever built, and it was splendidly serviced. It was ventilated by passing air, heated in winter, through ducts discharging through adjustable registers. Belper North Mill is six storeys high, the top floor reserved for a Sunday school for the young workforce.

The Bage mill had a Boulton and Watt steam engine and these engineers, Matthew Boulton and James Watt, were not slow to realize the developments that were taking place. When they were commissioned to construct a new mill in Manchester for the Salford Twist Company, they developed the cast-iron frame for a much larger building than Bage's and to a much greater degree of sophistication. It was heated by steam passing through hollow columns and beams, and lit by gas. The completion of a building of such quality in Manchester set the standard, and cast-iron construction became normal.

All of these mills had outer walls of brick or stone. There are various claimants to being the first to construct the completely metal-frame multistorey building. In 1840, the greatest of the English mill builders, William Fairbairn, built a prefabricated mill with outside walls of iron plates and shipped it to Istanbul for erection there; and in 1849 the American, James Bogardus (1800-1874), built a factory at Center and Duane Streets in New York entirely in glass and iron, Italian Renaissance in style.

Fairbairn's Istanbul mill and Bogardus' factory both disappeared long ago and few

Right *Sheerness Boathouse* (1858-60, Colonel Greene). It is probably the oldest multistorey building in existence to be completely framed in iron including the outside walls. It is also the first building where use was made of H-sections and I-beams – shapes which have since been standard for metal-framed buildings.

records remain, but it is probable that both buildings used masonry to take wind and other non-vertical loads. The oldest all-metal frame multistorey building, with rigid connections to take wind loads, is probably the four-storey Sheerness Boathouse of 1858-60, a magnificent building, which is unfortunately difficult to visit as it is in the Naval Dockyard. The designer of the boathouse, Colonel Godfrey Greene, had previously employed the contractors who built the Crystal Palace and had been influenced by their expertise. The Boatstore is clad in corrugated iron, and it was the first building to use the I-sections which are standard in structural steelwork today. A dozen years later, the Menier Chocolate Company built a factory, the Turbine Building, astride three turbines in the river at Noisiel-sur-Marne in France. Here the frame uses diagonal members to ensure rigidity without elaborate connections.

In 1790, Robert Owen had successfully spun American cotton by machine. At once it became obvious to Americans that they could emulate this British success, and spin their own cotton in their own country. In 1793, Sam Slater, who had been employed in Arkwright and Strutt's Belper mill, built America's first cotton mill at Pawtucket, Rhode Island, powered by water from the Blackstone River. Slater had left Belper

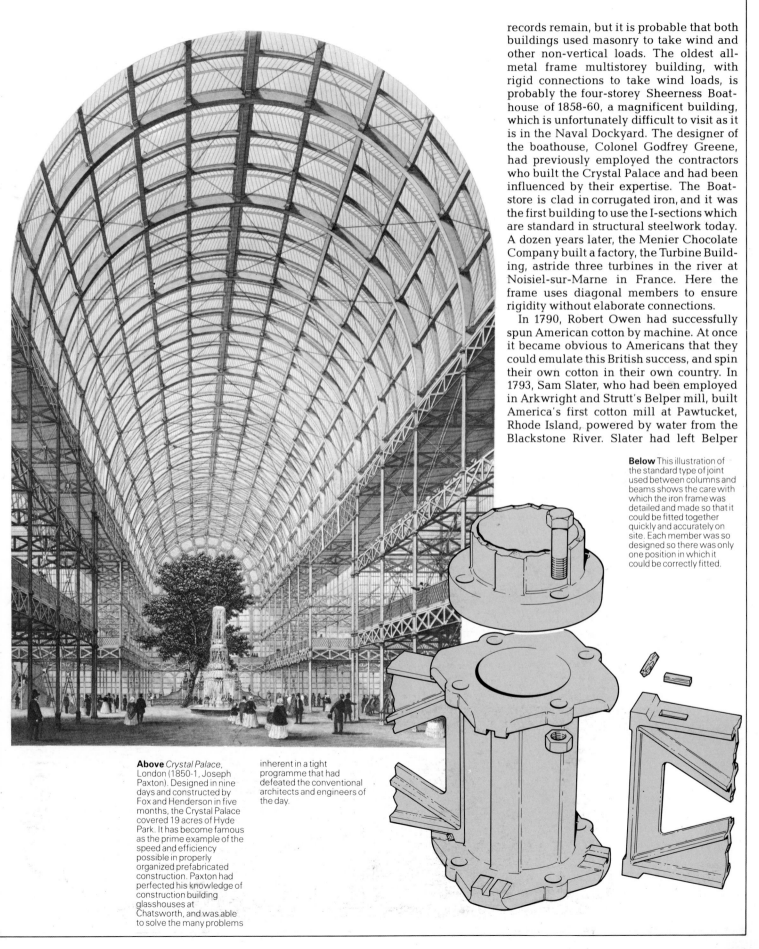

Above *Crystal Palace*, London (1850-1, Joseph Paxton). Designed in nine days and constructed by Fox and Henderson in five months, the Crystal Palace covered 19 acres of Hyde Park. It has become famous as the prime example of the speed and efficiency possible in properly organized prefabricated construction. Paxton had perfected his knowledge of construction building glasshouses at Chatsworth, and was able to solve the many problems inherent in a tight programme that had defeated the conventional architects and engineers of the day.

Below This illustration of the standard type of joint used between columns and beams shows the care with which the iron frame was detailed and made so that it could be fitted together quickly and accurately on site. Each member was so designed so there was only one position in which it could be correctly fitted.

before the arrival of the fireproof mills, and the Pawtucket building was built out of heavy timbers. The early American mills had outside walls of timber with shiplap boarding and the fire hazard in New England proved to be just as great.

When iron construction did come to American mill builders, fresh problems were in store for them, for the young republic did not have the skills, either at calculating or casting iron, that existed in England at that time. Columns were cast on their sides, and this meant that the core mould could slip out of alignment, so that a column taking a heavy load might have paper-thin iron on one side. Such columns, cast by the Eagle Iron Foundry, were used in the interior construction of Pemberton Mill, Lawrence, Massachusetts. The structure was perfectly fireproof, but, in 1860, it collapsed under its own weight, killing 200 people. This disaster discouraged builders from using iron; American mill engineers preferred timber construction until the end of the nineteenth century.

Office Buildings in Chicago

The great American contribution to building in iron was not made in mill construction but in office buildings, and not on the East Coast, but in Chicago in the 1870s and 1880s. Mid-nineteenth century Chicago was a boom town. Buildings were constructed of timber, with some cast-iron columns and beams, and with little serious study of the problem of fire. In 1871, the centre of the city was burnt to the ground in 48 hours, and in the heat of the fire, iron

Above left *Fisher Building* Chicago (1895, Daniel Burnham). More decorative than most buildings of the Chicago School the Fisher Building shows elements of that style – a clearly expressed regular frame, and bay windows to catch the light in narrow city streets. By 1895 the metal framing technique had been mastered in Chicago: once out of the ground the framing to the Fisher Building went up at the rate of a floor a day.

Above right and right *Statue of Liberty*, New York (1883-5). Beneath the green copper covering is the first large steel frame in the world. Designed by the sculptor Bertholdi and engineered by Eiffel, the Statue of Liberty was made in Paris and brought piece by piece, for re-erection at the entrance to New York harbour.

structural members melted, the running molten iron contributing to the spread of the fire. The city centre was destroyed and 100,000 people made homeless.

In the ruins of the city stood the nearly completed Nixon Building, designed by Otto Matz, at La Salle and Monroe Streets; the builders cleaned it down and completed it in two months. The triumphant success of the Nixon Building was due to its masonry external walls, and to the fact that the iron members of its internal frame were fireproofed with a layer of concrete or plaster. The next year, hollow terracotta blocks were introduced for floor construction, for building partitions and for encasing the structural iron. Efficient, economical fireproofing had arrived and was first used for the Kendall Building at 40 North Dearborn Street, completed in 1873.

Among those engaged in the frenetic rebuilding of Chicago's commercial district was the engineer William Le Baron Jenney (1832-1907). His First Leiter Building of 1879, still standing at Wells and Monroe Streets, takes some of the loads on the outside walls on iron members – almost true skeleton construction. It also shows mastery of the architectural expression of this type of construction – all windows and piers on all floors look alike, indicating the repetitive nature of a framed building, as opposed to traditional load-bearing structures, where walls became thicker nearer the ground.

In 1885, Jenney built the Home Insurance Building at La Salle and Adams Streets, a building best-known for its use of steel. The architectural expression of the iron frame is not nearly so clear as the First Leiter Building, but the structure was "pure" skeleton – all loads were taken on the metal frame. The building was no beauty, but Jenney made two great contributions; he instigated safe metal framing, whereby subsequent skyscrapers were and still are constructed, and he trained in his office the men who would design the beautiful Chicago skyscrapers of the next generation – Louis Sullivan (1856-1924), William Holabird (1854-1923), Martin Roche (1855-1927) and Daniel Burnham (1846-1912).

Development and Application of Steel

First Uses

Cast-iron as a building material arrived in the laissez-faire world of eighteenth- and early nineteenth-century Britain, but by the time steel arrived a century later, governmental control affected the use of the material. While the use of cast-iron had spread rapidly and indiscriminately, and was used with great flair leading to some dramatic disasters, the spread of steel was a

Above, left and below
Chrysler Building, New York (1929, Van Alen). New York skyscrapers in the years before the Wall Street Crash grew taller and taller. Sometimes they were dull, but sometimes, as at the top and the bottom of the Chrysler building, all is Art Deco styling carried out with verve.

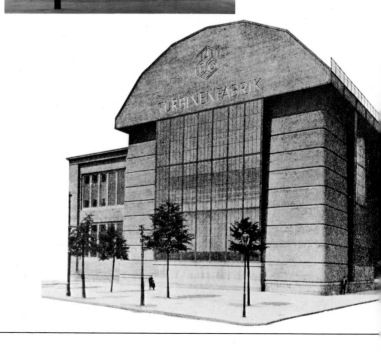

Above and right *Chrysler Half-ton Truck Plant*, Detroit (1937. Albert Kahn). The factory's exterior (*above*) and interior (*right*) are typical of the later designs of Albert Kahn, whose massive design organization served the motor industry. The roof profile gave extra light from above, and space for mezzanines and mechanical services.

slow and carefully monitored process, mercifully free from disasters, but often inhibited by bureaucratic obstinacy. In 1859, the engineer John Hawkshaw (1811-1891) proposed to use structural steel for his Charing Cross railway bridge in London, but he was refused permission by the Board of Trade who, for the next 20 years, would not allow steel to be used for shipbuilding or for structural work. It was left to the Dutch and the Americans to pioneer the use of the new Bessemer steel.

The first bridge using Bessemer steel was built in Holland in 1865, and the qualities of the material were fully demonstrated by Captain James B. Eads (1820-1887) in his beautiful bridge over the Mississippi at St. Louis, opened in 1874. The Eads bridge used Carnegie-Kloman chrome steel and launched Andrew Carnegie's career as a steelmaker. Some of the structural members of the Eads bridge were iron, but four years later, General William Sooy Smith spanned the Missouri at Glasgow, South Dakota, with a bridge entirely constructed of steel members.

In Britain, the Admiralty were not affected by Board of Trade restrictions and, after 1870, all major warships were built of steel. In 1877, the Board of Trade realized that steel could not be banned forever and appointed a committee (of only three men) to advise on the use of structural steel; the committee reported favourably on the merits of the new material. Arguments continued, but the use of steel was finally permitted in time for its use on a grand

Below *A.E.G. Turbine Factory*, Berlin (1909, Peter Behrens). In the early years of this century, architects started to admire simple structures and industrialists wanted something better then the Victorian mill. This shared interest is apparent in the clear structure of the Turbine House, the first building where a distinguished architect has enjoyed the design of the factory for its own sake.

The Ritz Hotel, London (1906). British government regulations had delayed the use of steel for building construction, but it was the completion of the Ritz Hotel that marked the beginning of its popularity. The British had been concerned with rust and the probability of deterioration of hidden frame members. However, in 1903 there came an opportunity to investigate the problem when the extension of New York's rapid transit system necessitated the demolition of a 12-storey steel-frame building at the corner of Broadway and 42nd Street. The magazine Scientific American reported on the excellent condition of the steelwork which had been painted with paint made from carbon and linseed oil, with white lead and tallow on machined surfaces. The steel was built into brickwork and terracotta and the only deterioration was found where the finish had been damaged during erection. The British were encouraged by these discoveries, and plans for the Ritz were begun. Although the London Building Act of 1894 did not permit the use of rivetted connections between beams and columns because the authorities were worried about thermal movement and required slotted holes to allow for the expansion and contraction of the beams, Mr S. Bylander, the engineer, persuaded the council to relax this requirement. The building went up with cleats shop-rivetted to the beams. However, the wall thickness requirements of an Act that envisaged load-bearing walls could not be modified so although the walls of the Ritz are carried on the frame at every floor level, they thicken as they descend.

The steel frame was recommended by the structural engineer because of the design freedom it gave, which was welcomed by the architects for their interiors (for example, partitions on different floors did not need to be directly above or below each other), but it seems that they were a little frightened of its implications for the exterior, and maybe relieved to have to design the outside of the building like a load-bearing masonry wall. But if the walls have to be thick enough to carry the load of the building, one might be prompted to question the necessity of the steel frame.

The building of the Ritz was started in June 1904 and completed in October 1905. The architects were French, the engineers were reference books, the erection foreman and the building tackle were American. The construction style proved popular, and many office buildings followed in the next years, with steel frames and load-bearing front elevations. It was to be some time, however, before steel construction was celebrated as something specific to our age, and could be enjoyed for its own sake.

Above right Second Leiter Building (1889-91, William Le Baron Jenney). Designed by Jenney, the greatest pioneer of high-rise frame construction, the Second Leiter Building takes a few tentative steps along the road to finding an appropriate expression for the metal-framed building.

scale in the Forth Bridge (1883-90), designed by John Fowler and Benjamin Baker.

The expense of setting up a rolling mill was so great that steel was marketed in standard sections, unlike cast-iron where special moulds for individually designed pieces presented no problem. The use of standard rolled sections, combined with the very high degree of reliability of the material, led to codified design procedures, and tables in which engineers could look up the load-bearing capacities of different steel members. The Phoenix Iron Company produced the first such handbook in the United States in 1869. This was followed by the Carnegie *Pocket Companion* in 1873, which became the manual for steel designers around the world.

In 1883, construction was started on the Statue of Liberty, which had a copper skin over a steel frame designed by Gustave Eiffel (1832-1923) and reaching up 147 feet (45 m). However, the first major use of steel in a conventional structure was probably William Le Baron Jenney's Home Insurance Building in Chicago, completed in 1885 and demolished in 1931.

Skyscrapers and Factories

In Jenney's Home Insurance Building, often claimed as the first true metal-framed high-rise building, the first five floors were built with cast-iron columns and wrought-iron beams, but the next five floors were built with Carnegie steel beams. Two additional steel floors were added in 1889.

Jenney followed his success with the Second Leiter Building (later the Sears Roebuck store) at State and Van Buren Streets. This building has a much more relaxed appearance than the Home Insurance and lacks the heavy base. Jenney's Fair Store at Adams and State Streets (1891) used steel for columns as well as beams. His Manhattan Building of the same year at 431 South Dearborn Street had a lighter structure, so that wind loads became a more significant factor – these are accepted through the frame by deep connections on the upper floors and by concealed steel diagonals at ground level. It was another 50 years before architects became brave enough to expose the diagonals needed to brace the tall frame.

Jenney was the structural innovator, but it was the young men trained in his office who gave clear architectural expression to the technical expertise he taught them. The Tacoma Building of 1889 by Holabird and Roche introduced rivetted connections. They followed this with the Marquette Building, still standing at 140 South Dearborn Street. Daniel Burnham's office produced the beautiful Reliance Building (1894), a facetted glass tower at 32 North State Street. But the most skilled of all were Dankmar Adler (1844-1900), and Louis Sullivan, whose Wainwright Building at St. Louis (1891), Guaranty building at Buffalo, New York (1895) and Carson, Pirie, Scott store in Chicago (1898), brought the fireproofed metal frame to as clear an expression as was possible with the means of the time.

The first complete steel-frame high-rise building in New York was probably the American Surety Building at Broadway and Pine Street designed by Bruce Price. Its 20 storeys took it to a height of 295 feet (90 m).

Following the success of the Tacoma and the American Surety, there was nothing to stop skyscrapers from growing and growing – and that is precisely what they did. The scene of this development was New York, where the buildings were more highly styled and less structurally innovative than their predecessors in the Midwest. In 1913, Cass Gilbert's (1859-1934) Gothic-style Woolworth Building reached 60 storeys, followed in 1929 by William van Alen's Chrysler Building, its 77 storeys capped by a flamboyant Art Deco topping. In 1930, Shreve, Lamb and Harmon's Empire State Building was completed. It had 102 storeys and there, for 40 years, the record stood. The Depression made sound financial planning more important than breaking height records, but skyscraper building went on.

Concern for the canyon-like streets between the skyscrapers led to zoning ordinances requiring set-backs – buildings with stepped-back storeys. The Finnish architect Eliel Saarinen's (1873-1950) entry for the Chicago *Tribune* competition of

Right *Farnsworth House,* Plano, Illinois (1946-50, Mies van der Rohe). Architecture comes no purer than this. All that is solid is the steel frame; all that is not structure is glass. Designed as the weekend house for a single person, the functional requirements were minimal, so the architect could concentrate on a poetic statement of the beauty of ordered structure.
Below *Eames House,* Santa Monica, California (1949, Charles and Ray Eames). Built for their own use by the creators of this century's most famous chairs, this house is very different from the Farnsworth House. Here the steel frame is light, almost playful; colour and diaphanous materials abound. This is the "kit" approach, not the fixed world of classicism.

1922 set a style, and the era of set-backs and ziggurats began. The 1930 Daily News Building by Raymond Hood (1881-1934) and John Howells was a pacesetter, but the next year the same architects built the McGraw-Hill Building, the first American skyscraper to show clear awareness of the European Modern Movement, with highly emphasized horizontals and an Expressionist top. In 1932, Howe and Lescaze built the Philadelphia Savings Fund Society building in Philadelphia, which had real architectural distinction, in Modern Movement terms.

The skyscraper is a very dramatic building, and steel made it possible. Less dramatic, but equally important, is the refinement of the single-storey factory, a development that took place in America in the 1920s and 1930s. The industry that forced the pace was the automobile industry, and the architect who led the way was Albert Kahn (1869-1942). Kahn was a new kind of architect. His clients saw him as a businessman, not as an artist; the demand was for cheap buildings, built quickly and finished on time. Albert Kahn built up a vast office which produced designs for major buildings in a matter of a few days, yet from commercial requirements he created some beautiful buildings. A typical Kahn factory has a steel frame, shop-welded and site-bolted, with a bay size 40 x 60 feet (12 x 18 m), and a roof line with alternate bays, raised to give clearstorey lighting and to provide additional height for lavatories, offices and service runs. The production floor is left clear for practically any industrial activity, to ensure that the building will not be obsolete when the process changes. Ford's River Rouge plant outside Detroit is Kahn's biggest work, his Chrysler half-ton truck plant at Mound and Eight Mile Road in Detroit, the most elegant. Both are extremely successful functional buildings.

The Modern Movement

While the Americans developed the steel frame, and the English built their first tentative steel buildings, the Europeans, in the early years of this century, were taking the first steps towards the creation of a new architecture. A faith in new technologies was a cornerstone of the new Modern Movement. Steel and concrete were to be enjoyed for their own sakes. The cloaking of a steel frame in traditional stonework was seen as a crime.

First, however, the tenuous forms of Art Nouveau provided inspiration. The curvaceous steel of Victor Horta's (1861-1947) buildings in Brussels, Charles Rennie Mackintosh's (1868-1928) in Glasgow and H. Guimard's (1867-1943) Paris Métro stations had their moment of glory before the world of fantasy gave way to the puritan seriousness of the Modern Movement.

The Dutch architect Hendrick Berlage's (1856-1934) Amsterdam Stock Exchange,

Left *John Hancock Center,* Chicago (1968-70, Skidmore, Owings and Merrill). This is one of the world's tallest buildings, but its structural weight was reduced by trussing the facades with diagonals. The resulting structural efficiency is also dramatic.

Above *Métro Station,* Paris (Hector Guimard). Designed at the turn of the century, these underground station entrances contain all the long, tenuous curves in iron so favoured by the architects of the Art Nouveau.

completed in 1903, has exposed steel trusses in an expensive, sophisticated space. Berlage's passionate belief in revealing materials and construction led him to display the trusses as they were – undecorated and uncovered. As roofs do not need fireproofing, the trusses did not need to be clad in another material.

Peter Behrens' (1868-1940) Turbine House (1909) for A.E.G. on Berlin's Huttenstrasse is a first on many counts. The city had known steel structures before – overhead railways, factory roofs, the glasshouses at Dahlem – but it is at the A.E.G. Turbine House that exposed steel is at last reverently treated by a major architect. Although large, the building is single-storey. As it is generally assumed that single-storey buildings do not need fireproofing, Behrens was able to expose the steel. The rivets, the glazing bars and the hinged bases to the frames are all treated confidently, expressing the material. The massive concrete corners, however, are a reminder of masonry construction.

Behrens' pupil, Walter Gropius (1883-1969), took the next step with the Fagus Shoe Last Factory (1911) at Alfeld-an-der-Leine, where the corners of the building are all glass. Gropius said of the steel-framed building, "the role of the walls becomes restricted to that of mere screens, stretched between the upright columns of the frame to keep out rain, cold and noise".

The heyday of this International Style was marked by a preference for smooth white buildings. Concrete could give this, steel could not; many important modern buildings were framed in steel, and the structure and skin were then plastered over to look like concrete. For an architectural movement dedicated to truth to materials, this development was decidedly odd.

Arthur Korn and Ludwig Mies van der Rohe (1886-1969) broke away from the confines of the International Style to explore the possibilities of expressing the steel structure. Mies' 1929 Barcelona Pavillion and his Tugendhat House (1930) in Brno, Czechoslovakia, used cross-shaped columns and sheathed them in chromium-plated steel to emphasize the luxurious qualities of the material.

Arthur Korn's Fromm Rubber factory (1930) at Kopernick deserves a key place among the heroic buildings of the Modern Movement. Constructed of red-painted steel with white glazed brick infill, it is the

Right Cummins Engine Company, Darlington (1965). Designed by American architects, this factory was the first major building in Britain built of weathering steel. The steel rusts and the rust adheres to form a protective patina. This is the only modern material that weathers with age like stone.

first building to express the steel frame as a regular cage. With this building, the architectural expression of multistorey steel structure had gone as far as it could go until the acceptance of welding.

During the Second World War, the structural steel industry in America was compelled to build big and fast. The construction of plants like Henry Kaiser's at Fontana and Willow Run were miracles of speed and organization. However, at the end of the war, it was a small domestic building that acted as a revelation to architects and designers the world over.

In 1947, the West Coast Magazine *Arts and Architecture* commissioned Charles and Ray Eames, the designers of Eames furniture, to design a case study house for their own use. The Eames House uses steel with ease and lightness. All the elements –

frame, decking and windows – are standard products out of catalogues. The lightness is achieved by taking the skin to the eaves over the fascia beam, by taking horizontal forces on clearly expressed diagonals and by using the same bar-joists as were later used in the Hertfordshire schools in England. The first domestic building to really express steel, the Eames House is one of the most cheerful houses of the Modern Movement.

Modern Steel Building

In spite of its fame, the Eames House inspired no copyists at the time. However, the steel architecture of Mies van der Rohe spread round the globe. The campus he designed for the Illinois Institute of Technology, most of which was built during the 1940s, was unified by a grid spread over the

site. The buildings had black painted steel frames which fitted on the grid.

The design of exposed steel frame and brick infill dates from Arthur Korn's Kopernick factory, but in the intervening decade the all-welded structure had become feasible. This meant that the detailing at I.I.T. could be neater and waterproof joints could be made, enabling rolled sections to be built up and exposed on the outside of the building.

The Minerals and Metals Research Building (1943) was the first I.I.T. building to be completed and set the grammar of the structural frame which is expressed inside and out. The Library (1944) was the greatest of the I.I.T. designs, using the same design in a more sophisticated way. It has rolled sections joined by continuous welds to give members a complex profile, which hold the brick infill clear of the columns, emphasizing the direction of span.

The Alumni Memorial Hall (1946) was, however, the most influential of the I.I.T. buildings. As it is a two-storey building, Mies had to face the problem of fire protection. At that time, Chicago architects believed that technology would soon give them a fire-resistant steel and students designed buildings on the assumption that this already existed. Mies could not wait for this development, however, and the Alumni Hall went up with the structural steel encased in concrete. This fireproofing concrete was faced with steel which formed part of a light steel framework on the outside of the columns. Architectural purists were horrified; the details did lack the clarity of the Library, but at last a fireproof steel building had been built which looked like a steel building.

After the Alumni Building, Mies went on to create the Farnsworth House near Pliano, Illinois (1950), 860 Lake Shore Drive, Chicago (1951) and the Berlin National Gallery (1969). He had made steel a major architectural material and given it a language of its own.

Mies's love of the clearly expressed steel structure was taken further by his pupil Myron Goldsmith (*b.* 1918), who became a partner in the large practice of Skidmore, Owings and Merrill. Goldsmith was fascinated by the structure of the very big building. As a student he had designed economically structured, highrise buildings by taking the horizontal loads on clearly expressed diagonals. Ever since the Manhattan Building of Jenney, steel-framed buildings had relied on diagonals to take the horizontal loads of wind or earthquake, but these diagonals had been hidden. In 1958, Goldsmith had proposed a design for a Seattle office building which had diagonals across the facade, but at 17 storeys, the building was easy enough to build by conventional means.

In the 1960s, Goldsmith and Fazler Khan

Top and right *Sainsbury Centre for the Visual Arts,* University of East Anglia, Norwich (1976-7, Foster Associates). The Sainsbury Centre is one of the most dramatic of modern English buildings. A steel space structure (*i.e.* a structure with beams and columns shaped like prisms and made up of numerous small members) contains the big volume within and forms a "service zone". Within this service zone inside the framing are lavatories, service rooms, ventilation, heating, lighting and access ways for the engineers. There is also a light filter so that sunlight can be baffled and gives an even light in the galleries. Both end walls are of glass, and this glass is without framing to emphasize the openness of the ends under the great structure above.
Above Until the Nissen Hut, walls and roofs were considered inherently different. At the Sainsbury Centre, they are identical and consist of metal panels, corrugated for rigidity and held in plastic gutter strips. Here two men are seen placing a panel on the roof. The panels are made removable so that solid may be changed to window.

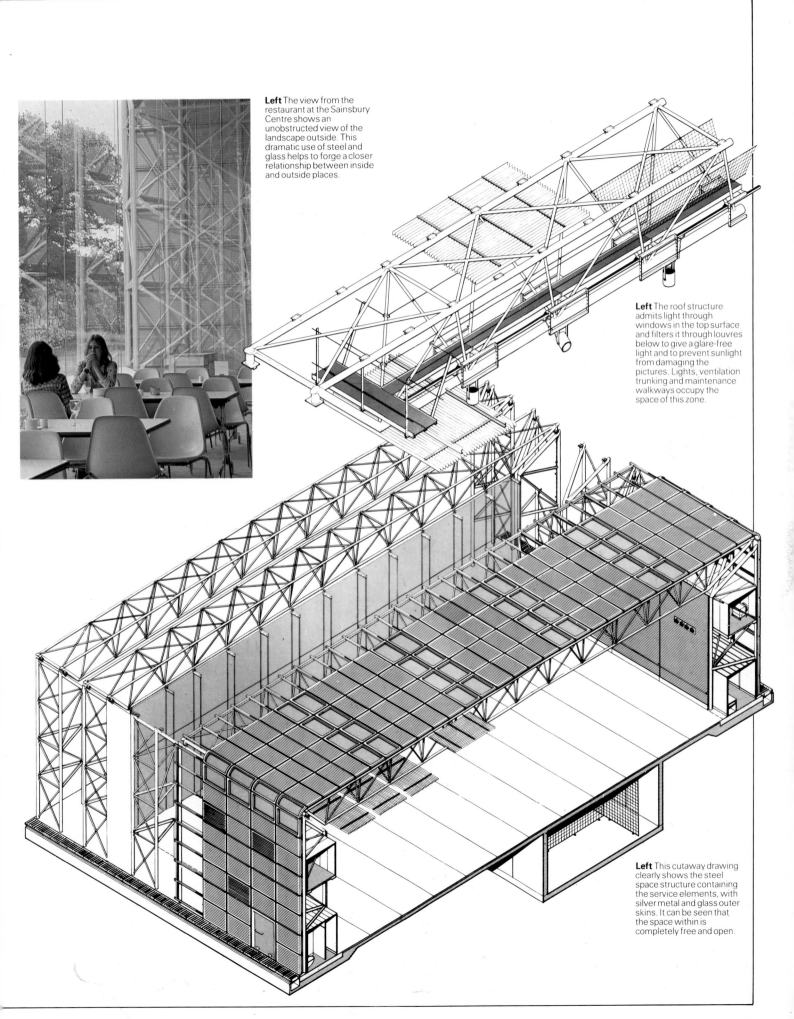

Left The view from the restaurant at the Sainsbury Centre shows an unobstructed view of the landscape outside. This dramatic use of steel and glass helps to forge a closer relationship between inside and outside places.

Left The roof structure admits light through windows in the top surface and filters it through louvres below to give a glare-free light and to prevent sunlight from damaging the pictures. Lights, ventilation trunking and maintenance walkways occupy the space of this zone.

Left This cutaway drawing clearly shows the steel space structure containing the service elements, with silver metal and glass outer skins. It can be seen that the space within is completely free and open.

(b. 1929), with their students at the Illinois Institute of Technology, investigated the possiblies of very tall buildings, and showed that lighter steel could be used if horizontal loads were taken by diagonals. This study coincided with an interest by developers in increasing height beyond that of the Empire State Building. The result of this coincidence of architectural, engineering and commercial desires was the construction of Skidmore, Owings and Merrill's Hancock Building on Chicago's north side in 1972. This was followed by the tower for Sears by the same architects, currently the world's tallest building at 109 storeys. The design of this building, which relies on a cluster of nine cellular tubes, gives it its structural efficiency. The completion of these two buildings marked Chicago's century of leadership in the techniques of highrise steel construction.

The tall buildings of nineteenth-century Chicago had exterior columns covered in brick, stone or terracotta for protection against the elements and fire. Following Mies' Alumni Memorial Hall where steel is put on the outside of the fireproofing, a generation of buildings was constructed with metal used both for cladding and for structure. Skidmore, Owings and Merrill's Lever House completed on New York's Park Avenue in 1952 was sheathed in glass and shining stainless steel. To a postwar generation it seemed to promise a better world, but its success was its undoing, as crude and badly built copies erupted in every major city in the world.

For those who did not take to the sleekness of Lever House, there was a steel alternative. In the John Deere Building at East Moline, Illinois, Eero Saarinen (1910-1961) used "Cor-ten", a steel which has a high copper content so that, after some years, surface rust adheres and protects the steel underneath. This was a modern material that would weather and become more beautiful with age, and more buildings followed using weathering steel, including the Chicago Civic Center, the Ford Foundation in New York and the Cummins factory at Darlington, England. However, the weathering of this material is difficult to forecast, and the difficulty of detailing a building so that it weathers well has deterred many architects from using Cor-ten.

The energy crisis of 1973 led to a change in attitudes. Faith in infinite growth was over, and each unit of energy, each piece of building material became precious. This gave rise to two architectural responses: the neo-vernacular, believing that "peasants" touched world resources lightly; and those who believed that only intelligent and highly sophisticated ways of building would allow economic use of resources. Architects of the second persuasion, though few in number, have emerged in England

Right 49A Downshire Hill, Hampstead, London (1977, Michael Hopkins). Designed for the architect's own family, this elegant house sits very happily amongst the neighbouring 200-year-old houses.

in the last decade with a series of influential buildings. Influenced by Mies, they take pleasure in the machine-made structures and in the hard edge; from Eames they take a love of structures made economical by the use of a multitude of tiny parts; from the space programme, a love of services, pipes and high technology imagery. To all this is added colour and sheer playfulness which is completely new to architecture.

The most famous building which exemplifies this approach is in Paris. A competition for a modern arts centre was held in 1971 and won by a team led by Richard Rogers (b. 1933) from England and Renzo Piano (b. 1937) from Italy. When the Centre Pompidou was completed in 1977, it aroused controversy and strong reactions, but few denied that it had style. As a reaction to the type of modern architecture that covered the structure with a curtain wall and a suspended ceiling, everything at the Centre Pompidou is on display — brightly coloured air handling pipes, circulation routes and a very complicated but clearly revealed steel frame.

The next year, Piano and Rogers finished the PATS Centre for a research organization in Melbourn, Cambridgeshire. Research organizations are continually changing, and Piano and Rogers adopted the usual solution of a light steel frame for the working floor, so that rooms and work patterns could change. Less usually, the exterior can change too. Maintenance men

can unzip a gasket to change glass for porcelain-enamelled steel. For centuries, architects have composed fixed facades; here a system was set up to accept random change.

Rogers' former partner, Norman Foster, has produced fine buildings in the hard-edge tradition. His Sainsbury Centre for the Visual Arts on the University of East Anglia campus at Norwich (1978), uses a deep structure of thin steel members as a service zone to contain mechanical equipment, both above and at the sides of the gallery. Lined on the inside with white louvres, through which structure and services can be glimpsed, the centre is a majestic and serene space. Less serene, but far more dramatic is Foster's proposals for the Hong Kong and Shanghai Bank, 590 feet (180 m) high, supported on massive steel columns.

Throughout the 1960s and 1970s, a series of beautiful small houses were built in England in the Miesian idiom. When Michael Hopkins, once an architect in the Foster office, completed his own house in Hampstead's Downshire Mill in 1977, the overtones were more of Eames than of Mies. Small spans, open web joists, and corrugated metal were used, a vocabulary later extended by Hopkins in his racking plant for the Greene King Brewery at Bury St. Edmunds, Suffolk.

Steel technology is evolving fast. One development still in its infancy is the use of suspended structures. The great bridges are now all suspension structures, and it may be that there are advantages to be gained from suspending the roofs of long-span buildings. There are certainly difficulties with uplift and flap (similar to those experienced in a tent in a high wind). Skidmore, Owings and Merrill's canteen building for Baxter Laboratories, (1976) north of Chicago, has a roof suspended from two masts, held down with internal cables and with more cables in each window mullion. Richard Rogers followed his 1981 suspended roof at Quimper, Brittany, with a factory for Inmos at Newport, South Wales. The roof is hung on cables from a bright blue open service spine. Foster's proposed Renault warehouse at Westlea Down, Swindon, has steel umbrellas hung from tubular steel towers, and, like Rogers' buildings, the appearance of the building is dominated by the towers and hangers. Steel continues to evolve, not only as a technology, but also in the way that that technology is expressed.

Left and above left *PATS Centre*, Melbourn, Cambridge (1976, Piano and Rogers). This research centre is constructed in steel to give a building that is light and flexible. Internal partitions can be changed, and also, on the outside, walls can be changed for glass and fixed glass can be changed for opening lights. For lightness, see the staircase up from the reception office with handrails of steel cables, tensioned like the rigging of a small yacht. It shows the elegance of steel.

Concrete

Concrete is a plain and unpretentious material, already some 2,000 years old. Reinforced concrete, on the other hand, has a relatively short history and is quite a different sort of material. Brash and versatile, it has stamped its image all over the modern world. In the twentieth century, reinforced concrete has been used to perpetrate both unspeakable eyesores and structures of great economy, ingenuity and delight.

Though surrounded by much evidence to the contrary, most of us still tend to think of concrete as invariably grey, dirty and stained: the epitome of soul-destroying ugliness. No epithet is intended to be more derogatory, when directed indiscriminately against contemporary urban buildings, than "they all look like concrete boxes". The effects of weather and pollution reinforce this innate prejudice – yet Portland stone, which stains abominably, is revered. However, it has to be admitted that *béton brut,* the waning architectural fashion for bare concrete, is not ideally suited to the damp grey climate of northern Europe.

To all but the purists, one way of avoiding this criticism is to apply tiles to the concrete surface, as the Romans did. Small white mosaic tiles, for instance, look like pristine concrete from only a short distance away. Another solution is to model the building so strongly that surface imperfections are of secondary importance and are scarcely noticeable.

Much development has been concentrated on improving the appearance of "visual" concrete – the type of concrete that is designed to be seen, rather than to be covered up. Attempts to achieve a significant difference in the colour of cement, by the addition of pigments, has not been very successful: time and exposure result in fading. The shades of grey, however, can be brightened by using white cement, silver sand and a near-white granite when making up the concrete. More importantly, the surface texture can be treated in interesting ways. Finishes can be varied by treating the surface directly or by applying different types of aggregate. The marks of shuttering can be left on the surface to give a board-marked finish; profiled and patterned finishes can be created by the use of special linings such as ribbed aluminium. One of the most effective profiled finishes is deep vertical ribbing, which encourages rainwater to run down the recessed grooves. Concrete is also a perfect sculptor's medium. With sufficient skill and dedication, the artist can model entire facades in bold relief, by casting it against carved polystyrene forms.

The Material

Mass Concrete

Of all the major building materials, concrete is the real hybrid. Like the latest group, plastics, it is a composite; unlike plastics, its constituents are to be found in their natural state. In its simplest, mass form, concrete is a cheap and efficient substitute for masonry. (Initially, it was seen as such and the artificial stone label still lingers.) There are only three basic components and all of these are available worldwide: cement, aggregate and water.

The cement, nowadays, is almost invariably a grade of "Portland" — so-called because its inventor likened its appearance to Portland stone — composed usually of limestone, silica, aluminous clay and gypsum. Portland is far superior in strength and durability to its predecessor lime cement, and has largely superseded it. High-

Above *Gatti Wool Factory,* Rome (Pier Luigi Nervi). Nervi's considerable skills as an engineer, and intuitive design sense, led him to develop the mushroom column, an elegant yet economical method of construction. The icostatic ribs — following the lines of stress — are both more attractive and less wasteful of material than flat slab construction.
Left This monument built in Como in 1936 by Cataneo is an exuberant demonstration of the engineering feats possible with reinforced concrete. Each band of concrete is marked with vertical lines, adding to the illusion.

Far left and below *Villa Savoye,* Poissy, France (1928-31, Le Corbusier). Villa Savoye is one of the private houses Corbusier built in and around Paris: these have had an immense influence on modern architects. This house displays all the features most associated with Corbusier's work. The roof terrace is treated as a space in its own right; the main floor is raised on pillars (*pilotis*) so that the garden can extend under the house; the windows are treated as horizontal strips. This formal, even classical style owes a lot to the particular qualities of reinforced concrete.

alumina cement (HAC), which contains bauxite instead of clay, is even stronger.

The aggregate is composed of fine sand and, in most cases, various sizes and shapes of coarse stone or gravel. Lightweight aggregates such as pumice, foamed slag, expanded clay and vermiculite are also used, particularly for precast building blocks. Cellular concrete, lighter still, is obtained with air-entrained bubbles.

The exact nature and proportioning of these ingredients is of vital importance to the performance of the finished product. There is good, bad and indifferent concrete; and the "mix" will vary according to the job that it is called upon to do. (A typical specification for a slab, for example would be written as 1 : 3 : 6 – the respective proportions of cement, fine and coarse aggregate.)

Above Boulder Dam on the Colorado River, Nevada (1931-6) is an example of the type of pure engineering structure which makes the greatest single use of mass concrete. The dam is 45 feet (14 m) thick at the top, 660 feet (200 m) thick at the base and 726 feet (220 m) high. Over 3,250,000 cubic yards (2,480,000 m³) of mass concrete were used.

Right To construct the GPO tower in London, 580 feet (177m) high, a core of reinforced concrete was first built up, around which concrete was poured with the aid of sliding shuttering. The structure, in effect, lifted itself. Unlike most tall structures, the building does not sway at all, due to the strength of the foundations. (The Empire State Building moves as much as 2 feet/4 m). It was particularly important for this building to be stable because of the transmitters and receivers at the top.

The essential feature of concrete is that it has great strength in compression, but very little in tension or shear. While it can withstand a massive axial load, it will not hold together under any comparable sort of pull. The modulus of elasticity of concrete is also exceedingly low and inconstant: that is to say, there is a tendency to shift or creep – a not entirely damaging phenomenon, technically known as "plastic flow".

It can take several hours for concrete to set, and four weeks to fully harden and develop ultimate strength. Other limitations include the fact that its denseness affords little resistance to impact sound and in its raw state it is not very attractive to look at. However, concrete is fireproof; it provides excellent sound insulation against airborne noise; and, in its initial semi-fluid state, it can easily be moulded. The fact that it can take up virtually any shape is a unique advantage.

Reinforced Concrete

The insertion of steel rods, wire or mesh into the concrete matrix completely transforms the performance of the material. Previous deficiencies in tension and shear are made good, so that the material is capable of spanning. Thanks to the continuity of the steel reinforcement, separate elements of a building become homogenous and monolithic. In that all the components act together, a reinforced concrete beam-and-slab system is structurally more efficient than, for example, a wooden floor composed of separate joists. When a series of beams and columns are rigidly connected together they form a frame which distributes the loads and stresses of one part to all the others. Effectively, the entire framework becomes a unified whole.

A comparison with traditional post-and-beam construction highlights the technical advance offered by reinforced concrete. Supports are smaller, spans are wider, and there is almost no upward limit to height. Reinforced concrete walls can also be thinner. The comparison with steel, on the other hand, is more a matter of degree. The choice between a steel-framed structure and one of reinforced concrete is often made on grounds of local expediency or even the personal predilection of the designer. Considerations of weight, assembly method, speed of erection, required lifespan, site access and many other factors will help to determine which is selected. For a straightforward conventional building such as an office block, reinforced concrete has two potential advantages – it will not need further fireproofing and, since floor slabs, roof and walls can all be brought into structural play, it is much more likely to be earthquake-resistant. There is, too, a total freedom in the size and shape of beams and columns (as well as other elements), whereas steel is normally restricted to a limited range of standard profiles.

The act of reinforcing concrete does not remove the basic limitations of concrete, and a new danger – corrosion of the steel – is introduced. Bad workmanship apart, this contingency is relatively remote since all building codes stipulate a minimum thickness of protective concrete "cover" (customarily two inches (5 cm) or so) which also maintains fire-resistance.

The behaviour of reinforced concrete is still unpredictable to some extent. Unlike mass-produced components such as steel or brick or even timber, reinforced concrete continues to change and age. Initial shrinkage and deformation, neither of which is uniform, progressively declines but may take several years to stop altogether. Quality of materials, mix ratio, rate of evaporation, dimensions, exposure and climate are just some of the factors that contribute to the uncertainties of performance. These uncertainties are exacerbated by "statical indeterminacy" – an engineering phenomenon where the precise conditions of equilibrium can never be positively identified because of the many alternative ways in which a reinforced concrete structure can elect to carry its loads. Stress concentrations, particularly at junctions, defy advance calculation.

The exceptional weather resistance of reinforced concrete, coupled with the

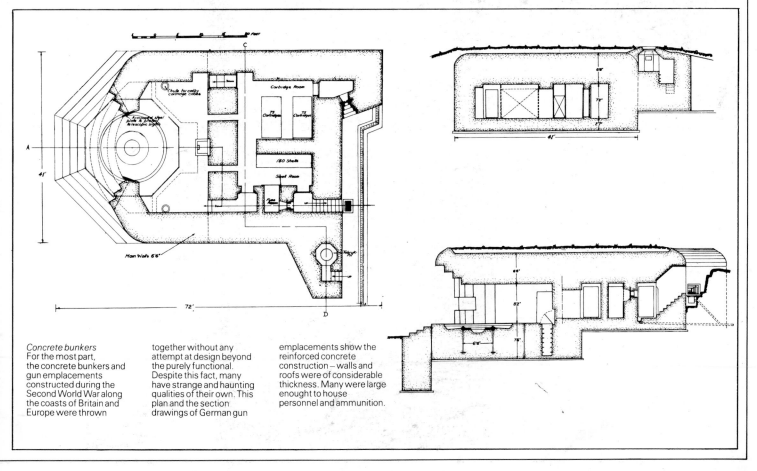

Concrete bunkers
For the most part, the concrete bunkers and gun emplacements constructed during the Second World War along the coasts of Britain and Europe were thrown together without any attempt at design beyond the purely functional. Despite this fact, many have strange and haunting qualities of their own. This plan and the section drawings of German gun emplacements show the reinforced concrete construction – walls and roofs were of considerable thickness. Many were large enought to house personnel and ammunition.

extreme hardness of its materials, makes it nearly indestructable. In an age addicted to demolition, this feature is not always regarded as a benefit. However, the material does have one overriding advantage. The imaginations of architects and engineers are set free from all manner of time-honoured constructional constraints – they can innovate, as never before.

Basic Techniques

The proper construction of a reinforced concrete beam, column or slab ''in situ' – that is to say, poured in place on the job – calls for a great deal of care and attention to detail. There are many factors, not forgetting the human element, that will affect the finished product.

The denser the concrete, the stronger it will be. Varying the type and quantity of cement also affects ultimate strength, and especially the rate of hardening. High water content reduces strength and increases shrinkage. There should be no more water than is necessary to achieve the correct chemical reactions and minimum workability.

Consolidation, preferably by mechanical vibration, increases density and is essential where the closeness of steel reinforcement inhibits the flow of the concrete. (Vibration, usually applied by special poker, to some extent overcomes the problem of thin mixes resulting from over-watering.

Concrete mixed at or below freezing point will simply not set; and the rate of drying also requires careful control.

Design of the shuttering against which the concrete is poured is crucial: it has to be rigid, well supported and without leaking joints. Every surface imperfection will be accurately transmitted to the concrete – for good or bad, depending on the designer and the contractor.

Concrete cannot, in most circumstances, be continuously poured. At the end of the working shift there will be a construction or ''day'' joint.

Achieving the planned objectives and attending to all the related site operations is labour-intensive and time-consuming. The clear need to economize in site labour, time and cost, as well as the desire to reduce inexactitudes, led to two early developments – permanent formwork and precasting.

Right This church in Heremence, Switzerland by W. M. Foerderer is an example of the strongly modelled sculptural effect possible with concrete. The celebration of angles is particularly well expressed in the corner apertures. Foerderer is an architect who trained originally as a sculptor, which accounts for the interest in modelling expressed here. This was carried out by unskilled local villagers.

Permanent Formwork

Although shuttering can be reused, basically by treating the casting face with a release agent, there are limits to the number of times that a piece of timber, ply or even metal can safely be employed again. Eventually, the shutter must be replaced; throughout its period of use it is necessary to take it down, clean it, and reassemble it in new locations.

The obvious alternative is to pour concrete against a lining which remains an integral part of the building. This idea is not new; the practice of depositing concrete between outer skins of brick or stone goes back centuries. Virtually any material that is keyed or rough on the unseen side is suitable, providing its coefficient of expansion is not too dissimilar from concrete. Materials most commonly used today include thin elements of precast concrete, woodwool, and glass-reinforced cement (GRC). Woodwool is the rather inappropriate name given to slabs of compressed wood-shavings bound in cement – a cheap insulator, frequently left unplastered as a ceiling. Glass-reinforced concrete is a lightweight composite material consisting of Portland cement and alkali-free glass fibres. It is sometimes used as a cladding material.

Over recent years, considerable strides have been made with both reusable and permanent formwork. Steel, aluminium, GRP and GRC have to a great extent superseded timber, though the initial expense of these materials calls for a high degree of repetition. However, obvious benefits result from comparative indestructability, accuracy and ability to be shaped.

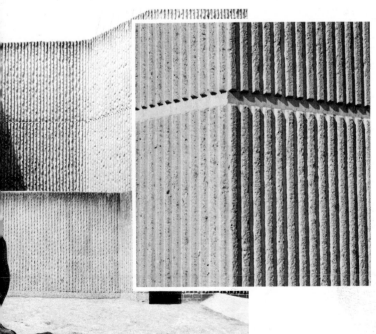

Above A persistent problem with concrete is staining – and it is this that has helped to give the material a bad reputation. In this London school, the disfigurement of staining has given the building a forbidding appearance, inappropriate for its function.

Above right Considerable care was taken during the building of the South Bank arts complex in London to keep the concrete as white as possible, but staining is still evident.

Left *Elephant and Rhino Pavilion,* London Zoo (1965, Casson and Conder). One half of this pavilion provides pens for elephants; the other houses white rhinos. The external walls are made of reinforced concrete, cast with vertical ribs and hacked to expose the aggregate. This creates a strongly modelled and textured surface which goes some way to disguising staining. Another benefit is that the water will run off down the back of the grooves in the surface.

Several moving formwork systems have emerged, notably sliding shuttering. Now commonly used for high-rise service cores, stair and lift enclosures, this system permits continuous pouring by using vertically sliding metal forms. Hydraulic or similar mechanisms raise the shutters at a sufficiently slow rate (a foot an hour, or less) to allow the concrete to set by the time it emerges from the shuttering.

An ingenious way of overcoming the problems of high-level staging and formwork is the lift-slab technique, in which all the floors are cast at ground level and subsequently lifted. Columns are first poured, the floor slabs are cast around them – one on top of the other, with a suitable means of separation – and then these are hydraulically jacked up to their correct position and connected to the columns.

Precast Concrete

Precasting, in common with so many other technical advances, demands standardization and repetition (disciplines which, in themselves, reduce cost and time). Compared with casting on site, there are formidable advantages: industrialized production methods are more efficient; factory conditions improve quality control; the designer is offered a wider range of finishes; the manufactured component is superior in accuracy, strength and weathering; and on-site time is drastically reduced.

However, given the need for continuity in the finished structure, new problems can arise on site with the jointing of the

Far right *Town Hall,* Kurashiki, Japan (1960, Kenzo Tange). This building displays a very Japanese treatment of concrete. The traditional timber details (such as overlapping beams) are replicated in concrete. The use of precast elements gives a very disciplined appearance.
Below *Olympic Sports Hall,* Tokyo (1964, Kenzo Tange). This suspension structure uses steel cables in tension with very strong concrete pylons to achieve the organic shape. The principle is similar to that of a suspension bridge.

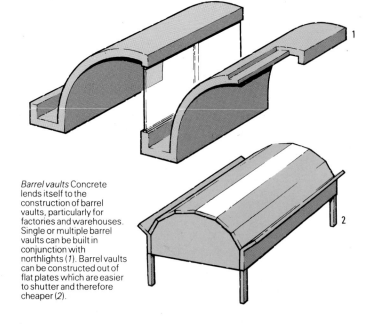

Barrel vaults Concrete lends itself to the construction of barrel vaults, particularly for factories and warehouses. Single or multiple barrel vaults can be built in conjunction with northlights (*1*). Barrel vaults can be constructed out of flat plates which are easier to shutter and therefore cheaper (*2*).

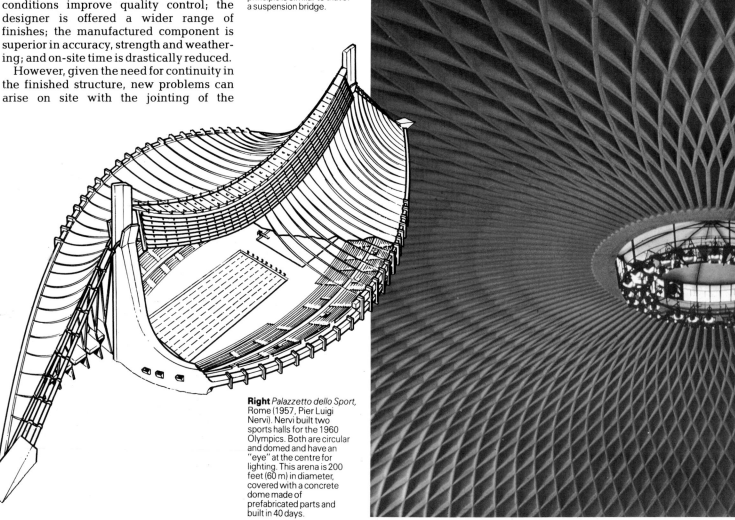

Right *Palazzetto dello Sport,* Rome (1957, Pier Luigi Nervi). Nervi built two sports halls for the 1960 Olympics. Both are circular and domed and have an "eye" at the centre for lighting. This arena is 200 feet (60 m) in diameter, covered with a concrete dome made of prefabricated parts and built in 40 days.

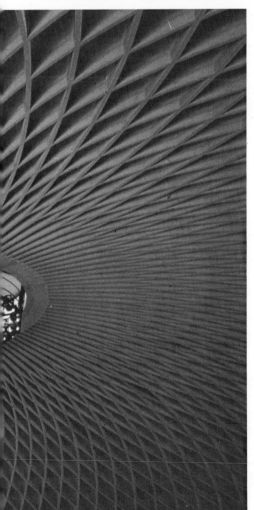

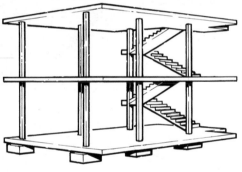

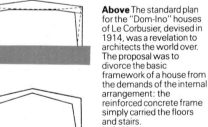

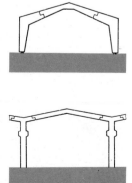

individual components. Structural engineers tend to view the whole construction process as primarily revolving around the connections, for it is these which must transmit stress, take up movement, and exclude weather. A great amount of effort has been directed at designing perfect systems of connection – yet contemporary buildings still leak and occasionally collapse.

In a structure composed of precast frame elements, continuity across the joints can be achieved by leaving projecting reinforcement and pouring concrete around it, or by bolting where there is least stress. In simple portal frames, for example, these joints will occur at the points where there is no bending moment. Similarly, as may be witnessed by anyone driving along a motorway, the main span of a precast concrete bridge (in all likelihood, prestressed also) is supported, at these points, by open joggled joints that incorporate rollers, permitting the beams to take up thermal movement.

Against the benefits of factory precasting must also be set the problems and cost of transportation – a not inconsiderable factor. For certain large jobs of a sufficiently repetitive nature, it pays to set up a suitable temporary enclosure and precast on or adjacent to the site itself. Since the advent of the tower crane, the final act of lifting the finished units into position is relatively easy.

Though the most interesting developments in precast concrete have taken place in the realm of custom-designed units, it should not be overlooked that a vast industry has grown up for the production of a host of off-the-peg components. These range from basic shed frames for light industrial and agricultural use, through domestic garages, to such humble everyday items as lintels, sills, copings, posts, kerbs, bollards and paving slabs.

Reference should also be made to the universal wall block, which, because of its superior thermal performance and relative cheapness, has largely superseded brick for partitions and the inner face of cavity walls. Solid or hollow, of varying density, surface texture and colour, it performs a yeoman service. The idea of inserting steel reinforcement and poured concrete into hollow blocks goes back several decades, and there has been a recent resurgence of interest in the application of structural reinforced blockwork.

Prestressing

In the short history of reinforced concrete there has been no more far-reaching and exciting technical achievement than the successful application of prestressing. Yet again, like all the best structural concepts, the underlying principle is simple, clear and far from new. Over the centuries,

Above The standard plan for the "Dom-Ino" houses of Le Corbusier, devised in 1914, was a revelation to architects the world over. The proposal was to divorce the basic framework of a house from the demands of the internal arrangement: the reinforced concrete frame simply carried the floors and stairs.
Left Simple precast concrete frames form the basis for many structures, from factories to bridges.

wheelwrights and coopers have bound their wheels and barrels with heated iron bands; and, on cooling and shrinking, these bands have compressed and tightened the underlying timbers.

Mass concrete has negligible tensile strength and placing steel reinforcing bars in the bottom part of a beam, for example, makes good this lack, enabling the beam to span horizontally and to carry superimposed loads. However, where sheer weight of the material and depth of beam is incompatible with the load and span – as occurs in wide-span structures such as bridges – this standard solution becomes unwieldy, uneconomic or even impossible. The reason behind this incompatibility lies in the imperfect interaction of two totally dissimilar materials. If the steel were to be stressed to its full capacity, the surrounding concrete would be in excessive tension. As a result, deflection would increase, the necessary bond would give way, and unacceptably large cracks would appear. A more effective bond can be obtained by deforming or twisting the bars, and high-tensile steel is often used in this way. However, the fundamental mismatch of steel and concrete still remains.

Above and right The government buildings in Sydney (*right*) and M.L.C. Centre in Canberra (*above*), both by Nervi and Harry Seidler, are very economic in their use of concrete, using prestressed beams.
Above left Ronan Point was built using an imported large-scale prefabricated system. When a gas explosion occurred high up in the building, causing the death of four people, there was not sufficient structural continuity to keep the various parts of the system together and the whole collapsed like a house of cards.

Right The fundamental principle of prestressing can be illustrated by the example of lifting a row of books by pressing them together. If pressure is exerted too near the top of the row, it will collapse; if pressure is exerted at the middle, the books can be carried; if pressure is exerted a little below the midpoint, the row will act as a beam and will even support other loads on top.

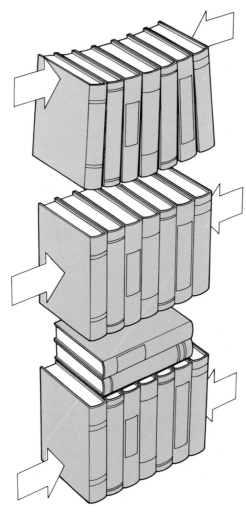

Below *Casa del Popolo*, Como, Italy (1932–6, Guiseppe Terragni). This beautifully proportioned building typifies the work of the Italian Rationalist School. The headquarters for the Italian Fascist Party, it makes effective use of the contrast between the expanse of material and the fine grid of windows and frame.

A way had to be found to balance the internal forces more closely. A Berlin builder, Doehring, took out a patent in 1888 for compressing mortar in small floor elements with iron wires tensioned by a screw-jack. Other experimenters took up his screw-jack idea, but it was to be some 40 years before Eugène Freyssinet (1879 –1962) and the Belgian engineer Magnel succeeded in transferring this principle to reinforced concrete.

What happens in a prestressed concrete beam is that the tensioned, extended steel attempts to revert to its original length and, in so doing, compresses the surrounding concrete. When bending takes place under load, the concrete will not be in tension until all the gratuitous compressive stress is used up. In practice, the amount of prestress applied is carefully set so that the concrete is effectively free from tension and the "dead load" or weight of the beam itself has been eliminated. (The downward load has been transmitted to a horizontal one, the stresses being taken up internally in the steel cables.)

The immediate result is that cracking is minimal and controlled, and there is an improvement in elasticity, resilience, structural continuity and weather resistance. Above all, a higher strength to weight ratio means that far longer spans become possible, and with less material. In comparison with conventional reinforced concrete, up to 70 percent concrete and 85 percent steel can be saved. Since, in their stressed condition, the two materials are balanced – and as all the concrete is now contributing – the profile of a prestressed beam begins to resemble a conventional I-section steel joist.

The fundamental nature and characteristics of a prestressed beam is most eloquently portrayed by Magnel's analogy of a line of shelved books. It is an experiment which anyone can do and unwittingly often does. When we come to lift a row of books, we instinctively press with our hands at both ends, fairly low down, and up comes the row of books as if they were glued together. The separate books, which would otherwise slide apart, have been unified by compression and the row acts as a composite beam – a "beam", moreover, that will carry an additional load on top. (If you were to apply pressure centrally, or near the top, then your instinctive grasp of the principle would be faulty: the books would collapse.)

The prestressing steel elements, commonly high-tensile wires or cables, can be tensioned in one of two ways: before the concrete is poured, or after the concrete has hardened. Prestressing is by no means confined to horizontal beams. It can be equally applied to lattice girders and trusses, to cylindrical forms such as silos, to dams, and to vertical masts and tower structures.

Other Advanced Techniques

Ferro-cemento is the name coined by its inventor, Pier Luigi Nervi (*b.* 1891), for thin slabs of cement reinforced with steel mesh. Nervi's wartime experiments included the design and building of boats, in a time of steel and timber shortage, with hulls of cement mortar trowelled in through steel mesh and then smoothed – a method used today by countless yacht enthusiasts. These hulls weighed no more than timber ones and cost a little over half; comparisons with steel were even more favourable. After the war, Nervi used the material most effectively in his Turin exhibition halls and many other structures, enabling these to be erected and completed in record time. Several layers of very fine mesh, saturated with cement, produced a homogenous material of exceptional flexibility and strength. Precast off plaster moulds, ferro-cemento was used for moveable shuttering, permanent formwork, and for structural units. The finished surface was extremely smooth, needing no additional treatment or maintenance.

Gunite is the application of concrete pneumatically sprayed onto steel mesh or an "inflatable". There was some experimentation in the United States during and after the last war, with sprayed "bubble" structures; but these do not appear to have been viable. Sprayed concrete continued, however, as a worthwhile technique for irregular, complicated double-curvature shapes and for light-weight shell structures. The apparently solid and very thick front wall of Le Corbusier's Chapel of Notre Dame, Ronchamp (1955) is, in fact, faced with a gunite skin. Sprayed concrete combines well with steel cable suspension nets, and its special properties include high strength and density due to the velocity of placement and the low water-to-cement ratio.

Development and Application

Roman Use of Concrete

The Romans, who must be credited with inventing concrete, mixed lime, water and pozzolana – a volcanic ash containing silica and alumina – to create a cheap and primitive material to which they applied stone or brick. With this early type of concrete, they constructed arches, domes and vaults that were often cast in one solid mass. In terms of roof-spanning, this was a significant advance on the unmortared post-and-lintel methods of the Greeks. Notable examples include the Pantheon (A.D. 120-4) and the *thermae,* or baths, in which the outward thrust of the roof was absorbed by transverse walls – comparable to the action of Gothic buttressing. Lime cement, gravels and quarry debris were plentiful; as was the supply of unskilled slave labour. Considerable engineering skills gave rise to the rapid and widespread expansion of arch and vault construction

Left *Weaver's Mill,* Swansea (1898, François Hennébique). The first large reinforced concrete framed building in Britain, this warehouse was built to withstand tremendous floor loads. The cantilever above the loading bay would have been impossible without reinforcement.

Above *Chapel of Notre Dame,* Ronchamp (1950–5, Le Corbusier). Built around a hidden reinforced concrete frame, which was filled with rough masonry and rendered with gunite, this chapel uses concrete not to express the purity of the Modern Movement, but to suggest a traditional type of folk building. The soft contours and sweeping roof echoes the site of the church in rolling countryside.

throughout the Roman empire.

Apart from continuing rudimentary usage for rubble and concrete-filled walls, concrete virtually disappeared after the decline of the empire. The expertise, for the design and assemblage of formwork, appears to have been lost; only to reappear, centuries later, with the advent of the pointed arch and the increasingly elegant application of stone ribs and vaulting. When, for example, the Early Christian builders were working on the tomb of St. Theodoric in Ravenna, around A.D. 530, they elected to cap it with a shallow dome 35 feet (11m) in diameter, shaped from a single stone slab – a prodigious, yet unsophisticated, feat.

Engineering Advances

In 1794 Joseph Aspdin started producing Portland cement and this was to pave the way to the large-scale adoption of concrete, initially in Britain and France. Suddenly, during the late stages of the Industrial Revolution, there was a rash of patents which included: a floor construction of concrete infilling and iron girders (Dr. Fox, 1844); "fireproof construction" in the form of concrete reinforced with wire rope (W.B. Wilkinson, 1854); and the basic principles of reinforced concrete (François Coignet, 1855). Though the reinforcement of concrete is often attributed to a French gardener, Monnier, who in the 1860s stiffened concrete water basins with a network of iron rods, the historian Sigfried Giedion has pointed out that the concept was not new – Henri Labrouste (1801-75) for instance, had formed the vaults of the Bibliothèque Sainte Geneviève (1845-50) of wire-reinforced plaster.

The latter part of the nineteenth century

Left *Notre Dame*, Le Raincy (1922–3, Auguste Perret). This is one of the first buildings where concrete is expressed as a material in its own right. The flat concrete vault is supported by thin pillars. The walls are made of precast concrete elements, making a trellis effect. All the structural concrete in the church is left unfaced.

witnessed the introduction of reinforced concrete to frame and slab buildings, often warehouses or mills, where the load-bearing requirements could more efficiently be satisfied than with timber or cast-iron. However, it was not until the early 1900s that the full potential of the new material began to be explored seriously. The first trials of strength were directed at obtaining greater spans, primarily in bridges.

Despite prior claims, it was indisputably François Hennébique (1842-1921) who established the art and science of "steel concrete", or ferro-concrete as it came to be called. Hennébique was not only an excellent engineer and contractor, but also a great entrepreneur. After establishing his credentials with various patents in the 1980s, he went on to set up an international organization with agents throughout North and South America, Africa and Western Europe. By 1917 his business could boast of 35,000 separate contracts. His own house, built in 1904 at Bourg-la-Reine, exploits the potential of reinforced concrete cantilevers and well illustrates his prodigious skills.

The new ideas spread fast. In the United States, William Ward was building houses of reinforced concrete on the East Coast as early as the 1870s, and in 1902 E.L. Ran-

some erected a 16-storey skyscraper in Cincinatti. In 1904, John Brodie, Liverpool city engineer, put up a three-storey tenement block that anticipated "large panel" systems by nearly 50 years. Each of the six sides of the rooms was precast, conveyed to site by traction engine and erected by block and tackle.

The next quest was the search for a way to reduce the amount of material and the depth of construction. This was to lead to the concept of the beamless slab, reinforced in two directions and carried by columns whose flared caps not only reduced the effective span of the slabs but also facilitated stress-transference from the horizontal to the vertical plane. Flat slab construction and mushroom columns were first introduced by the bridge-builder Robert Maillart (1872-1940) in 1908. The transition from a one-way to a two-way system had been made.

The Modern Movement

After the achievements of the great engineers, a new generation exploited the potential of the material: Perret and Le Corbusier in France, Lloyd Wright in America, Behrens, Gropius, Steiner and Mendelsohn in Germany, Loos in Austria, Maillart in Switzerland, Torroja in Spain,

Right *Johnson Wax Company*, Racine, Wisconsin (1936–49, Frank Lloyd Wright). The interior of the administration building has reinforced concrete mushroom columns holding up an illuminated ceiling. These graceful lily-like forms are arranged so that each just touches another. The columns have hollow cores which act as storm water drains. Wright even designed special office equipment and furniture for use in this buiding.

Above *Lovell Beach House*, Newport Beach, California (1925–6, Rudolf Schindler). A partner of Richard Neutra, who built the Health House for Dr Lovell one year later, Schindler was also an exponent of the International Style. Their open plan buildings which were characterized by the use of glass with gleaming white walls had an enormous effect on architecture on the West Coast. Schindler had originally worked with Frank Lloyd Wright.

Right *Rue Franklin apartments*, Paris (1903, Auguste Perret). This is one of the first buildings where a reinforced concrete frame is clearly expressed, although the concrete itself is covered up with decorated ceramic tiles and mosaic. The deep recess at the centre of the façade brings light into the building.

Candela in Mexico, Niemeyer in Brazil, and Nervi in Italy. It is unnecessary to distinguish between architects and engineers, inventors and builders: most combined a variety of skills. While the earliest forms of reinforced concrete had understandably followed the pattern of iron and timber construction, these master builders developed structural solutions and shapes that were entirely novel, stretching the performance of the new material to limits scarcely exceeded today.

The startling new departures in art, music, and to a lesser extent in literature, were paralleled by a radical purism in architecture. This purism, eschewing ornamentation in favour of broad expanses of concrete and glass, ushered in the Modern Movement.

Ornamentation did not disappear overnight, however. Quite early on in a working career that spanned over 70 years, Frank Lloyd Wright (1867-1959) used highly modelled concrete blocks in his idiosyncratic designs, particularly effectively in the Millard house of 1923. Meanwhile in France, Auguste Perret (1874-1954) was breaking new ground in a restrained transitional style. His Rue Franklin apartments, built in Paris in 1903, exhibit a patrician elegance, and the Church of Notre Dame, Le Raincy (1922-3) reinterpreted stained glass windows with a splendid open tracery of concrete.

Others, notably Rudolph Steiner and Erich Mendelsohn (1887-1953), exploited to the full the plastic quality of concrete; producing, in Mendelsohn's Einstein Tower (1920) and Steiner's Goetheanum (1925-28), a disturbing and potent imagery that must in part have stemmed from the Expressionists.

Above *Goethenaeum* (1924, Rudolf Steiner). Steiner's mystic philosophy expressed itself here in organic imagery. This institute looks like it has been moulded out of clay. Like Mendelsohn, Steiner was part of the Expressionist movement in Germany which saw the goal of all art as the representation of powerful emotions.

In the civil engineering sphere, Eugène Freyssinet remained in the forefront until the 1950s: building wider and wider bridges across the rivers of France and Belgium and developing the science and techniques of prestressed concrete. In 1916 he built two gigantic parabolic airship hangars at Orly which, unfortunately, were destroyed in the last war.

In 1933, Robert Maillart spanned the Schwandbach gorge with graceful curves that complemented the mountainous setting. In this, as in most of his other bridges, he introduced thin vertical planes of reinforced concrete to support and stiffen the slightly arched plane of the road-deck, with the result that the whole construction is an elegant unity. By comparison, many of today's bridges seem disjointed.

The architect to whom the discovery of reinforced concrete meant most, however, and who in turn contributed more to its entrenchment as the prime building material and aesthetic of the century, was Le Corbusier (1887-1965) (born Charles-Edouard Jeanneret in Switzerland). His writings, notably *Vers une Architecture*, 1923, and theoretical projects had an immense impact, but for many years his genius was unfulfilled. The sweeping Ideal City concepts – with thousands of people housed in skyscrapers above an endless, gridded parkland – were clearly too grandoise, too Utopian (and, paradoxically, too inhumane) to be realized. However, Le Corbusier did suceed in putting up more than one Unité d'Habitation (1946-52) and in 1952 his campaigning zeal was at last rewarded with the master plan and key buildings for Chandigarh, the new capital of Punjab.

It was, however, the less ambitious early buildings of Le Corbusier that have had the greatest influence. His private villas in and around Paris, and the Swiss Hostel, Paris (1931-2), were stunningly innovative in plan, section and appearance. Smooth square-edged facades, broken only by bands of glass and roof-terraces, are poised on *pilotis* (heavy, reinforced concrete columns). Inside, traditional room divisions

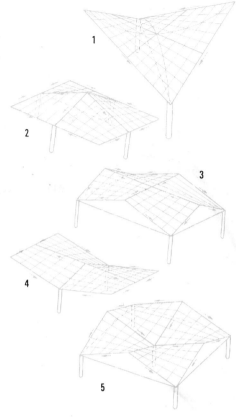

Hyperbolic parabaloids
The basic hyperbolic parabaloid, although double-curved, is straight-line generated: that is, it can be made using straight formwork that is simply twisted to produce the warped shape. This warping gives the resulting concrete cover it strength. The basic hyperbolic parabaloid (*1*) can be combined in a variety of ways to make different shapes (*2, 3, 4, 5*). These thin shapes are often used as covers for filling stations, garages and other simple structures.

Right *Schwandbach bridge*, Canton Berne, Switzerland (1933, Robert Maillart). Unlike many of today's inelegant motorway bridges, this structure has a grace which complements the drama of its setting. Maillart was the first to use thin planes of concrete vertically.

Above This roof, designed for a factory in Mexico by Felix Candela, is composed of four square domes, each composed of four thin shells in the form of a hyperbolic parabaloid.
Left *"Los Manatiales" restaurant,* Mexico (Felix Candela). The use of thin undulating concrete shells is a striking example of the powerful shapes possible with this material.

Left *Airship hangars,* Orly (1916–24, Eugēne Freysinnet). These huge airship hangars, each 984 feet (300 m) long and 205 feet (63 m) high were parabolic in section and made of reinforced concrete. The ribbing in the concrete gave it stiffness and strength. Unfortunately, these monumental structures were destroyed in 1944.

give way to open planning. Painted white, and proportioned by the "Modulor" (Corbusier's version of the Golden Mean), these houses were, and remain, consummate works of art. Invariably they were constructed in reinforced concrete, the only suitable material.

Corbusier's influence and prestige, undiminished by later works such as Ronchamp and La Tourette, was tremendous. The so-called International Style was largely his creation. By contrast, Frank Lloyd Wright developed his organic style in isolation: the closest he came to his European contemporaries was in Falling Water (1936), the house he built for Edgar Kaufmann.

This period of development saw the thin beamless slab transformed into the even thinner shell. Warped, curved and undulating roof membranes were designed, but the necessary traditional timber formwork for such curved and complex shapes was costly. Pier Luigi Nervi addressed himself to this problem and solved it with the use of permanent or reusable "ferro-cemento" shuttering. Nervi was an innovator of the very highest order. Throughout his lifetime he preached and practised economy of material, cost and time. A continuing search for greater efficiency in structure and erection methods led to a succession of impeccably engineered buildings that were as handsome as they were original. Strangely enough, volumetric geometries that followed the lines of stress, while at the same time obeying the dictates of prefabrication, brought back an intricacy of detail that was functionally decorative. One has only to look at the hangars, factories, exhibition and sports halls that he designed to get the measure of his achievement. Later, his unique talents were combined with those of Marcel Breuer in the Paris

Right This Volkswagen assembly plant under construction in Venezuela was designed by architects working in the Candela tradition. The 50 thin hyperbolic parabaloids are cantilevered from the columns and tilted for clearstorey lighting.
Below This motorway garage on the M1 in Nottinghamshire, England, has a rudimentary cover in the form of a hyperbolic concrete shell. This type of structural gymnastics looks dramatic, but is in fact economical and simple to produce.

Left *Cistercian Monastery of La Tourette*, Eveux, France (1960, Le Corbusier). One of Corbusier's last major works in France, this monastery combines a public church with a private cloister. The building is elevated from the ground and has a quality of austerity and simplicity emphasized by the rough board-marked finish to the concrete.

Below *Villa Savoye*, Poissy France (1928–31, Le Corbusier). These stairs with curvilinear screens provide access to the roof garden at the top of the house. Corbusier believed roof gardens were important as they replaced the area taken up by the building. The main living area of the house is on the raised first floor rather than the ground floor: the first floor is reached by a ramp. The smooth planes of concrete show a delight in pure form.

Left *Aircraft hangar*, Orbetello, Italy (1939, Pier Luigi Nervi). This shows the precast reinforced concrete ribs before the erection of the cladding. The delicate lattice was supported by only six buttresses; a striking example of Nervi's daring engineering. Unfortunately, the hangar was destroyed in the war.

UNESCO headquarters (1958), and Harry Siedler (who had once worked for Breuer) in several prestigious Australian projects.

Modern Applications

By the 1950s, almost every conceivable shape that reinforced concrete could accomplish had been accomplished; and many of these shapes are very beautiful. There are others, such as wartime gun-emplacements, which also possess a strange and haunting quality of their own. Though reinforced concrete continues to be used in higher and higher structures, for example in telecommunication towers, and though the Japanese, in particular, continue to make innovative use of the material, it is disquieting to realize that all the major technical advances were established over 20 years ago. Two supreme achievements of reinforced concrete have been designed since the Second World War, one in 1957 and the other eight years later. Arguably, neither have been surpassed in the intervening years.

Perhaps the most astounding spectacle in the field of large, precast units, is Moshe

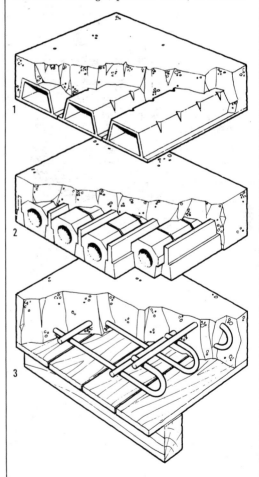

Types of concrete floor
1. Precast reinforced hollow beams are covered with a layer of concrete.
2. Solid precast reinforced concrete beams, alternating with lightweight hollow blocks, are covered with a layer of concrete.
3. Steel reinforcement is covered with concrete.

Left *Sydney Opera House* Sydney (1957–73, Jørn Utzon). The pristine appearance of the concrete shells is achieved by the application of white ceramic tiles which preserve the sharpness and clarity of the original design. The building stands dramatically on reclaimed land in Sydney Harbour.
Below left *TWA terminal*, Kennedy Airport, New York (1962, Eero Saarinen). The gull's wing shape of this airport building expresses some of the excitement of air travel.

Above and right *Habitat '67*, Montreal, Canada (1967, Moshe Safdie). Designed for Expo 67, Habitat is a setpiece which illustrates the potential of precast units for housing. Although Habitat remains in use, there have been no comparable schemes, possibly because of the large costs of transporting the units and lifting them into position (*right*).

Safdie's Habitat, built as a permanent housing complex at the Montreal Expo of 1967. Its designer has referred to it as a "handmade" prototype for a fully mass-produced three-dimensional building system. Yet this township of nearly 400 box units rising to 12 levels, called for the most sophisticated techniques of precasting and transportation, together with engineering expertise of the highest order. The magnificent array of piled-up boxes and street girders (which service, stiffen and partially support the units) is structurally knit together by prestress rods and post-tensioned cables.

Whereas Habitat is a rational, disciplined assembly, Sydney Opera House (1957-73) is representative of a more individual and poetic architecture. The engineering and manufacturing problems of Habitat were nothing compared with the Danish architect Jørn Utzon's masterpiece.

The Opera House was so expensive (about A$ 100 million) that it needed a state lottery to finance it. A very large proportion of the cost went, not just on the fabrication and erection of the giant shells, but on the engineering design process. It was a process that took six years, 2,000 computer hours, and something like 500,000 man hours. The shells went through many geometric permutations – pointed arches that did not follow the line of thrust, elliptic and cubic paraboloids, and ellipsoids – before the final design was reached – spherical triangles derived from the same 246-foot (75m) diameter sphere. Though the story may be apocryphal, the solution is reputed to have suddenly struck the architect as he was about to peel an orange.

Despite many promising schemes, there have not been any projects to equal Habitat, and the famous Opera House (which was so nearly a disaster) could never be repeated. Doubtless there are lessons to be learnt: about design over-reach, inflexibility, irrecoverable cost, and the diminishing taste for architectural "monuments". Several well-publicized structural failures involving reinforced concrete – from the Ferrybridge cooling towers, Ronan Point and Aldershot barracks, through to the Berlin conference hall and San Francisco convention centre – have also added tarnish. The unpopularity of high-rise system-built flats has done nothing to improve the image of concrete.

In the future, designers will need to be conscious of the causes of failure, and be aware of the continuing gulf between theory and performance. Computerized design aids will augment laboratory and model analyses and back up further innovations in a material whose formal and technical potentials can not have been exhausted.

Glass

The discovery that the three common materials – sand, soda and lime – could be fused together by heat to form a hard transparent material is generally thought to have originated in the Middle East, sometime before 1500 B.C. Glass was at first used only for decoration, but when it was realized that in its molten state it could be cast or blown into shapes, simple hollow vessels were also produced.

The Romans did much to perfect these techniques and were even able to make a type of flat glass for use in buildings by rolling out the hot glass onto a hard flat table. The surface of this glass was rough and it was not very transparent.

Crude glass is coloured by traces of iron impurities, giving it a green or brown tint, which can be removed by adding small quantities of manganese dioxide, or a mixture containing selenium. The Venetians developed this technique in the fifteenth century and became famous for ornamental and mirror glass.

During the Middle Ages, larger panes of flat glass were produced by the cylinder process, but the quality was poor and by the eighteenth century, this type of window glass was superseded by crown glass. Improved cylinder methods developed in the nineteenth century were in turn displaced later that century by mechanized sheet processes, which allowed the glass to be drawn continuously from the furnace.

The surface finish of this sheet glass was still of poor quality and whenever fine quality was required, the plate glass process was used. This technique was developed in the seventeenth century by the French, at first by laying out the molten glass on a table. Later the cylinder process was used, and then in the twentieth century a continuous pouring process was devised. The inherent disadvantage in all these processes was that the glass had to be ground and polished to impart a good finish.

This very costly technique of grinding and polishing was not supplanted until 1959, when float glass was introduced, which gave both continuous production and a fine finish in one operation. By altering the additives to the basic glass mix, and by combining the glass with other materials, a whole range of glasses for special purposes can be obtained.

Right The special qualities of reflective glasses have led to their increasing use in modern architecture. At night, or when light is behind the building, the glass becomes transparent and reveals the interior.
Below *National Gallery of Art,* Washington (I. M. Pei). Glazed roofs or rooflights are often used in galleries and museums in conjunction with filtering systems to distribute glare-free light in an exhibition space. Here the dramatic form of the glazing provides a suitable setting for modern sculpture.
Bottom During the daytime, reflective glass when seen from below can make a building seem to dissolve and form part of the skyscape. Weather conditions other than bright sunshine can make such buildings look monolithic.

Above Stained glass was commonly used in medieval churches for a variety of reasons. Light had a metaphysical importance: the quality of light in cathedrals and churches took on a religious significance. Stained glass could be used to portray Biblical scenes, which was important when most of the population were illiterate. More practically, glass could not be made clear enough at that time or in large enough pieces to give a clear view of the outside: it was sensible to use small pieces of coloured glass in a vivid pictorial way.
Left *Crystal Cathedral*, Garden Grove, California (Philip Johnson). Another useful chameleon effect of mirror glass is its ability to reflect the environment. This church employs reflective glass, not only for the purity of its line, but also to suggest a communion with the world outside.

The Material

Types of Glass
Flat drawn sheet glass The Romans made flat glass by rolling out molten glass onto a hard flat table, but modern sheet glass techniques date from developments made late in the nineteenth century, in the United States. The basic glass mix or "frit", consists of 15 parts sand (silica), five parts soda, and four parts limestone, to which up to one-third as much again of scrap glass or "cullet" is added, to assist the melting. The function of the limestone is to harden the glass. The soda or soda ash, (sodium carbonate or bicarbonate) is added to help make the silica melt at a lower temperature.

The glass mix is fed into a tank and after it has been melted at a temperature of around 2700°F (1500°C), it is drawn up out of the tank on a bar of glass called the "bait". As soon as the glass has cooled enough and the surface is sufficiently hard not to be marked, it is passed between pairs of rollers which pull the glass and flatten it to the required thickness. At this stage, the rollers can be patterned to give decorative or obscured glass. The glass, whether patterned or plain, is then drawn up through a cooling tower or "lehr", and cut off in sheets.

Above Crown glass was widely used until the nineteenth century. The surface had a high polish, but only small panes could be cut from the flat circular plate the process produced.
Right The potential of shaping glass is still not fully explored. In the past it was more common to create irregular shapes by cutting, or domed forms for arcades by blowing glass.
Far right The oriel window was designed to maximize light for the interiors of northern European houses. Because individual panes were quite small, it was necessary to brace them with lead reinforcement to create the necessary large glazed area.

The surface finish of glass produced by this method is smooth and has a natural brilliance, without the need for grinding and polishing. However, the drawing process does impart strains on the glass which show as distortions. Such glass cannot be used where great clarity is required and although the process is inexpensive, and is commonly used in horticultural and domestic applications, it is gradually being replaced in general use by float glass.

Crown glass This method was widely used in the Middle Ages. Glass was formed into the shape of a small pear by blowing, heating and rolling on a polished metal surface, until it formed a sphere. This sphere was broken off from the blowpipe and its base was sealed onto an iron rod or "punty", and the whole was reheated and spun, the centrifugal force pulling the glass out into a flat circular plate up to about 5 feet (1.5 m) in diameter. As the glass did not touch another surface in its malleable state, the surface had a high polish and lustrous appearance. On the other hand, only small

panes could be cut from the circle and both the "crown" or bull's eye in the centre and the outer parts were usually wasted. The process was widely used until the nineteenth century, when it was replaced by improved versions of cylinder glass.

Cylinder glass This process involves blowing hot glass into a cylinder shape which is then slit along its length, opened out, flattened and cut to size. Up until the end of the seventeenth century, it produced both ordinary window glass and, after grinding and polishing, plate glass, but the process could only produce lengths of 4 feet (1.3 m) or so, before the glass became too thin to polish.

In the eighteenth century, improved techniques made it possible to produce larger panes. The cylinder was allowed to cool before being slit from end to end with an iron or diamond, then it was reheated just sufficiently to open it out onto a flat piece of polished glass. This gave an acceptable finish to the glass surface, without the need for subsequent polishing.

Although the larger cylinder resulted in larger panes, the transparency of window glass produced by this method was still marred.

Plate glass In the seventeenth century, the French made large "plates" of glass by pouring liquid glass onto a metal table and rolling it flat. The table and roller gave the glass a rough finish which had to be made smooth by grinding and polishing, first with sand and water, then with felt pads charged with rouge.

The term "plate" glass derives from its original use in the seventeenth and eighteenth centuries as coach glass or mirror glass – the silvered glass being known as "looking-glass plates". By 1701, plate glass 6 x 6 feet (1.8 x 1.8 m) was being sold in England, but the high cost of the process plus a tax on glass by weight, made it uneconomical for general use.

In the 1920s, a method was devised for pouring a continuous ribbon of glass. With continuous grinding and polishing, this improved the speed at which plate glass

could be made. However, this remains an expensive process and is gradually being superseded by float glass.

Float glass This process was introduced in England in 1959. It consists of a continuous ribbon of molten glass up to 11 feet (3.3 m) wide, which is poured out of a melting furnace, to float along the surface of a bath of molten tin. The ribbon is held in a chemically controlled atmosphere at a high temperature to melt out the impurities. The ribbon is gradually cooled on the tin so that the surfaces are hard enough not to be marked by the rollers in the annealing lehr. The glass produced by this method has a uniform thickness which can be varied to suit particular requirements and has a bright, fine polished surface, without the need for grinding and polishing.

The process was further modified in 1967 to allow metallic ions to be driven into the glass as it passes through the float bath. This produces the bronze-tinted glasses so widely used in modern buildings.

Laminated glass This is a safety glass made by sandwiching a thin layer of transparent plastic between two sheets of glass. It was originally developed for car windows because when the glass breaks, the pieces are held safely in place by the plastic. Today, the middle layer is usually a vinyl plastic. A combination of toughened and laminated glass in multiple layers produces bullet-proof glass.

Wired glass A wire mesh fed in between the rollers when the glass is made gives the glass the tensile strength that brittle glass lacks. The combination is tough and is extensively used in rooflights or as a fire barrier, where the heat would expand and shatter other types of glass.

Toughened glass Glass breaks because, when it is bent, the brittle surface layers are unable to stretch sufficiently. The remedy is to compress the surface beforehand, so that when it is subsequently stretched, all the compression stresses will first have to be released before the glass will reach its breaking point. The way this is done is by heating the glass and then chilling it

Above *Hall of Mirrors,* Palace of Versailles (1661-1756, Le Vau). The Hall of Mirrors, designed by Mansart and decorated by Lebrun, uses mirror glass to give an illusionist effect. The daylight from the windows on one side is reflected to create the impression of a symmetrical classical interior, and to add depth to the hall. Mirror glass is used today to similar effect in entrance foyers.

suddenly, so that after the outside has set solid, the inside will continue to cool more slowly and as it cools, it will shrink, thus pulling, and thereby compressing, the outside surfaces. This strengthens the glass considerably and the result can be used in many structural applications including doors and ballustrades. However, if the surface of the glass is damaged in any way, the stresses will cause the whole piece to shatter into tiny fragments. To prevent this, the glass must be cut and shaped before it is toughened.

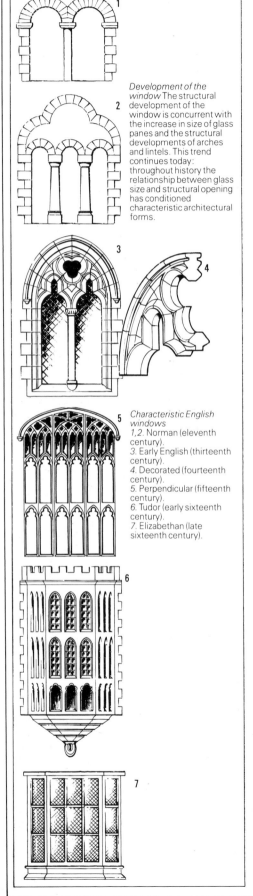

Development of the window The structural development of the window is concurrent with the increase in size of glass panes and the structural developments of arches and lintels. This trend continues today: throughout history the relationship between glass size and structural opening has conditioned characteristic architectural forms.

Characteristic English windows
1,2. Norman (eleventh century).
3. Early English (thirteenth century).
4. Decorated (fourteenth century).
5. Perpendicular (fifteenth century).
6. Tudor (early sixteenth century).
7. Elizabethan (late sixteenth century).

Development and Application

Early Civilizations

In the hot, sun-drenched climate of the Middle East, providing daylight for the interiors of the great buildings of Mesopotamia and Egypt was not difficult. The sunshine was so bright and the surface of the stonework was so reflective, that even very small openings illuminated interiors to an acceptable level. With little rainfall and no need to seal the buildings for warmth, it was sufficient simply to leave holes in the roof or to provide clearstorey openings. Nor was it a great disadvantage that the builders had difficulty in making large openings in stonework, because deep narrow holes served to keep out the hot rays of the sun and made the interiors refreshingly cool. Glass was known to the Egyptians, but not as flat glass suitable for glazing. Its use was confined to jewellery and the making of small bottles and jars.

As civilization moved north across the Mediterranean, and improved techniques for glassmaking made flat glass available, glass was gradually introduced into buildings. By Roman times, it had found a particularly useful application in the *thermae* (hot baths) where its value in allowing light in, while preventing heat from escaping, was quickly recognized by Roman engineers. Nevertheless, window glass remained something of a rarity, for, as in the Middle East, the bright sun and relatively

Left *Hagia Sophia,*. Istanbul (523-7). A precursor to medieval stained glass, glass mosaic was used to decorate, inform and reflect light around the interior of Byzantine churches. The window area was kept small because of the bright light and heat. The use of mosaic capitilized on whatever light reached the interior.

Above and right *Chapel, King's College,* Cambridge. The medieval metaphysics of light, particularly as interpreted by Abbot Suger of St. Denis, linked the neo-platonic idea of the "oneness" and "luminous aliveness" of the world, with Christian dogma. In medieval thought, God as creator of the universe became known as the "superessential light" and Christ as "the first radiance". Suger interpreted these references to light literally and soon the new concept was adopted by others. In northern Europe, the desire for greater light, for religious and for practical reasons, was allied with a development in masonry construction which permitted larger spans. Walls became infills to the structure and were composed of brightly coloured windows, supported by delicate traceries of stone.

mild climate still made it practical to leave openings small and unprotected, even in such major buildings as the Pantheon. Where openings needed to be protected, it was far more common to use curtains, animal skins, or waxed paper; and if a permanent effect was required, it was often easier to cover openings with stone trellises or translucent marbles.

The Byzantine Interior

The development of the Roman arch dome and vault which characterizes Byzantine architecture, had little immediate impact upon window design, but glass did come into its own in a new way, during this period.

The great interiors of Santa Sophia (A.D. 532-7) in Constantinople and San Marco (twelfth and thirteenth centuries), Venice, show the immense, billowing wall surfaces almost entirely covered in different marbles and brilliant glass mosaics. The glass was not just a highly decorative device, it was also functional. The mosaic pictures depicted religious scenes for the education of the populace, in much the same way as stained glass was later used in Gothic churches, and in the dark Byzantine interior, these highly reflective surfaces took what little light came through the lanterns within the dome, and bounced it from surface to surface, giving an ethereal glowing quality to the space, and making it seem even larger than it was.

When the Venetians made mirror glass widely available after the fifteenth century, the effect of "depth" in glass could be explored more fully. In conjunction with the Renaissance delight in optical illusion, the mirrored wall became a popular device. At the Palais de Versailles (1661-1756), the Hall of Mirrors (1678-84) uses mirrors on one side of the hall to repeat the window openings on the other, confusing the source of light and giving matching visual depth to both sides of the room.

Gothic Attitudes to Light

From the ninth century onwards, following the decline of the Roman Empire, there was a considerable growth both in secular and ecclesiastical building throughout Europe. In France, the Abbey of St. Denis was a major religious centre, the focus of pilgrimages to the shrine of the patron saint of France, and the burial place of the French kings. By 1124, it was exempt from feudal and ecclesiastical domination and subject only to the king.

The Abbot of St. Denis, Suger, a brilliant and energetic organizer, was also a flamboyant opportunist who saw a way of attracting still more custom to his church by reconstructing the building. Suger loved splendour and while he knew it would appeal to the pilgrims and to the king, his patron, he was afraid that the church would

Above *Little Moreton Hall, Cheshire (1550-9)*. Historically, there have been three types of ways in which a window is related to structure: as a hole in a masonry wall; as glass filling in a cage of structure; or as an integral part of the structure, where the window and the wall are the same element. Medieval timber buildings showed a unity between the main structure and the windows – both elements were suffused into one decorative and functional whole.

object to his extravagance. Consequently, he justified his expenditure by referring to the medieval metaphysics of light. In medieval thought, the universe was unified by "the superessential light" or "invisible sun", with God the Father as "the father of the lights."

Suger interpreted the metaphysical references to light in Christian dogma quite literally, and quickly set about rebuilding St. Denis as a monumental expression of this vision. Rejecting the Romanesque architecture of the time, he brought in craftsmen from abroad and began reconstructing his church with much larger windows and with bright stained glass to instruct the pilgrims, in the same way as the mosaics at Santa Sophia.

Soon this new concept of light and space was adopted by others, first in France and then elsewhere throughout Europe. It fitted well with the northern climate with its dark

winters and consequent need for larger apertures to let in light. As the craftsmen gained confidence with stone, churches sprang up ever more daring and lighter.

By the end of the fifteenth century, buildings such as King's College Chapel, Cambridge, were being built, in which the wall itself was no longer necessary as a support. The vault and buttress could carry the roof loads and the wall became an infill between the structural supports, requiring only sufficient bracing to support itself and the coloured glass with which it was glazed.

The Renaissance

In northern Europe, the Gothic style continued well into the sixteenth century, but by this time, the characteristic tall, pointed, arched window was being gradually replaced by the more practical flat arched or square-headed window. This was par-

Above In the warmer climate of the Mediterranean, windows did not need to be so large. The architects of the Italian Renaissance treated the window as a punctuation point in the solid mass of the wall. The size and proportions of windows were subservient to the overall harmony of the elevation.

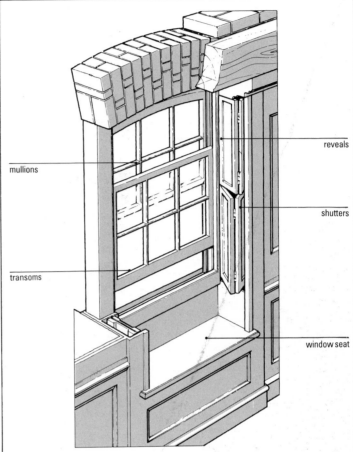

mullions

transoms

reveals

shutters

window seat

The sash window
The north European classical window – the Georgian sash window – was larger than its Mediterranean counterparts, but had the same classical proportions. In contrast to the casement window, the sash window remained flush with the facade when open and preserved the symmetry of the design. The sliding sash operated by counterbalance weights made the window easier to clean from the inside. Other features included: folding wooden shutters for insulation; chamfered mullions and transoms painted white and kept as thin as possible; splayed reveals to admit more light. The window seat provides a clue to the development of glassmaking. Up to the eighteenth century, glass was only translucent, not clear. The commercial availability of clear glass meant that there was some point in providing a seat to look out of the window.

ticularly true in domestic buildings where the height of rooms was restricted, and the greater glazed area at the top of a squared window gave valuable additional light to the interior. As clearer types of glass became available for general use, and it was just possible to see through it, there was an added incentive to bring the window sill down to a convenient level.

At this point, window glass was still restricted in size to small panes which were set in lead frames and its effectiveness for lighting interiors was hampered by relatively low transparency. To offset these limitations, it was customary in northern Europe to chamfer the window reveals and frames to present the least obstruction to the light, to project the windows out from the face of the building in the form of oriel or bay windows, and to make these bays as wide as practical. The increase in width made transoms (crossbars) more necessary and by Elizabethan times, windows in timber-framed houses, such as Little Moreton Hall (1550-9), Cheshire, were both structurally and aesthetically integrated with the walls.

In southern Europe, this problem of maximizing the available light did not arise. The Renaissance of classical humanism in the fifteenth century, which saw the revival of Greek and Roman architectural forms, also changed the whole relationship of the window to the wall. The result was that the window reverted to its previous subordinate role as a punctuation in an otherwise solid mass. Used as an element of surface modelling, its form was now more determined by aesthetic rules of proportion and massing, than by functional necessities.

However, as the influence of the Renaissance spread through northern Europe, not unexpectedly, it underwent considerable change as it was modified to meet local conditions. In particular, the window area again gradually increased in proportion to the wall until by the eighteenth century, the town houses of the newly affluent English middle classes had elegant windows of some considerable size. These windows, which we call "Georgian", had a sliding sash operated by a counterweight. This gave a flush, more classical, appearance than the casement and made it much easier to clean the windows from the inside.

By the end of the eighteenth century, it was possible to obtain crown glass of good quality of a reasonable size and price, so each pane could be larger, and to increase still further the amount of light from such windows; the reveals were often splayed and the glazing bars made of extremely fine timber sections. The resultant window had a delicacy and refinement which has proved popular to this day.

2 *Transparency and translucency*
The availability of large sheets of highly transparent glass profoundly affected building in the twentieth century. At the same time, the translucency of glass has fascinated architects, since the earliest times, from the time when skins, waxed papers or thin marbles were the only materials available to cover windows.

1. Palm House, Kew Gardens (1845-7, Decimus Burton). The development of the iron frame in the nineteenth century permitted very large spans. The lightness and relatively low cost of flat glass made it ideal as a covering material for winter gardens, conservatories and arcades. The Victorian vogue for these structures reflects the new wealth brought by industrial processes and a spirit of civic awareness.

2. In this interior of a Frank Lloyd Wright house in Hollywood, glass is a transparent mediator between the inside and outside. When larger panes of clear glass became available, the relationship between the window and the wall changed – the window could become the wall, bringing the outside landscape into the interior. Wright was one of the first to exploit glass in this way, leading to what is popularly known today as the "picture window."

3. Robie House, Oak Park, Chicago (1909, Frank Lloyd Wright). One of Wright's "prairie houses", demonstrating Wright's attempt to create an American organic architecture, the interior shows fascination with the soft, even lighting reminiscent of Japanese interiors.

4. Maison de Verre, Paris (1931, Pierre Chareau): In Japanese houses, the use of carefully proportioned translucent paper panels gives a lightness and delicacy to the interiors that many modern architects have sought to emulate. When the Japanese influence was at its height in the first decades of the twentieth century, European architects used glass blocks to produce gridded translucent interiors.

Right *York Station,* York (1871-7, T. Prosser, B. Burleigh and W. Peachey). This station is noted for its curved roof, with glass used in conjunction with ironwork. The delicacy of the ironwork takes it beyond a mere engineering material. Many Victorian railway stations had glass roofs – this station is particularly striking because of its double curve.

Victorian Use of Glass

In England, by the middle of the 1820s, the boom in industrial production, together with social and agrarian reforms, brought a dramatic increase in prosperity and population, concentrated in the new industrial townships. The need for new housing and factories and the growth of the railways in the 1830s led to a building boom which accelerated demand for window glass.

This demand was intensified when the pioneers for sanitary reform campaigned successfully for light and airy houses. The window was no longer considered a luxury for the rich, but a necessity for all. In the 1840s, the excise tax on glass was repealed which had the immediate effect of reducing the manufacturers' costs by half. In the next decade, the window tax, too, was repealed. Although the effect of this tax should not be exaggerated, as it mainly applied to larger residential properties with more than seven windows, and not to commercial or industrial properties at all, it was, nevertheless, an important psychological step forward.

As the century progressed, new building types emerged, requiring fresh architec-

tural solutions. James Hartley's patent of 1847 for cheap rolled plate glass produced a product admirably suited for skylight glass, which was used for the new railway station roofs, covered markets and greenhouses. Further improvements in glassmaking furnaces produced great savings in fuel and led to further reductions in cost. At last glass was commonly available for use in buildings and could be seen as a practical alternative to other materials.

Glass had already been quite widely used for horticultural purposes in the eighteenth century, to exploit the "greenhouse" effect. This is the effect whereby a high proportion of incident shortwave solar radiation is transmitted through clear glass and heats up objects, walls and floors. These then reradiate energy as a longwave radiation to which the glass is opaque, causing a buildup of heat. By 1817, J. C. Loudon had reviewed the developments in this field and was researching optimum angles for glass roofs to make use of this effect. He wrote enthusiastically of the advantages of the wrought-iron glazing bar, and the "ridge and furrow" glazing

techniques, later used by Sir Joseph Paxton (1801-65) on the Crystal Palace of 1851. He showed how glazing bars could be formed to a curve, and used charts to demonstrate that the new glazing bars blocked a great deal less light than the wooden alternatives.

Ever since Elizabethan times, glazed galleries had been a popular retreat in bad weather, a place outside, yet protected. The new technology of glass and iron made it possible for this idea to be extended, allowing house and garden to merge. From conservatories, it was a short step to the glazed courtyard and to entire structures spanning many acres enclosing landscape and people, under one cover. Winter gardens, railway stations, exhibition halls and museums proliferated. Loudon even envisaged a new style of architecture, "beautiful without exhibiting any of the orders of Grecian or Gothic design", and forsaw whole towns covered with "immense teguments of glass" in an artificial climate. The glass roof became the hallmark of the Victorian era, easily recognizable in design and style.

Left *University Museum,* Oxford (1855-9, Benjamin Woodward). A forerunner of the atrium of today, the internal courtyard in this natural history museum is covered with a glass roof, supported by decorated cast-iron pillars and cast-iron ribs. The skeletal framework and "natural" ornament on the pillars relates to the building's exhibits. The museum is a fine example of Victorian Gothic.

Below *Corn Exchange,* Leeds (1851-3, Cuthbert Brodrick). Another example of the High Victorian enthusiasm for glass, this roof shows how glass can be adapted to more traditional spatial forms, such as the dome.

Modern Applications

In the twentieth century, glass has become still cheaper. With the advent of the flat-draw continuous manufacturing process and the continuous plate glass grinder, the size of glass sheet increased dramatically and the quality improved to such an extent that by the 1920s, large plate glass was already an economic proposition for many buildings.

When float glass was introduced in 1959, the quality, variety and size of glass was again significantly improved. Today, normal manufactured sheet sizes of up to 11 x $26\frac{1}{2}$ feet (3.3 x 7.11 m) are available, and can be made in a bewildering range of colours, patterns and shapes, laminated or toughened, wired, or treated with coatings and films, to meet a variety of specific requirements. Large sheet glass has had a great influence on housing design.

When the Victorians attached glazed verandas and conservatories to their houses, the landscape and the houses had remained separate. By the beginning of the twentieth century, Frank Lloyd Wright (1867-1959) was building houses around Chicago where the traditional subdivision of the home into separate rooms was challenged. Each space was linked together and integrated with the landscape outside. Influenced by Japanese architecture, this concept gained ground. As it became possible to build large frameless glass walls, glass lost its horticultural associations and became a symbol of the clean fresh lines of modernity.

Ludwig Mies van der Rohe (1886-1969) produced an "idealized" version of his house without walls for the Barcelona exhibition of 1929, where the inside and outside are continuations of the same space. In his Farnsworth House (1950), Mies used large sheets of clear glass for the entire enclosure, in effect making the walls invisible. His assistant at that time, Philip Johnson (b. 1902), built his own house shortly after, and, using the same principles, made the glass wall sit flush with the ground so that the room appeared to be part of the landscape. Such is the transparency, the room seems to be bounded by the surrounding trees rather than by the glass walls.

Left Farnsworth House, Plano, Illinois (1950, Mies van der Rohe). The drawings for this house had an influence on Johnson's Glass House, but here the composition is more that of a classical pavilion. The house is set up on a platform, like a podium.
Right Internally, the Farnsworth House is composed of a central core, containing bathrooms, a fireplace and heating system, with open-plan areas surrounding the core. Areas are divided by partitions which do not reach the ceiling.

Left *Glass House,* New Canaan, Connecticut (1949, Philip Johnson). The ability of steel frame to span large distances without support means that the wall is reduced to a mere infill between structural elements, providing thermal and acoustic insulation. As larger glass sizes became available, designers followed the Japanese precedent with timber construction and filled the frame in with glass. In one of the most dramatic examples of this approach, Johnson's Glass House has glass walls which are flush with the ground – the rooms are not bounded by walls, but by the landscape beyond the house.

Below This pavilion in the garden of the Katsura Imperial villa at Kyoto, Japan, shows some of the features of Japanese design that had such a powerful influence on Western architects.

At the turn of the century, engineers were developing the principles of the steel frame for construction, which, allied with the introduction of electric lifts and central heating, made high-rise buildings possible. The new framed structures did not need walls for support, so these became merely infills, and what better material to use for infilling than glass. Glass was light, which kept the size of steel needed to support the building to a minimum; it was thin, which maximized the useful floor space within the building; it was durable, and, to a certain extent, a self-cleansing material.

In 1919, Mies van der Rohe suggested that glass be used over the entire facade. His proposals for an office building in Berlin showed a 20-storey tower entirely sheathed in glass, the sheer cliff uninterrupted by any visible frames or panels. It took several decades for architects to realize this type of design.

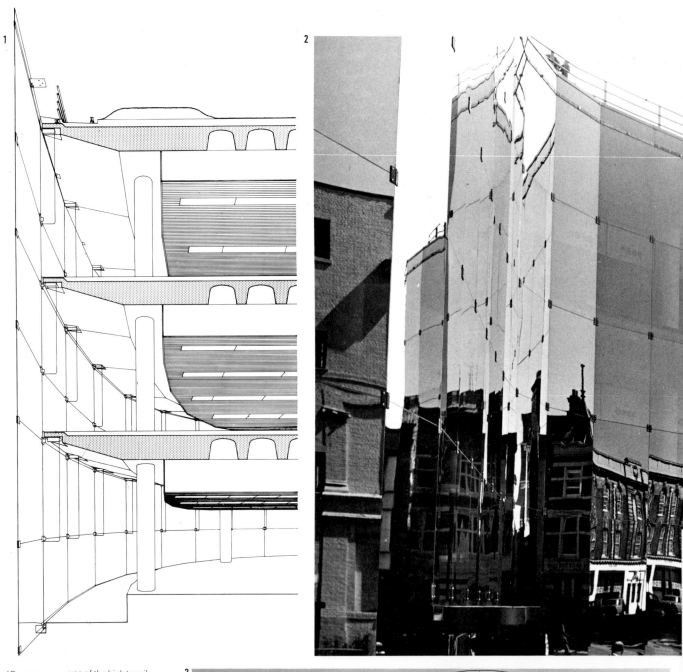

Willis, Faber and Dumas Offices, Ipswich (1974-5, Norman Foster). The building was designed to provide an enjoyable workplace for 1,300 people, which respected the scale of the historic market town where it was to be located. Because "most people are happier being able to see the outside", as the architect remarked, it was decided to clad the building in glass – either by supporting the glass with steel or suspending it like a curtain. At the last minute, the suspended glass wall was approved (5). This makes use of the high tensile strength of toughened plate glass in suspension. In the final design, the structural members – floors and columns – are separated from the enclosing glass (1). The joints between the glass are translucent silicon sealant and the only visible connections are the patch fittings. In the daytime, the building looks like a dark crystal – it is possible to see out but not in (2). At night, the reverse is true (3). The organization of the building reflected the informal style of the company and its concern for the welfare of

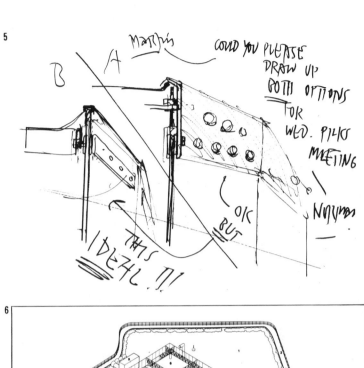

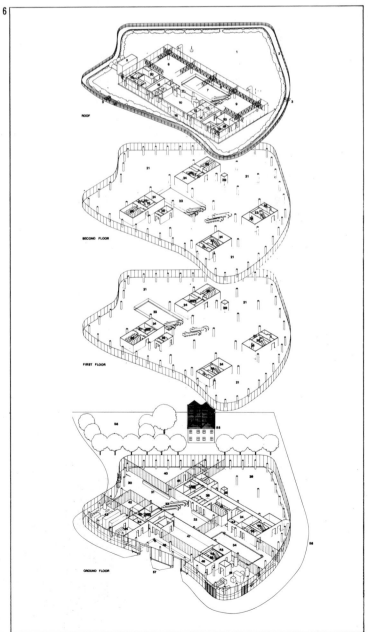

4 its staff. The ground and upper levels house amenity areas such as a gym, swimming pool, coffee bar and restaurant. Two office floors are sandwiched between (6). The floors are linked by open banks of escalators, lit by daylight through glazed roof tiles (4). The roof has a glass restaurant pavilion set in a landscaped garden.
Despite its innovative and generous design, the building is economical and easy to maintain. The glass is virtually self-cleaning and the turfed roof provides excellent insulation, cutting energy costs.

First, was the problem of structure. Steel frames produce structures composed of rectangular bays, with the columns on the outer edges. Many buildings of this type have been sheathed in glass, but the clarity of Mies' design depended on the floor planes being free of such structural restraints and independent of the columns. In 1914, the Swiss architect, Le Corbusier (1887-1965), had shown the way ahead using the newly developed techniques of reinforced concrete constructions. His Domino house project was a clear statement of the principle of column and slab; the diagram only needed the enclosing element of glass to be capable of being realized. Unfortunately, at this time, although glass was available in quite large sheet sizes, it still required mullions and transoms both for support and to resist the high wind loads imposed on tall buildings. These mullions were inevitably so thick that effectively they became small frames themselves. Despite all the improvements that the advent of steel and aluminium had made in reducing the size of such components, by the 1950s the totally transparent wall was still some way off. One problem was that the mullions had proved useful, as convenient posts against which to abutt the internal partitions. Until the partitions could be dispensed with, the wall would never quite be free.

There were other problems, too. Although glass has many advantages, it also has certain limitations. It is waterproof, but it must be joined, and the joint must be sealed. Traditionally, this is achieved with putty, or by compressing some caulking material between the frame and a capping piece. Such frames are quite cumbersome, and the bigger the glass size, the bigger the frame. The frames are also doubled where the windows need to be opened, making them even thicker. The development of rubber and neoprene gaskets made this simpler and more reliable, but it was not until translucent silicone sealants became commercially available in the 1960s that a nearly invisible joint could be made. Even so, only when air conditioning had become a practical possibility could buildings at last dispense with this requirement.

Air conditioning is not a perfect solution, however, as it is expensive, both to install and to run. On any facade exposed to the sun, but particularly on the east and west facades where the sun is low in the sky and can penetrate deep into the building, the greenhouse effect can be a problem, causing a rapid buildup of heat. In large volumes, the heat can be dissipated, but in offices and homes, other measures must be taken. Internal blinds or curtains will help, but heat will still build up in the gap between the blinds and the glass. A much more effective technique is to shade the glass.

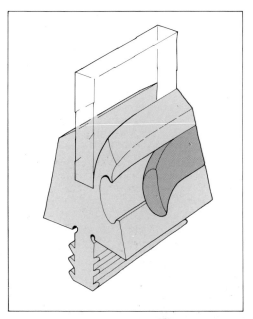

Left This steel building by Skidmore, Owings and Merrill – Chicago's first stainless steel and glass office block – shows another way of handling the expression of windows in a modern high-rise. The structural beam is shown independently and windows form an infill between the frame and beam.

The problem of heat can only be overcome by increasing the heat absorption or reflectivity of the glass itself, to throw more heat outside than is allowed in. The early tinted glasses that became available in the 1950s could absorb a certain amount of heat energy but it was not until the mid-1960s that truly reflective glass was developed. It was not surprising that architects found this simple development so appealing. It not only answered a particular technical difficulty, it gave rise to some unexpected advantages. Buildings could be opaque and transparent at once; they could subtly reflect the environment or they could be blatantly revealing. The possibility of future developments – glass which can change density as the light varies and glass panels that can be made opaque at the flick of a switch – suggests that the potential of glass is far from exhausted.

Ironically, by making glass reflective, the light passing through it is reduced as well as the heat. This encouraged still larger

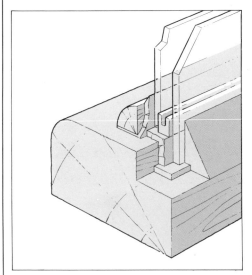

Above As glazing takes up more area, the thermal performance of the building becomes more critical. The problems of energy conservation make this a crucial consideration today. Double glazing – trapping air between two or more skins of glass – is one way of dealing with this problem.

glass sizes to be used but glass is not a very good insulator, except in its fibre form, glass quilt. Large areas of single sheets of glass lose heat to the outside by conduction and will cause cold down-draughts and excessive condensation on the inside. Trad-itionally, this problem was resolved by means of thick internal curtains or folding wooden shutters set into the window reve-als, but as this is not always practical in new buildings, an early modern remedy was to blow warm air over the inside glass surface. A more efficient alternative is double-glazing. This works on the principle of trapping air between one or more skins of glass, preferably with the air gap being hermetically sealed to prevent air move-ment and internal condensation. It also overcomes to some extent another problem of glass, in that it is fairly transparent to sound, but unfortunately, the maximum gap required between the glass for thermal insulation ($\frac{4}{5}$ inch/2 cm) is considerably less than the minimum needed for acoustic insulation (6-8 inches/15 - 20cm) and as yet, no adequate combination of these charac-teristics has been achieved for general use in building.

There are still other problems to be faced in the search for the perfect glass covering. Building codes in some countries demanded a fireproof separation between each floor of a building, and, until the codes were relaxed to take account of fire protec-tion and sprinkler systems, it was often necessary to use fireproof backup walls behind the glass or to provide projections on the outside of the facade. Safety meas-ures also had to be taken to protect people from falling glass. Only when toughened or laminated glass became available, was frameless clear glazing a practical proposi-tion.

Above This department store in Stockholm shows how effective glass walls can be at night. The store is revealed as a giant mechanism, with its working parts on display.

Right *Engineering Building,* Leicester University (1959, James Stirling and James Gowan). For the roof of the laboratory block, translucent glass was used to create strong, sculptured forms. Taking influences from vernacular brick buildings and the Modern Movement, these architects have created a modern university style.

Cleaning and maintaining the glass presented fewer difficulties. Until non-stick coatings are perfected, the most common methods for cleaning will remain motorized platforms which run in guides along the window mullions and overhead cradles suspended from the roof of the building.

It is not surprising that Mies van der Rohe's 1919 design for the all-glass building took so long to realize. Fifty-six years later, in 1975, Foster Associates completed the Willis Faber building in Ipswich, a building that matches the clarity of structure and elegance of that early design.

The sharp rise in heating costs precipi-

tated by the oil price rises of the 1970s has encouraged a fresh look at energy conservation. Buildings account for a great percentage of a country's total energy requirement and research is currently underway to improve their thermal performance. This will undoubtedly change the physical appearance of future buildings, perhaps quite markedly. Three of the most promising applications for glass in this field are in the better insulation of buildings by means of double glazing and glass quilt; in the production of solar collector devices; and in the exploitation of the "greenhouse" effect.

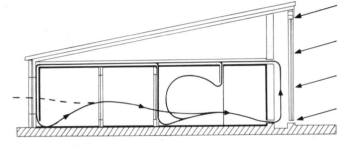

The greenhouse effect The design of this building exploits the greenhouse effect for increased thermal efficiency. The inner wall is insulated and painted black. Heat rises, drawing in cooler air from the house; the warm air passes into the house to heat it, cools and is drawn out again.

Left This use of mirror glass in Minneapolis shows how buildings can be made to appear to dissolve into the sky. Where high-rise developments could otherwise dominate the skyline, such effects can be useful to create a lighter, less claustrophobic feeling.

Plastic

Plastic is not just the newest of the primary construction materials available to the building designer today, it is also the most challenging. The basic building materials – brick, stone and timber – are natural raw materials with a history as long as man. Even metal, glass and concrete are processed from natural materials and their basic principles have been understood from ancient times. Plastic has no such pedigree. There is no deep wealth of experience in its use, nor is it yet associated with any clear cultural meaning. It is unique in being an entirely manmade material, a product essentially of the twentieth century, and of the last few decades in particular.

To most people, the word "plastic" means something that can be easily shaped, like plasticine or putty. Such materials do exist naturally, in the form of resins secreted by plants. Shellac, animal horn, amber and the latex from which rubber is made, are well-known examples and it was because of the similarity of these to plastics that the term "resin" is still quite widely used as a substitute for the term plastic.

The earliest artificially made plastic material was celluloid, produced in 1855 and later famous for its connection with the film industry. It was highly inflammable and was superseded by the invention of the safer cellulose acetate in 1894. Three years later, in 1897, casein was produced. None of these plastics were fully synthetic. Celluloid was derived from cottonwool and casein from milk.

The first truly manmade plastic was invented in 1907. Called phenol formaldehyde, or more commonly known as Bakelite, after its discoverer, the Belgian chemist Leo Baekeland, it was only available in its natural dark-brown colour and was rather brittle. Up to this point, plastics were still something of a novelty, and, although Bakelite became well-known in connection with early radio cabinets, its use was generally confined to small objects such as buttons and toys.

The First World War precipitated a rapid expansion of the European and North American chemical industries, and by the 1920s and 1930s, a plethora of other plastics materials had been invented, including acrylic, polystyrene, nylon, polyethelene and PVC. These inventions were accompanied by the development of new forming techniques, such as injection moulding. By the outbreak of the Second World War, plastics were already finding a use, albeit specialized, in a wide variety of products.

The Second World War also provided the impetus for the development of plastics and as chemists turned from using gas as the primary feedstock to oil, a massive escalation of plastics types followed. Today, just 40 years on, plastics materials are so commonly available and so widely used, that they enter into every aspect of our life.

Bakelite
One of the first common uses of plastic was for everyday items like this 1934 Bakelite radio. Bakelite was only available in its natural brown colour and was very brittle. The design of this radio case uses plastic as if it were wood: these early uses tended to promote the notion that plastic was a cheap substitute for other more worthy materials.

The Material

There are two basic categories of plastics, distinguished by their behaviour when heated. The first category, "thermosetting" plastics, become soft when heated and can be shaped, but upon further heating, they become stiff and solid and cannot then be softened again.

The second category, called simply "thermoplastics", soften when heated and become stiff and solid again when cooled. Unlike the thermosets, by further heating and cooling these states can be repeated. Generally, whereas both plastics remain sensitive to variations in temperature, the thermosets are less so, have better resistance to stress, better fire endurance, and can be made more rigid, while the thermoplastics can be processed into more complex shapes. Both types of plastics have many different applications in building.

The Chemistry of Plastics

Materials such as glass, concrete or steel may have a certain number of fundamental characteristics that can be modified to create special variants for specific purposes, but only within fairly restrictive limits. The better qualities of these materials can be improved and their weaknesses ameliorated, but they cannot be changed altogether. The basic properties of plastics, on the other hand, can be changed. Plastics can be made that are rigid, or flexible, opaque or transparent, cellular or solid, soft or hard, and so on. It is the ability to engineer the substance to meet specific performance requirements that differentiates plastics from other materials.

The chemistry of plastics hinges upon the element, carbon, and its exceptional ability to form compounds with other elements, particularly with one or more of the five elements, hydrogen, oxygen, nitrogen, chlorine and fluorine. Every element consists of small particles, or atoms, unique to that element. To form compounds, the atoms of the elements involved must combine and the resultant combination of atoms is called a molecule. Most molecules consist of only a very few atoms. Water, for instance, has just three, two of hydrogen and one of oxygen (H_2O). Plastic molecules however, can consist of many thousands of atoms, and it is the size and shape of these molecules that differentiate plastic compounds from others.

To make these large molecules, chemists start from quite simple molecular structures called monomers. Ethylene is a monomer, having just six atoms, two of carbon and four of hydrogen. By linking these simple structures together into a pattern, a more complex molecular combination can be formed called a polymer. The process is called polymerization. When the basic ethylene molecule is polymerized so that it has 4,000 carbon atoms and 8,000 hydrogen atoms, the resultant polymer is a plastic material, polyethelene or polythene.

Left and above Plastic, as a new material, has no formal convention of usage unlike the more traditional construction materials of timber, stone and brick. When using plastic in their buildings, architects have tended to borrow imagery from other fields of design, particularly from aerospace engineering and the automobile industry. The housing at Runcorn New Town, England (*left*), designed by James Stirling, uses GRP panelling and portholes styled in a way that if reminiscent of aircraft design, as in the Junkers airplane of the Second World War (*above*).

The large size of the plastic molecules and the way these are arranged lead to several important properties. When the molecules are joined in long chain-like structures, with few cross-linkages, the resultant linear configuration produces thermoplastics. Similarly, when networks of essentially linear molecules are connected together by many cross-linkages, then thermosetting plastics are produced.

Because these structural arrangements can be controlled by the chemist and engineered to give a particular range of properties, plastics compounds have proved to be remarkably versatile and useful materials. One the other hand, this very versatility has created its own difficulties.

The building designer, familiar with the relatively limited physical properties of traditional materials, and the few processes whereby these may be shaped to suit his purpose, is now confronted with a bewildering range of different basic plastics. There are permutations within the ranges, between the ranges, and different shaping techniques, which vary widely according to the plastic or plastics selected.

Right and below right The streamlined, high technology design of modern transport has inspired architects in their use of plastics. The covering of this pleasurecraft bears some similarity to the covered walkways at Charles de Gaulle Airport in Paris. The advent of clear plastic sheets which can be heat-formed in different shapes, and are virtually unbreakable, have led architects to dispense with the way arcades and covered areas are traditionally constructed. The approach here is more like product design than architecture.

Development and Application

After centuries of usage and refinement, the many vices of traditional building materials have become so well known that they have been largely accepted. Yet timber rots, metals rust, brickwork and concrete are neither good insulators nor impervious to rain, tiled roofs are prone to cold and damage, and even stone can degrade in polluted atmospheres. It took many generations of trial-and-error to build up a knowledge of acceptable practices which could cope with these failings.

Thermoplastics	Uses
Polyethylene (Polythene)	packaging components – films for greenhouse covers and inflatable structures – insulation for outdoor cables – piping – ropes – metal coatings – swimming pool linings.
Polypropylene	chairs – baths and sinks – piping – ropes – ironmongery.
Polyvinyl Chloride (PVC)	floor finishes – suspended ceilings – rooflights – damp-proof membranes – metal coatings – chair covers – cable insulation – shower curtains – piping – foamed for window frames and furniture components – inflatable structures – pool linings – pool linings – panel facings – weatherproofing seals – skirtings.
Polystyrene (including ABS – Acrylonitrile Butadeine Styrene)	expanded for insulation, and as lightweight concrete aggregate – shutter linings – foamed for window frames and furniture components – suspended ceilings – ironmongery – covings.
Polymethyl Methacrylate (Acrylic e.g. "Perspex")	glazing – baths, sinks and shower cabinets – furniture – fascia panels – suspended ceilings.
Polycarbonate	glazing – furniture – household goods
Polyvinyl Acetate	emulsion paints – adhesives – floor finishes – admixtures for mortars and fillers:
Nylon (Polyamides)	door furniture – curtain rails – fabrics – ropes.
Polytetrafluorethylene (PTFE e.g. "Teflon")	coatings to kitchen utensils and roofing fabrics.

Thermosetting plastics	Uses
Phenol Formaldehyde Resins (e.g. "Bakelite")	phenolic paper honeycomb covers to sandwich panels and shells – with tung oil for sealing cork, wood and linoleum – with melamine in decorative laminate panels – glues for plywoods – fuse blocks and meter housings – telephone handsets – saucepan handles – knobs – drawer pulls – desk equipment.
Urea Formaldehyde (e.g. "Beetle")	foamed for cavity insulation – glues for plywood – electric plugs – tableware – lighting reflectors – floor sealers – for waterproofing papers.
Melamine Formaldehyde (Melamine)	decorative laminates – electric plugs – tableware – cladding panel facings.
Polyester Resins	with glass fibre to form fibreglass (GRP) – ropes – admixtures for mortars and fillers – floor finishes.
Epoxy Resins (e.g. "Araldite")	structural adhesives – metal coatings – admixtures for mortars, fillers and renders – floor finishes.
Polyurethane	foamed for insulation, sealing strips, cushion and mattress linings – underlays and as core material for sandwich panels – paints – varnishes.
Polyorganosilicone (Silicone)	cushioning and caulking – weatherproof seals – waterproofing films – polishes, paints, varnishes.

The appearance of our buildings today has largely been determined by these corrective practices.

It is not surprising that when plastics became available, their introduction followed the time-honoured route of development of all new materials. The first applications of plastics were supplementary to traditional materials, providing better paints for wood, protective coatings for metals, insulants for brick and concrete, damp-proof membranes for roofs, sealants for stone, and so on. However, as industrialization tempted skilled craftsmen away from the construction sites to the better conditions and pay in the factories, labour costs began to rise and hence, the cost of traditional materials rose as well, since the production of these were labour-intensive. This development coincided, in the 1950s and 1960s, with a massive increase in building output and a higher standard of living, which led to a demand for faster, cheaper construction with better thermal performance and lesser maintenance. As the properties of plastics became better known, they developed from being supplements to traditional materials, to actual replacements for them. At first plastics could only win acceptance by appearing to be something else, since plastic was a material despised at the time for its association with cheap products. Decorative laminate panels, plastic fencing and wall claddings were all made to look as much like timber as possible. Plastic fireplace decorations, Georgian-style architraves and rainwater gutters, still imitate traditional materials, even today.

An understanding of the future of plastics can be gained by examining the ways in which plastics are made into products. The polymerization process results in a variety of forms of raw plastic – in basic forms such as powders, granules and liquids or in semi-finished forms, such as sheets, films, foams, rods or tubes. A number of different shaping techniques are needed to make these into articles and these techniques have a strong influence on the use to which the plastic can be put and the shape of the final product. These different shaping techniques are also already beginning to change the appearance of buildings.

Plastic Sheets and Films

Plastics such as acrylic can be simply formed into sheets by heating the raw material with a catalyst to form a viscous liquid. When this is poured between two polished surfaces, such as glass, and allowed to cool, it will harden to a sheet of even thickness with a smooth, flat surface.

Transparent acrylic sheets made in this way are widely used as an alternative to glass. Although they are flammable, can scratch easily, are not good insulators and cost more, in some cases disadvantages

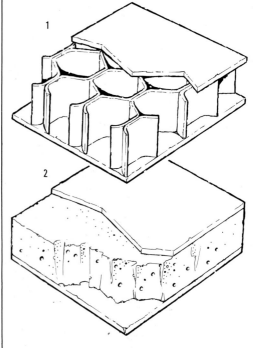

are offset by their lightness and resistance to breakage.

Both the acrylics and the more expensive but more scratch-resistant polycarbonates have been used primarily as a replacement for glass in windows, walkway covers, ballustrade panels, and so on, in areas prone to damage by vandalism, particularly in schools, shopping centres and other public places. The flat sheets may be machined to shape, or formed by heat-bending into simple one-way curvatures. More complex double curvatures require heat-forming techniques.

Flexible films and sheets can be made in two ways. PVC sheet is made by mixing the raw plastic with plasticizers, pigments and stabilizers, then heating it to about 340°F (170°C) and drawing it through a row of hot rollers. The continuous sheet of thin molten plastic which results is cooled; it then solidifies and can be trimmed.

Polythene, on the other hand, is made into a thin sheet by drawing out molten plastic into a tube. Cold air is blown into the tube to make it into a thin continuous balloon-like film which is solidified by cooling and then flattened and wound onto rollers. By cutting one side of the tube along its length, it can be opened out to form a flat sheet.

Apart from ancillary applications, such as shower curtains or chair covers, the main uses for such sheets in building are as waterproof membranes for swimming pool linings, damp-proofing, and as protective covers. They are also being used increasingly for temporary covers to structures, particularly in horticulture, because of their low weight relative to strength, and their high transparency. These covers are made either by stretching the sheets over a metal or timber frame or by inflating them with air. In these applications, the relatively short life of the material when exposed to ultraviolet light is compensated

for by cheapness, ease of replacement, and the reduction in shading afforded by the lighter structure required for support.

Ordinary PVC has an average life of one to two years and with an ultraviolet inhibitor, up to four years, but as the sheet widths are narrow and may require electronic welding, it tends to be more expensive than polythene. PVC also attracts dust, and can be subject to fungal attack. Polythene can degrade in about nine months in a sunny climate, but it is available in continuous sheet widths of 40 feet (12 m), which is sufficient for many small enclosures. A characteristic of the film is that it allows infrared energy to escape at night, so in many greenhouse applications, it is made into a double skin. The condensation which forms between the skins becomes a useful barrier to heat loss.

One of the ways to make plastic sheets less elastic, other than reinforcing with high-strength fibres such as glass or carbon, is to bond the sheet to a more resilient base. Laminated panels, such as Formica, are made this way. If, however, plastic sheet is bonded firmly to each side of a low density core material, such as rigid polyurethane foam, the structural forces in the resulting panel operate much like a lattice beam; but the surface sheet is prevented from buckling by its adhesion to the core. The core is more than just a spacer, for it not only stabilizes and unites the structure to provide resistance to shear but is also a good insulator.

Such panels can be flat, with smooth or embossed surfaces, or they can be moulded into shapes to give greater strength. However, not all sandwich panels are made entirely of plastics. The fact that plastic is vulnerable to fire has encouraged the use of alternative facing materials including metals, wood and plasterboard, for external wall cladding panels, floor and roof panels, and partitions.

Above Plastic has an important, though everyday, use in sandwich panels. The honeycomb panel (1) has a honeycombed core – in doors, the core is paper impregnated with resin. Honeycomb panels made of two skins of reinforced plastic are used for the floors of 747s – these are very strong and very light. A foamed plastic core (2) can be used as a spacer and for insulation.

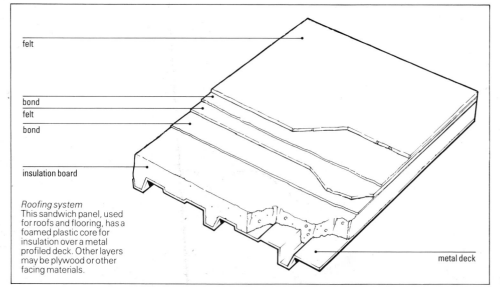

felt

bond
felt
bond

insulation board

Roofing system
This sandwich panel, used for roofs and flooring, has a foamed plastic core for insulation over a metal profiled deck. Other layers may be plywood or other facing materials.

metal deck

Right *Centre Pompidou,* Paris (1975–7, Piano and Rogers). The clear plastic tubes which carry the escalators on the outside of the Centre Pompidou are a good example of the way in which architectural detailing can resemble product design. All the mechanical services in this building are exposed rather than hidden from view, and are treated as objects to be admired in their own right. By having the main escalators running up the outside, valuable exhibition space is saved and visitors to the arts centre are provided with a dramatic view of Paris.

Drawn and Moulded Shapes

To make drawn shapes or extrusions in plastic, thermoplastic powder or granules are fed from a hopper into a heated barrel. Inside the barrel, a rotating screw forces the softened plastic out through a die which is shaped to give the required cross-section. Dies can be made to produce flat sheets, rods, bars or planks, both hollow and solid, and even coating for wire or other materials. The material which results has a uniform profile and thickness which cannot be varied along its length, but the length itself is limited only by the ability to handle it conveniently. The dies are not cheap but they are interchangeable.

Extrusions may be fabricated into larger components by making the long edges interlock side by side, by jointing the ends, or by using connector pieces. Typical of the many smaller applications for extrusions include trims for panel ends, wall mouldings, drawer inserts, skirtings and a wide range of draught excluders and gaskets. The ubiquitous neoprene gasket is an extruded section which, when bonded to a range of moulded junction pieces, forms a characteristic grid pattern.

Extruded PVC is also widely used as a replacement for metal and clay products in cold water plumbing, rainwater and underground drainage systems. It is relatively cheap, does not rot or need repainting, is virtually unbreakable and its smooth finish aids water flow. The disadvantage of the extrusion is that it cannot be made to form the more complex pieces required – such as clamps, traps, bends and inspection chambers.

A similar example of plastic replacing a traditional material can be seen in the growth of PVC extruded planks in place of timber. Hollow sections with moulded connectors are commonly used to make fences and posts wherever low maintenance and high durability required. Claddings can also be built cheaply in this way, using extruded planks to interlock or overlap on the face of a building, to resemble traditional timber "ship-lap" weatherboarding.

More recently, the characteristics of the hollow extrusion have been exploited not merely to give thickness and strength, but also to use the contained air space as an effective heat barrier. Insulated window shutters and the many transparent or translucent extrusions now being offered for roof glazing are examples of this use. This is an interesting development because the planks not only provide insulation with elegance and economy, but they are also quite rigid and capable of large spans without intermediate support. Many plastics have been used for this purpose, particularly PVC and acrylic, and with the introduction of the more durable polycarbonates, there are exciting possibilities for the future.

Another way of shaping plastic is by heat-forming. A flat thermoplastic sheet, formed by extrusion or casting, can be softened by heat. After it is pressed, blown or sucked (vacuum-formed) into a mould, it will take up the shape of the mould on cooling. The process itself is relatively inexpensive. Large one-way curvatures can be made without any reduction in the thickness of the plastic, but moulding a two-way curvature restricts the size according to how far the flat sheet can be stretched or drawn before it becomes too thin. Vacuum-forming produces a moulding with a flat base where the sheet has been clamped and with simple chamfered sides

Above The detail of the Expo 67 dome clearly shows the metal frame and acrylic panels. Made of standardized parts, these domes are capable of covering large areas efficiently. Buckminster Fuller even conceived a scheme whereby a large area of Manhattan would be encapsulated by a geodesic dome – providing a weatherproof, controlled environment.

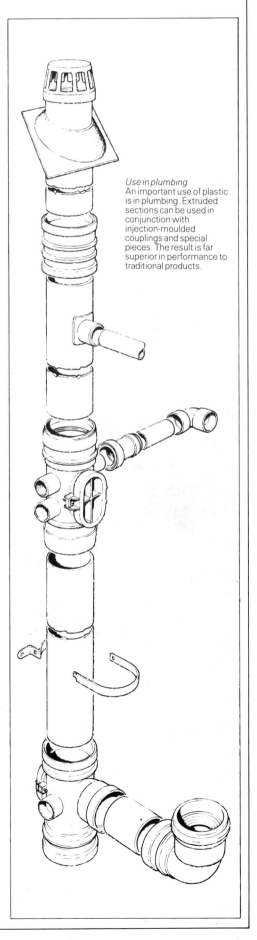

Use in plumbing
An important use of plastic is in plumbing. Extruded sections can be used in conjunction with injection-moulded couplings and special pieces. The result is far superior in performance to traditional products.

Above One of the problems with acrylic plastics is their flammability. After such disasters as the fire which destroyed the entertainment centre, Summerland, in the Isle of Man, the applications of these plastics are now restricted in modern structures.

Left *US Pavilion*, Expo 67, Montreal, Canada (1967, Buckminster Fuller). World's fairs and exhibitions have been the showcase for many innovative structures which might not have otherwise been built. This geodesic dome is constructed of a lightweight tube steel or aluminium frame with balloon acrylic panels.

Far left *Nakagin Capsule Tower,* Tokyo (1972, Kurokawa). The Archigram Group of architects in the 1960s envisaged a new city form composed of a permanent infrastructure onto which changeable components could be clipped. This capsule tower is the built version of that vision. The service core is fixed; the prefabricated bedroom capsules are made to appear as if they could be replaced when obsolete – rather like domestic appliances.
Left and below *Olivetti Training Centre,* Haslemere (James Stirling). Although GRP has the appearance of an industrial component, in fact its production is almost a handcraft process. Some architects exploit GRP's ability to create sculptural form, creating unusual shapes rather than using it in repetitive panels. The jointing on this building is reminiscent of automobile detailing.

to aid release from the mould.

Perhaps the most dramatic and attractive use of this technique is in the moulding of acrylic sheet. The plastic itself lacks stiffness and has a tendency to expand and to deform when subjected to heat, but by moulding it into a domed or pyramidal form, that is, by giving it strength by means of double curvatures, these effects can be minimized. Transparent telephone hoods and domed rooflights are good examples, and in the future, frameless moulded acrylic or polycarbonate windows may become commonly available for buildings. Since these plastics are far lighter than glass and developments in engineering have led to space-frame and geodesic structures, long-span trusses and cable suspension systems, it is possible to construct economic glazed roofs of considerable scale and delicacy. If these plastics were incombustible, the possible applications would be greatly increased.

Glass Reinforced Plastics

The larger plastics components used in building, such as wall and roof panels, are more commonly moulded from the rigid thermosetting resins. Polyester resin together with glass fibre reinforcements produces a material known better as glass reinforced plastics (GRP), or fibreglass.

The mould in this process is generally an open one. There is only one surface against which the plastic can be pressed, and, as this determines which side will receive the better finish, it first has to be established whether this surface will end up on the inside or outside of the finished moulded form.

Left This civic building in Marin County, California was designed by Frank Lloyd Wright towards the end of his career – a career that spanned almost 70 years. Even near the end of his life, Wright was still open to the possibilities of new materials – the plastic rooflighting in this building shows great sophistication.

Above *Olympic Stadium, Munich (1972, Frei Otto).* Like Buckminster Fuller's geodesic domes, this structure is an example of the potential of lightweight plastic panels used in conjunction with steel – in this case, steel in tension. Nets of this kind are quite capable of covering vast areas with delicacy.

A "male" mould is used for a good inside finish and a "female" mould for a good outside finish. Wall and roof panels normally require a female mould and this can be made of metal, plastic, or, more commonly, timber. The mould is first smoothed and is then sprayed with a releasing agent to prevent the plastic from sticking to it. A gel coat is added to form a hard finish. This consists of a polyester resin, with a promoter, catalyst and pigment. On top of this, alternate layers of polyester resin and glass fibre mat are pressed until the correct thickness has been established.

Unless more costly moulds are used, the form which results usually has just a simple curvature, and a lip at the top of the mould where the component may be jointed. In recent years, considerable improvements have been made in the mechanization of this process and hulls for naval mine-sweepers have shown how large these mouldings can be made.

GRP was the first practical plastic material that could be used for making sizeable building components. However, early attempts to translate the experience of boat builders and car body manufacturers to building projects were not always successful.

Right *House of the Future,* "Daily Mail" Ideal Home Exhibition, London (1956, Alison and Peter Smithson). This early application of plastics in a domestic interior was intended to demonstrate how an entire building could be prefabricated. The project aimed to show that a variety of shapes and forms could be used if interiors were mass-produced: the alternative is using standard components, which can lead to uniformity.

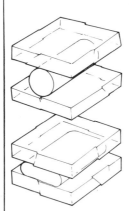

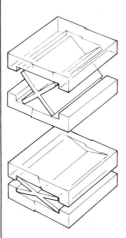

Above An unglamorous but ubiquitous use of plastics is for gaskets and sealants where the flextural and weatherproofing properties of the material are used to seal all kinds of materials simply and economically.

Fire resistance was a problem which it was hoped could be cured by modifying the resins or by adding fillers, but as these were found to affect the curing, mechanical and weathering properties of the material, other techniques had to be devised. In some situations, fire-retardant laminates were introduced beneath a gel coat, but elsewhere, it was necessary to add separate incombustible linings. GRP is also not entirely impervious to water and the strength of the material reduces in time and with temperature increases.

Nevertheless, the material is light, promising savings on structure and foundation costs; it comes in various colours; and most importantly, it can be shaped relatively easily. Shaping or reinforcement is necessary to increase rigidity. Reinforcement can be done within the moulded form by increasing the thickness of the material, by moulding in metal, timber or foam inserts, by adding in higher strength fibres such as carbon fibres, or by filling the moulded shape with rigid foams.

Where plastics are used for light, non-loadbearing purposes, such as cladding panels, the shaping needed to resist wind forces and to keep the panel rigid is not very great. As these panels need to be jointed at their edges with the main structure, and the back of the panels should be flat, any sculpturing tends to be fairly restrained.

Designers have been very influenced by automotive and aerospace design and have used GRP to make the shiny finishes, round cornered window inserts and ribbed surfaces associated with these industrial products. Today, most moulded cladding panels are of this type.

Where plastics are used to form larger complete enclosures, the need for greater rigidity means there must be more pronounced shaping. Bathroom units are a good example: the rigidity is given by the moulding of the bath, shower and other accessories into the structure itself. An early forerunner of this approach was the House of the Future interior, designed by Alison and Peter Smithson in 1956. Since then, there have been many examples of this approach. All are characterized by the notion of a "capsule", a complete structural enclosure of plastic, heavily moulded for rigidity.

Taking this one stage further, in the 1960s, the British group of architects known as the Archigram Group saw capsules as an ideal way to exploit the advantages of plastic, particularly its lightness, while overcoming what were then its disadvantages, – poor sound and fire insulation and lack of permanence. Their proposals for a "plug in" architecture – housing capsules that could be lifted up by crane onto a support structure, and then detached and removed when they had outlived their usefulness – have had a powerful influence upon designers the world over.

Very different from either the cladding panel or the capsule home, is a third area where GRP is used in building. The good strength-to-weight ratio of the material and its translucency when used as a single layer, encouraged a number of studies for large-span structures, particularly swimming pool covers, and warehouses where good light and clear spans are an advantage. Here, a fundamental weakness was the elasticity of the material, and it could only be overcome by stiffening. There are two broad categories of structure which resulted: shell structures, with single or double curvatures, and folded-plate structures, like prisms or pyramids.

Somewhere between these three different approaches, a formal language for the design of moulded structures is in the process of development, but it is still far from clear what will result. It may even be that the relationship between shape and strength will not be such a critical factor in the future as it is today.

Fabrics

Most people associate plastic with the synthetic fabrics used in clothing, yet few realize how important these materials could be for building. Buildings are thought of as being synonymous with solidity and permanence, yet, through history, alongside stone, brick, timber and concrete buildings, there has always been the tent, the skin-covered enclosure of the nomad. We still think of the tent as temporary, as in the marquee or the circus big top, and forget that by a single technical development which would give longevity to the fabric, all that could be changed.

From the simple films used for greenhouse covers, newer materials have been devised, consisting of extruded filaments of nylon, polyester, or glass fibre, spun into threads and woven into tough fabrics, strong in tension, light and translucent. When such fabrics are coated with other, more durable plastics such as PVC, neoprene, hypalon or PTFE, a useful life of perhaps 25 years becomes possible. Fabrics need no longer be considered temporary and this realization has generated many new applications which promise to have a profound effect upon the art of building.

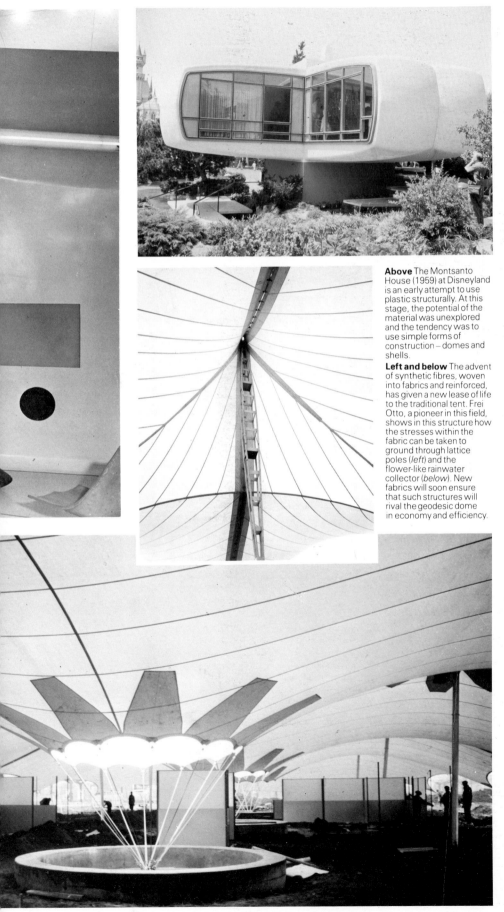

Above The Montsanto House (1959) at Disneyland is an early attempt to use plastic structurally. At this stage, the potential of the material was unexplored and the tendency was to use simple forms of construction – domes and shells.

Left and below The advent of synthetic fibres, woven into fabrics and reinforced, has given a new lease of life to the traditional tent. Frei Otto, a pioneer in this field, shows in this structure how the stresses within the fabric can be taken to ground through lattice poles (*left*) and the flower-like rainwater collector (*below*). New fabrics will soon ensure that such structures will rival the geodesic dome in economy and efficiency.

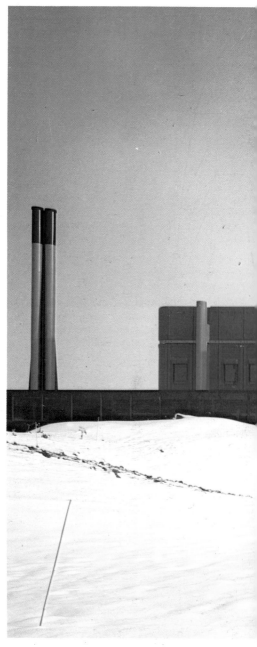

Above *Fuji Pavilion,* Expo 70, Japan. In this type of inflatable, the enclosure consists of tubular inflated ribs spanning like arches and tied together. The advantages of this system over single-skin inflatables are that puncture of the membrane does not cause collapse of the structure, there is no need for an airlock to maintain pressure and the double thickness provides thermal insulation. However, there is a limit to the size of the span.

Left Neoprene gaskets are now in widespread use, particularly in glazed facades, where they produce a characteristic gridded effect. Here they are used to hold panels together: one particular advantage is that panels can be interchanged. It would even be possible to change a solid panel for a window.

Above and left *Water Research Centre,* Swindon (Architects Design Partnership). The use of plastics in this building illustrates the variety of applications of the material in construction. Neoprene gaskets seal the glazing on the front elevation; plastic-based paints cover the external steelwork, and complex profiled GRP panels are used for cladding (*left*). The detailing here makes obvious reference to product and transport design.

Perhaps the most obvious is the tent itself. Because these new materials are so much lighter and stronger, the tent can be made much bigger. The traditional system of the fabric carrying the tension stresses to a pole or compression strut still holds, but with the high strength steel cables available today to support or supplement the fabric, vast gossamer-like tented structures are now possible.

For still larger enclosures, the flexible membrane may be supported without struts by compressing the air which it encloses. Such structures are known as "inflatables", and there are two basic types. The first contains the air in compression between two skins of fabric much like a balloon, and the "balloon" itself transfers the load to the ground. This type of inflatable can be designed as a simple, large, cushion-like envelope, or it can be divided up into separately inflated cells or ribs. The advantages are that collapse of one cell does not cause the collapse of the whole and the structure does not need to be sealed tight to the ground. The double skin also gives a measure of thermal insulation. The disadvantage is that such structures cannot yet be made to span very large areas.

The second type of inflatable supports the flexible membrane in tension by compressing the air which it encloses, the air itself transferring the load to the ground. Such structures, or single-layer inflatables, require a constant input of air to maintain the internal air pressure at slightly above that outside and, although the differential in pressure is barely noticeable, the structure must be sealed to prevent air loss: an airlock is needed at the entrance. In the event of the fabric being damaged, the low pressure and large volume allow the air to escape only very slowly so there is little risk of sudden collapse. Nevertheless, a lightweight secondary steel or cable structure is sometimes used to restrain the fabric against wind buffeting or to keep the volume to be pressurized to the minimum. This can also serve to prevent the deflated fabric from total collapse.

Right *Einstein Tower*, Potsdam (1920-1, Erich Mendelsohn). At the turn of the century, reinforced concrete seemed to promise a new freedom from the structural frame – in practice this was rarely realized. The Expressionist shape of the Einstein Tower was achieved by rendered masonry, rather than the concrete the architect had originally intended to use. Free organic shapes retain their powerful appeal for architects.

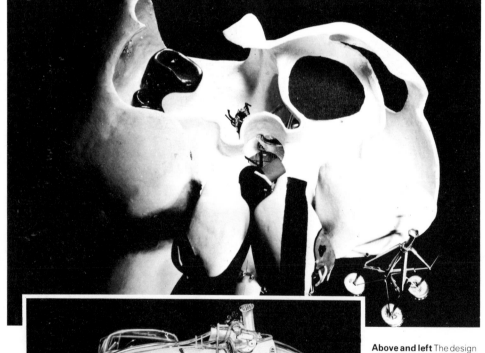

Above and left The design of this "living pod" by David Greene combines the notion of organic shape with the disposable and mobile capsule idea popular in the 1960s.

As the inflatable generally consists of a single layer of fabric, problems of condensation and high heat gain and loss can arise. This may be overcome by air conditioning, or, perhaps one day, by climate-control devices, but the cost of doing so will be high. These inflatables are therefore used mainly for large enclosures where thermal comfort is not critical. Exhibition pavilions, sports facilities and warehouses are typical current applications but despite their impressive size, this is merely the beginning. If landscapes and townships can be covered and protected from the weather as, Frei Otto and Buckminster Fuller have suggested, then the constraints of climate control which have helped shape our buildings for centuries past will no longer apply.

Foams

Foams, either flexible or rigid, can be made from polyurethane. Flexible foams are mainly used for soft furnishings and for

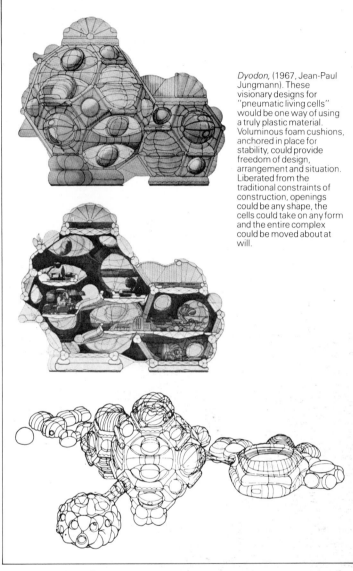

Dyodon, (1967, Jean-Paul Jungmann). These visionary designs for "pneumatic living cells" would be one way of using a truly plastic material. Voluminous foam cushions, anchored in place for stability, could provide freedom of design, arrangement and situation. Liberated from the traditional constraints of construction, openings could be any shape, the cells could take on any form and the entire complex could be moved about at will.

carpet underlays. Rigid foams are particularly useful as the core material for sandwich panels and are widely used as insulation for cavity brickwork, although some types have been banned in certain countries because the vapour given off can present a health risk.

Of all the foamed plastics, however, structural foams are particularly interesting. These are usually made from polystyrene, PVC or ABS. The thermoplastic granules are either mixed with a "blowing agent", a chemical which gives off a gas such as nitrogen when heated, or nitrogen can be forced into the molten plastic under pressure. Either way, when the plastic mix is injection-moulded, or extruded into a cold environment, the gas expands, causing the mix to foam. As the outer surfaces are cooled, they harden to a smooth rigid finish, while the inner parts continue to foam.

These mouldings and extrusions have a tough outer skin and a lightweight core,

which makes them very strong for their weight. They can be drilled, screwed, nailed or sawn like wood, but, unlike wood, they do not rot, warp, split or splinter and can be coloured. The fact that they can also be made in complex profiles or be moulded to intricate shapes has encouraged their use in a wide range of traditional joinery applications ranging from window frames to chairs.

In 1967-8, the architects, E.H. Brenner and Associates, working with plastics engineers in the United States, produced plans for buildings to be spun from foam. The foam was based on epoxy resin which was sprayed with a foaming agent. When the mixture came into contact with the cold surface of a mobile, rotating conveyor mould, it set hard on the outside to form a tough double skin, sandwiching the foam between. As the mould moved on, a ribbon of structural walling was left behind which could be laid vertically in the same way as conventional walling and carried over to

form roofs. It could also be sprayed in a spiral pattern to make domes or other free-form shapes. It seems likely that such a development will one day change our understanding of normal building practice.

Buildings have always been created by bringing small components together and jointing them. Not only is this time consuming, but the joints are both expensive and vulnerable to weathering. If joints could be eliminated, and, along with them, the need to control dimensions so that the small components can be integrated, then the size and shape of doors and windows, and the heights and shapes of rooms need not be restricted by traditional limitations.

Such freedom has long been a dream of architects. From the "organic" designs of Frank Lloyd Wright and the Expressionist structures of Erich Mendelsohn (1887-1953), to the visionary projects of Paulo, Soleri, David Greene and others, the advent of a truly plastic material has been long awaited.

Applied Decoration

An applied finish is, by definition, a secondary process. From earliest times, people have covered up, painted and decorated over the primary materials from which buildings were constructed. Finishes rarely play a primary role in building design but they always affect the result. Reasons for using finishes range from the functional to the aesthetic; from emphasizing a structure to deliberately covering it.

The decorative potential of a material is rarely left unexploited for long. The longest-serving finishing materials have owed their success as much to their use by artists and craftsmen as to their practical performance. At times, architecture has been dominated by the advantages of such materials. Stucco, for example, contributed a great deal to the appearance of seventeenth- and eighteenth- century Europe through its use as a cheap alternative to stone.

When applied finishes are used for functional reasons, they are usually considered for their ability to withstand weathering and wear and tear, and to provide sound-proofing. Other factors include how easy they are to maintain and how receptive they are to other materials. Decorative qualities are rather more subjective, but materials with interesting texture and colour which reflect light have obvious advantages.

The range of materials which can be applied to buildings, for either functional or decorative reasons, is vast. However, it is possible to distinguish three main categories of finish which have been in use since antiquity and from which most modern methods are derived. These are thick coatings, such as plaster; decorative finishes, such as paint; and layers and skins, such as mosaics and tiles.

Thick Coatings

Thick coatings generally consist of one or more coats of a prepared mixture of materials which bind together when mixed with water. This mixture can be spread or trowelled to a smooth or textured finish, or modelled or moulded, to subsequently dry hard in the atmosphere. The materials included in this category are usually worked by a plasterer, who is responsible for all work that involves spreading or modelling the material.

Unbaked Earth
The sympathetic relationship that usually exists between primitive vernacular buildings and the landscape is derived from the material dependence of the one upon the other. The oldest and most primitive protection afforded to simple earth or adobe building is a skin of mud. In the simplest situations this can be applied and deco-

rated by hand, as it still is in many parts of Africa.

In Europe, prior to the Industrial Revolution, the panels between the frames of timber buildings were filled in with lathing or wickerwork (wattles). These were then coated with daub – a mixture of local clay or mud dug nearby. If possible, the daub would be finished with a hard thin layer of lime plaster. Otherwise a lime or ocre wash had to suffice.

Plaster
Plaster is a general term which usually includes the different plasters based on lime, gypsum and Portland cement. It often also includes stucco, a term which tends to be loosely used to describe a more sophisticated mixture that has, from time to time, been based upon each of the other three types of plaster.

Their workable nature means that plasters are ideal for decoration, a field in which they come into their own. Most mortars and plasters lend themselves to moulding or carving and to being "run" to profiles. They are also in the vanguard of substitute materials, being cheap and effective.

The three main groups of plasters are lime, gypsum and Portland cement plasters. Limestone or chalk deposits are common throughout the world and these materials are important constituents of lime plaster. Lime plaster is obtained by heating chalk or limestone to produce quicklime.

Top Mud can be wedged into moulds to provide an in situ construction material (*pisé*). The use of such materials – usually local clay – makes these types of buildings blend in with their surroundings. Round huts are the simplest to make. The mud can be carved, moulded or modelled to provide decoration.
Above Another use of mud, which was common in areas of the world where timber construction was established, was as an infill for the gaps between the main structural members. For the "wattle and daub" technique, mud or clay was daubed over the basketwork of wattles which made up the structure. Limewash or plaster would then be applied as a finish.

Above In Ancient Egypt, gypsum plaster was used to cover rough stone. The interior of this shrine shows how the plaster was subsequently painted with scenes of religious or symbolic importance. Apart from the smooth surface this plaster provided, it was also cheaper than dressed stone and the decorations lasted longer. The decoration painted on stone around the doorway has not weathered as well as the frescoes in the inner chamber.

Left In some parts of the world, rough stone construction is finished with adobe or clay. This layer or skin improves weather-resistance and provides a surface for subsequent decoration – either by carving, moulding or modelling.

This is tempered, or slaked, by the controlled addition of water to form lime putty, which sets slowly as it dries.

Gypsum plaster is very fine, sets hard, and, if used to make stucco, can produce highly finished work. It is obtained by firing gypsum, a soft rock composed of calcium sulphate and water. Because gypsum could be fired at a lower temperature than lime, this plaster was preferred in Ancient Egypt where fuel was scarce. Firing drives off the water content to leave what the English termed "plaster of Paris", after the famous gypsum deposits beneath Montmartre. Gypsum plaster is laborious and demanding to use. After sifting, the wet mixture is stirred for long periods to make it set more slowly, and make it suitable for moulding or carving. It was also used traditionally to finish undercoats of rough lime plaster.

Portland cement, not commercially available until the mid-1820s, is an artificial cement made of crushed limestone or chalk and mixed with clay or shale. Most modern external rendering is a mortar of Portland cement and sand, sometimes with the addition of lime to reduce hardness and prevent cracking.

Techniques All plasters are made by a combination of three principal ingredients. These are cement, aggregate and a binding agent. Cements include lime, gypsum or Portland cement, from which the three main groups of plaster are derived. The aggregate is usually a local material, such as sand – the finer the sand, the smoother the finish. A binding agent, such as animal hair or straw, was often necessary to increase strength. To make the plaster harder, a coagulant such as ox-blood was often added. The plasticity and setting speed of plaster dictate how workable it is, and certain ingredients can be added to improve these characteristics. In the past, sugar and molasses would be added to retard the setting time and milk or egg-white to improve plasticity.

Most rendering and plastering is done by building up several layers of rough plaster and finishing with a fine layer floated off to a hard smooth surface. Long straight rules are used to regulate the overall flatness of the surface. Basic plasterer's tools have been in existence for centuries. The Roman architect Vitruvius described the spreading of stucco-duro with an iron trowel or float, and the smoothness of Egyptian plaster could only have been achieved with such equipment. The 1703 edition of Joseph Moxon's *Mechanick Exercises* describes and illustrates tools for plastering which are not unfamiliar to us today.

To make mouldings, plasterers use either "running moulds" or casting moulds. Running moulds are used to form continuous profiles such as cornices and skirtings. A

Right The relative cheapness of stucco, combined with its potential for modelling, made it ideally suited to the purpose of the Baroque architects, who aimed to create a sense of animation through space and on the surfaces of their buildings. The decoration on this nave ceiling in Speinshart Abbey, Germany, shows the combination of painted medallions and heavy plaster relief.
Below *Cumberland Terrace*, London (c. 1827, John Nash). One of the best examples of Nash terraces, Cumberland Terrace is one of those facing Regent's Park. These houses were basically typical London terraces, but fronted by impressive facades, largely created from stucco, in order to provide a picturesque backdrop in the landscape setting.

template is cut from zinc, in the reverse and exact shape of the required profile. This is then mounted on a wooden support known as a "horse", which is run back and forth over a mound of wet plaster. The consistency and accuracy of line is achieved by running the horse along a fixed ground or a rule. This type of moulding can be done either in situ or on a bench. Complicated sections are usually built up from different mouldings run in short lengths and assembled later. Very heavy or thick sections are run over a formwork to leave a hollow space behind.

Casting in moulds is a workshop activity. The Adam brothers, Robert (1728-92) and James, used to use moulds carved from box or pear wood. But usually gelatine, wax or plaster were used for internal work and wood, iron or plaster for external; today, PVC is also used. By the mid-eighteenth century fibrous plaster was introduced in France. This consisted of plaster of Paris reinforced by a coarse canvas known as "scrim", in conjunction with wooden laths, wire netting, tow, fibre, sawdust and slag wood. As well as facilitating lighter mouldings, it has excellent fireproofing properties, which resulted in a long association between fibrous plaster and early steel-framed buildings. Fibrous plasterwork has recently enjoyed a revival in the Middle Eastern building boom, being a cheaper method of achieving traditional Moslem decoration than stucco. However, the mass market in fake detail is more appropriately served by the plastics industry today.

Other, purely external, plastering techniques include roughcast, pebble dash and Tyrolean render. Roughcast is composed of crushed aggregate mixed with slaked lime or Portland cement. The wall surface is first rendered with a coat of coarse sand and either lime or cement. Then, while the render is still wet, another layer of slightly liquid roughcast is thrown on. For heavier textures, crushed stones or pebbles are used. Roughcast has had a long and widespread use as a covering material over porous or poor quality base materials. As well as providing additional weather protection, it has often been used to architectural effect, to provide contrast with stone or brick dressings. Charles Rennie Mackintosh (1868-1928) used a roughcast finish on the exterior of Hill House (1903) in Helensburgh.

Tyrolean render is a technique of applying thin coatings of aggregate in order to provide a smoother texture than roughcast or pebble dash. At least three coatings are applied by machine, the finishing coat being a mixture of Portland cement, silver sand and a colouring pigment.

Other less well-known plastering techniques include scagliola and sgraffito. Scagliola, popular in the eighteenth century, was a polished plaster composition

Above *Strawberry Hill, Twickenham* (1747-63, Horace Walpole). Walpole remodelled his home over a period of years in "Gothick" style, which used elements of medieval building to create an air of mystery and age. The exterior of the building is covered in pebble dash, a simple aggregate of small washed pebbles and Portland cement, thrown by hand onto a coat of wet cement render. This finish resembles stone but is cheaper – the stone in this building being reserved for the decorative details and window dressings. Apart from reasons of economy and weatherproofing, pebble dash lends an antique air to the facade. This type of finish was also used by C. F. A. Voysey in the late nineteenth century in his romantic vernacular designs – and as a cheap facing material between the two world wars to much less effect.

made from sand, lime, gypsum and crushed stone. It was used to imitate marble or stone. Batches of the basic composition were mixed in different colours and spread in layers. If a granite effect was wanted, the mix was pushed through a coarse sieve to give mottling. Veins were made by placing frayed strings soaked in dye across the surface; after the material set, these strings were removed and the streaks filled in. The results were often extremely convincing.

Sgraffito, popular during the Italian Renaissance and later in the decorative arts revival of the nineteenth century, involved building thin layers of coloured plaster and cutting each back before it set to expose the undercoats, according to a design. The usual preference was for a white layer over red or black. More colours were used in the nineteenth century, the design being transferred to a coarse coat by pricking through carbon paper. The different coloured areas were then plastered separately, so that too many layers did not have to be applied. Areas of work depended on what could be done in a day, before the plaster set. There was virtually no margin for error with this technique.

Stucco

The plasterwork that survives from antiquity is invariably what is now known as "stucco-duro". Early stuccoes were considered suitable for external and internal work, but by the eighteenth century, stucco was taken to mean external painted plaster, as the mixture and method had changed.

In ancient times, gypsum plaster was easily obtained and a tradition of gypsum stucco became established. To make the stucco, fine marble dust was fermented with a mature lime putty for a week. Curdled milk, lard, egg-white, ox-blood, fig juice or urine might be added, according to well-guarded recipes, to retard the setting or regulate shrinkage and hardness. The paste was applied layer upon layer, each beaten or rubbed into place for as long as three days, before being washed, brushed and polished. The manufacture and use of this material continues in the same way today in modern Yemen.

This stucco-duro tradition was lost until the mid-fifteenth century, when Cardinal Giovanni de Medici instigated a serious excavation of Roman ruins. After considerable experimentation and research, the skills were revived. When the Cardinal became Pope in 1513, he commissioned Raphael to build the loggia of the Vatican in which stucco was used again.

The influence of the Italian stuccoists spread to other parts of Europe, generating the early Renaissance stucco-duro style in France and England often known as "grotesque". The finish, portraying Biblical, classical, heraldic and natural themes, was produced by chisel or brush, and often

Above *Royal College of Organists,* London (F. W. Moodie). The Victorian sgraffito craftsmen had to be true artists, as the work was done directly onto the panels. The size of the panel was determined by what the artist could complete in one day. In this example, sgraffito is combined with plaster relief work.

displayed great character and individuality.

Stucco work in the Baroque period is noted for its exuberant and intricate scrolls, faces and caryatid figures. The details of such ceilings as that at Astley Hall, Chorley, were built over a structure of armatures (brackets and stems made of wood, leather and lead strips).

By the eighteenth century, native craftsmen had emerged in most European countries. In England, family firms, such as Joseph Rose and William Collins, began to work in close liaison with architects, such as the Adam brothers. A number of new recipes involving oils and alternative powders, such as cockle-shell lime, were invented. In 1777, the Adam brothers acquired the patents for two of the most important recipes and cornered the market in providing stucco decoration. Designs in similar style were made available through the general dissemination of pattern books. The stuccoed motifs were taken from boxwood moulds that could be used over and over again. The high relief exuberance of the Renaissance had been replaced by a technique that produced shallow relief of

great delicacy; a suggestive veneer rather than the full-bodied imitation of stone architecture or sculpture, and with little more spirit than wallpaper.

For external use, Georgian architects such as John Nash (1752-1835) and Thomas Cubitt applied patent stuccoes over brickwork to provide impressive facades imitating expensive masonry. The addition of statuary and architectural stone carvings, made from the secret recipe of Coade Stone, took the general effect of makebelieve a stage further.

The most famous of the patent external renderings was Parker's Roman Cement. It was said to have made Nash's architecture possible, due to its strength, durability and power to withstand damp. Carefully incised lines imitated stone coursing, and stone weathering was simulated with paint.

After 1824, Portland cement gradually took over from the patent lime-based stucco mixtures. Erich Mendelsohn (1887-1953) used Portland cement stucco as a substitute for reinforced concrete for his Einstein Tower (1920-1), and it proved an ideal means of achieving an expressive design.

Left Pargetting is a decorative plastering technique which originated in East Anglia during the fifteenth and sixteenth centuries. The wet plaster was cut or "raised" as in this example – Sparrows House, Ipswich – to form rustic relief work which would be modelled in situ by hand. In this building, pargetting was used to give a medieval timber-frame house a fashionable classical appearance. This type of decoration reflects the influence of Italianate architecture, which first appeared in England when Henry VIII imported the style for Nonesuch Palace. This modern pargetting motif *(above)* was produced by combing – a time-honoured technique of combing the wet plaster into designs.

Decorative Finishes

Apart from their decorative purposes, finishes such as paint also serve to protect and identify surfaces. Liquids designed to give specific protection against weather, damp, insects, fire, bacteria and fungi can be applied in thin coatings over many types of surfaces.

Colour is one of the most important aspects of decorative finishes. It can be used to identify architectural elements or whole buildings, and in this way, crucially affects the way we perceive space and surfaces. Another important role of colour is to unify where coherence would not otherwise be apparent.

It was not until the mid-nineteenth century that serious studies were made concerning colour perception. Whether or not to obscure the natural colours of building materials with paint became a major obsession in the late nineteenth century. In the twentieth century the rationalists of the Modern Movement sought a purity of expression that included colour only in its purest forms. An effect of these preoccupations has been an understanding of colour and its relationship with light, form and pattern.

Types of Finish

The basic composition of most surface coatings consists of a medium, a thinner and a pigment. The medium has drying and textural characteristics, adheres to the surface and provides specific resistance to water and chemicals. Thinners facilitate application and evaporate after use. Other ingredients in surface coatings affect drying time, plasticity and stabilization.

Limewash, or whitewash, was the traditional coating of vernacular building. It is a porous mixture of lime and water, thus allowing the structure to breathe. The addition of tallow improved weathering characteristics, but in northern Europe limewash required constant upkeep. In Mediterranean areas, limewash still works well because it reflects solar heat, suits the clear bright light, and is not subject to such bad weather. Colour can also be added.

Modern descendants of limewash include special masonry paints containing particles of cement, sand and mica and alkali-resisting pigments. Some are based on acrylic or vinyl copolymer resins. They are often textured and therefore likely to harbour stains and dirt in a polluted atmosphere, but they are still more durable then traditional materials.

Oil paint is preferred for coating stucco, because it is smooth and does not obscure the underlying texture. Thicker or more textured coatings would obliterate the intricate detail of stucco work.

Watercolour can be applied to stucco-

duro in a technique known as "fresco buono". The paint is absorbed into the plaster before it dries and lasts longer than a skin coating. This technique originated with the Romans and was subsequently rediscovered during the Italian Renaissance. Together with stucco-duro, it fell from use after the seventeenth century, but the Victorians made use of a similar technique on modern stucco–part of their general interest in historical revivals.

A basic problem with any paint is deterioration. Today, paints have been developed which, provided they are applied to a suitably prepared surface, are supposed to last up to 100 years without fading. These contain ground silicones and are very expensive.

Techniques

This type of finish is usually applied by brushing, rolling or spraying. The best brushes are made from boar's bristle or horsehair; the cheapest are made from fibres such as jute. Rollers covered in wool or synthetic fibres offer the advantage of speedy application but tend to leave a stippled effect. Spray guns provide an even coating, but accuracy of detail depends upon masking techniques.

Thin coatings are usually applied to a prepared surface. Primers are needed where paints need to resist chemicals present in the base material. Thin undercoatings and top coats are needed with oil-based paints, but modern paints are designed to be applied in thick, single coats. Finishes vary from high gloss to matt.

Above Whitewash, a mixture of lime and water, is a common decorative finish applied to vernacular buildings in many Mediterranean countries. In this square, use of whitewash gives uniformity to the different styles of buildings and provides a degree of harmony. Whitewash is well suited to the bright Mediterranean light; in northern countries it requires more upkeep.

Right *Last Supper,* Monastery of Santa Maria delle Grazie, Milan (c.1497, Leonardo da Vinci). Wall painting was a common form of decoration from Roman times onward; fresco – applying pigment and water to patches of wet plaster – reached its height in Italy during the Renaissance. The *Last Supper,* however, is not a true fresco, with the result that it had begun to deteriorate badly as early as 1517. Repeated restoration work has been carried out ever since, but much of the painting has been lost. Nevertheless it is still possible to appreciate Leonardo's use of perspective and the drama of the overall design. The mural is placed at exactly the right height in the monastery room and is perfectly suitable for its setting.

Layers and Skins

This type of applied finish is embedded or stuck on top of a prepared surface. Materials include mosaics, tiles and terracotta.

Mosaic

Mosaic is composed of small pieces of glass, stone or other materials, called "tesserae", set in mortar. The Romans originally used pieces of used marble and limestone; later, around A.D. 200, they imported gilt cubes from Egypt. Since then, materials have included clay and clay tiles, pebbles, crystals and minerals, broken pottery, shells and mirror.

Several types of glass are used today. The traditional type is called "smalti" and is made according to a process carefully guarded by a few families in the north of Italy. The glass splits unevenly to give it a highly valued reflective quality. There are many shades, permitting subtle colour gradations.

Other glasses lack the depth and richness of smalti. Vitrious glass is manufactured in Italy and Mexico. It comes in larger, thinner pieces which can be cut down. Stained glass can also be used, but a reflective backing is needed if it is to be effective.

Ancient mosaic was set in a mortar of slaked lime, combined with volcanic ash. Today, mortars of sand and cement are standard. Colour additives provide backgrounds which match the tesserae. A stronger alternative is magnesite, a hard cement used in composition flooring. Sometimes epoxy resin and casein glues are used. The joints are usually grouted with a mixture of lime putty and Portland cement.

There are two methods of laying mosaic. The direct method involves placing each tessera by hand into a setting bed of mortar. The consequent unevenness in the surface of the mosaic makes it more lively, the angles of reflection changing with each viewpoint. This was an essential ingredient in Byzantine architecture. The interiors of Byzantine churches were meant to suggest heaven, and the shimmering skin of mosaic helped to create a mysterious space in which columns appear not to carry weight and boundaries appear to dissolve.

The reverse method makes use of tesserae already pasted onto a piece of paper according to a design. This paper is then turned upside down and pressed into wet mortar. Once set, the paper is washed off and the mosaic grouted. The method ensures an even surface and allows for correction before being laid.

A firm background for a mosaic is important. Small designs can be laid on a wooden base over which a layer of non-ferrous lathing has been laid. Buildings often require larger works which are either made in the studio on precast panels of concrete, or are applied using the reverse method.

Mosaic perfectly suited the Roman preference for two-dimensional forms of decoration, their desire for a durable surface and their love of figurative imagery. However, Roman applied decoration was incidental to the overall architecture, unlike the Byzantine and Islamic traditions. In the latter case, mosaic was used to conceal the structure and reflect spiritual rather than architectural values.

Modern uses of mosaic have tended to

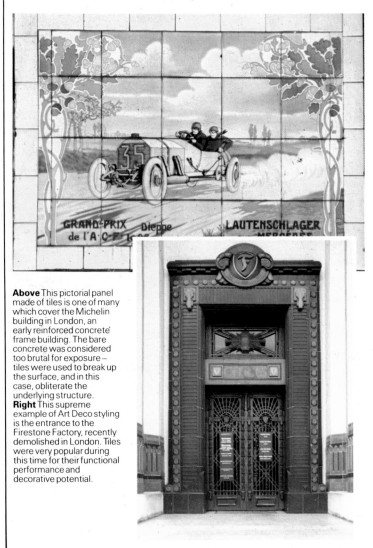

Above This pictorial panel made of tiles is one of many which cover the Michelin building in London, an early reinforced concrete frame building. The bare concrete was considered too brutal for exposure – tiles were used to break up the surface, and in this case, obliterate the underlying structure.
Right This supreme example of Art Deco styling is the entrance to the Firestone Factory, recently demolished in London. Tiles were very popular during this time for their functional performance and decorative potential.

Left This detail of a mosaic at Ravenna from the fifth century B.C. shows a typically Byzantine use of mosaic decoration. The mosaicists intended to create an impression of life, as well as inspiring a sense of mystery and awe. Subtle colour shading, the use of glittery metallic mosaics and the method of setting the mosaics at different angles created the shimmering effect.

Above *House of the Tragic Poet,* Pompeii. The Romans decorated their walls with paintings, chiefly frescoes, and mosaics. This panel shows a rehearsal for a satyr play – its theme and execution display the vulgarity of much Roman decoration. Decoration was not normally consistent with the architecture – just a way of implying space beyond the plane of the wall.

Right These thirteenth-century tiles from Chertsey Abbey illustrate signs of the zodiac. Tilemaking reached a high level of decorative sophistication during the medieval period, although most were poorly fired and did not wear very well.

reflect the subservient role played by the decorative crafts in architecture. However, in Mexico City are examples of modern mosaic decoration which are integrated into the whole design of the building. The tower of the library at the National University shows an exuberant use of mosaic on an otherwise blank wall.

Tiles

Tiles have been used since ancient times on floors, roofs and walls, both internally and externally. They can be plain or patterned, coloured or natural, glazed or matt, flat or profiled. Tiles are generally made from clay, with various additives. Encaustic tiles have colour mixed and baked into the clay. Ceramic tiles are glazed with colour.

The Romans bedded tiles in a mortar of lime combined with volcanic ash. In medieval times, brick dust would often substitute for the pozzolana. The modern practice is to bed floor tiles in a mortar of sand and Portland cement. The choice of bedding materials is very wide. For walls, cement mortars are less used than formerly, having been superseded by adhesives based on organic mastics and cement, which are much easier to use.

The primary value of tiling is protective, although its potential as a decorative medium has resulted in its continuous use as a means of aesthetic expression.

The earliest uses of decorative tiling appeared on walls and floors demanding resistance to heavy wear and tear. Medieval examples were poorly fired and did not wear so well. However, their value as a fireproof material accelerated the use

of clay tiles for roofing and interiors from the fourteenth century onwards. The use of glazed wall tiles to produce a decorative but fireproof finish behind fireplaces, kitchen stoves and around chimney pieces developed into a taste for covering entire walls, especially in such clay areas as Germany and The Netherlands.

Tiling is also impervious to water, dirt and staining. As the need for hygiene and easy maintenance in hospitals, butcher's shops and dairies came to be appreciated, tiling manufacturers prospered. The advances made in the nineteenth century are reflected in the abundance of the tiled shop fronts and interiors built by the Victorians and Edwardians. Their penchant for decoration and their interest in the revival of neglected crafts reinforced their interest in the material. Food shops, railway stations, domestic porches, pubs, swimming pools were all clad in clay tiles.

Terracotta tiles were an excellent fireproofing material much liked by the pioneers of steel-frame skyscrapers in the United States. Terracotta covers the steelwork of Burnham and Root's Reliance Building (1890-4) and uncannily resembles a cast-iron front. Louis Sullivan (1856-1924) also exploited terracotta for its ability to provide cheap and effective decoration as much as for its fire-resistance.

By the 1930s, tiling as a facing material was being used primarily as a functional surface. The art deco style continued to use tiles decoratively, but Modern Movement architects were not interested in that.

Postwar architects have tended to use tiling from a very functional standpoint —

primarily to privide durability and easy maintenance. Occasionally, the material is used to cover an otherwise bare concrete structure, as in the case of James Stirling and Gowan's Leicester University Laboratory. Such a feeling is not so far from the intention expressed in the greatest tile architecture of all, in Islamic countries. Designed to conceal rather than reveal buildings, the tile coverings also display an abundance of formal decoration.

The Use of Decoration and Ornament

An important architectural notion is that it is the nature and working characteristics of the primary materials which determine the appearance and character of a building, and that structure and construction must reflect these qualities in some way if there is to be architectural integrity. Most architecture can be evaluated in this way because these factors are also representative of the cost or effort of building, which are generally among the more critical determinants. However, occasionally such

practical considerations are outweighed by more abstract ones, sometimes to the extent that buildings become vehicles for the expression of very different values. Invariably, architecture reflects the preoccupations of the society.

The architecture of Islam is, among other things, a visual translation of Islamic mysticism. Again, the Byzantine church was just a device, or box, inside which was created another world of iconographic significance: a representation of heaven. The architecture of the picturesque in eighteenth- and nineteenth-century England was a response to the humanistic ideals expressed in poetry and romance. The building was seen as an object in a "natural" landscape, and (as with most dramatic scenery) this effect was achieved by using anything that would give a realistic effect within the available means. In each of these examples, the architecture is designed to convey purely spiritual or intellectual meanings. In each case, too, the use of a decorative or ornamental finish (a secondary material) provides the means by

Left These sixteenth-century tiles from Topkapi Palace, Istanbul, show the brilliance of Islamic ceramic decoration.
Right *Carlton Terrace,* London (John Nash). The Picturesque style in architecture coincided with a renewed appreciation of the natural landscape in the arts generally.
Below *La Muralla Roja,* Spain (1973, Ricardo Bofill). Here the building is itself a type of decoration, the bright sculptural form contrasting with the rugged setting.

Above *Masjid-i-Shah,* Isfahan (1612-38). The domed prayer hall of this building is covered with glazed earthenware (faience) decorated with calligraphic, geometrical and natural patterning. One of the finest examples of Islamic architecture, this mosque demonstrates a perfect attention to detail and form.
Right Interior decoration in mosques is reminiscent of an earlier period when the walls would be covered with patterned textiles.

which the effect is created, often with decoration taking precedence over the expression of structure and composition. In such types of buildings, surface ornament becomes fundamental, which is the opposite to the utilitarian attitude with which we are more familiar today, where decoration is considered to be superficial.

Islamic Decoration

In Islamic architecture decoration often seems to take over from all other aspects. From the earliest times the representation of living beings was forbidden. Abstract pattern and calligraphy provided the basis for what became a conventional framework of decoration capable of infinite variation.

There are three basic motifs, which are often layered over each other, weaving back and forth so that the precedence that one takes over another is constantly changing. These can be appreciated in the mosque of Sheik Lütfüllah, Isfahan (1601-8). The first motif is writing. The second is vegetal; leaves, fruit and flowers are used in repeating patterns, and prob-

ably have no greater significance than to provide surface cover. The third type of motif is geometrical. Geometry is also the governing principle of the other elements. The predominance of mathematical organization may have been due to an attempt by the mathematicians and scientists to explain and guide the work of the artesan. At any rate, the geometrical nature of the decoration reflects the mathematical creativity of Islamic civilization.

The layering of these motifs can be two- or three-dimensional. The geometry modulates the repetition of column and panel and decoration is used to identify the presence of a panel, window or door in an overall composition. The composition is derived from the tradition of hanging rugs and textiles on the walls. The shape and structure of such buildings is so obscured by decoration as to be denied importance. The sense of depth and extravagance (as is given by the stucco stalactites or *muquarnas* in the Mirador de la Daraxa in the Alhambra, Granada (1338-90)) is an illusion created by simple means.

Byzantine Decoration

In Byzantine architecture, decoration also plays a dominant role. The interior of the Byzantine church is of prime importance because upon entering the church, one is entering an image of heaven itself: the exterior and structure are only important insofar as they provide the means by which the interior is supported and protected. The image of heaven is achieved by covering a polygon or a square with a dome, which implies a vertical axis running from the centre of the church floor up to the sky (heaven). Inside the dome, God and the saints reveal themselves iconographically. When mosaic is used to depict the heavenly figures, the images have a shimmering quality that is part of the whole attempt to create a space which appears "dematerialized". This is done by "dissolving" the wall surfaces, through the indeterminate curvature of the dome and the creation of an awareness of indefinite spaces beyond and behind, but also by the use of light so that the shimmering surface appears to move. At the time the effect must have appeared unearthly.

Picturesque Decoration

The discovery, by the English architect John Nash (1752-1835) and his contemporaries, of the enormous versatility and economy of stucco coincided with the abandoning of the stiff and formal traditions borrowed from classical antiquity in favour of a genuine appreciation of local countryside and tradition. In late eighteenth-century literature, painting and music, artists and composers such as Wordsworth, Claude-Lorraine and Beethoven conveyed a pastural mood which was also reflected in the architecture. The appreciation of a more natural landscape included a serious re-evaluation of the role of architecture as part of the landscape.

One of the greatest demonstrations of this mood was the plan by John Nash for the Prince Regent in London. A "Royal Mile" was cut through London to connect the centre of government in Whitehall with a housing development for the new and affluent class of administrators built in the parkland to the north. The buildings themselves were really no more than long terraces of tall houses with narrow frontages in the traditional pattern. However, Nash applied grand facades to the whole group which made them look like great palaces set in a rural landscape, providing the owners with a flattering status-symbol. As with stage-scenery, the appearance was contrived on one side only. Not only are the buildings not palaces, they are not built from stone either. Nash used stucco instead, the only feasible method by which the result could have been affected within his means. The use of stucco as a cheaper substitute for stone meant that the classical

architectural style became generally available as a veneer.

Honesty of Expression

During the nineteenth century, there was a great debate in architectural circles about the purpose of decoration. Up to this point, decoration had been generally accepted, even though the emphasis placed on it had varied. Decoration had been a fact of architecture – Ruskin called it "the principal part of architecture".

Walter Crane, a follower of William Morris, divided decoration into two

Above *860 Lake Shore Drive,* Chicago (1948-51, Mies van der Rohe). These apartment buildings, which equally could be office blocks, demonstrate the purity of the steel and glass architecture of the International Style. The architect was reputedly alarmed when the inhabitants of the first building put up blinds and curtains which were not consistent with the elevation; when the second building was completed, smoked glass prevented such individual expression. Unfortunately, imitators of Mies' style went on to create debased versions of the International Style which lack the dignity of these examples. The subsequent dehumanization and anonymity of modern cities has recently led to a renewal of interest in decoration.

The lack of humanity in so much post-war architecture has arguably grown out of the failure of the Modern Movement to supply architectural symbols or themes which place buildings into a relevant social or cultural context. Reaction was slow but inevitable. The American architect Robert Venturi's slogan of the 1970s "less is a bore" reaffirmed the desire that buildings should provide continuity in a historical context and take delight in "complexity and contradiction".

An impression of a building is so often based upon its external form. Most people understand buildings as facades. Buildings in the spirit of the Modern Movement explain themselves in a language of structure, and the character of the primary materials. Those buildings say much about themselves, but there is little to satisfy the needs of the passerby or the individual user when it comes to understanding them. Current architecture is trying to recreate a language which stimulates response and conveys an understandable meaning. As an example of this approach, the Byker renewal project by Ralph Erskine in Newcastle was built following considerable participation in the planning process by those being rehoused in the scheme. Consideration for diversity and individual identity is achieved by a decorative mixture of materials and elements. These are combined to break down the scale of the huge monolithic "wall" into humanly acceptable proportions.

The whole building as decoration is clearly demonstrated by schemes such as La Muralla Roja (1973) and Xanadu (1967) by Ricardo Bofill's Taller de Arquitectura. At Xanadu, the building is displayed as a beautiful object in a setting, with strong colour and strong form being used to gain maximum contrast to natural rock.

In the Burns House (Charles Moore and Associates), colour, light and shade are used to create a series of illusions of depth and recession. The whole house is designed to delight, puzzle and entertain. References to precedent are deliberately employed.

If architects want people to understand and like their buildings, then those buildings must express themes, ideas and values with which people can identify. Today, decorative and ornamental aspects of architecture seem to be valued again. Their acceptance is, as always, a question of attitude.

categories: organic and inorganic. The former was "an essential and integral part of the structure, to which it gives final expression". The latter he described as mere surface ornament, intended to conceal a structure, not emphasize a design. A. W. N. Pugin (1813-52) maintained that the only, Christian architecture was Gothic, which was essentially decorated. But as well as putting forward a moral case for Gothic in particular and decoration in general, he also inveighed against "all mechanical contrivances and inventions of the day, such as plastering composition, papier-mâché and a host of other decorations which only serve to degrade design". The whole issue of using materials honestly was a vital part of the argument which questioned the moral purpose of decoration.

The Industrial Society

By the turn of the nineteenth century, patronage of major building projects was moving away from a wealthy minority of individuals into the hands of corporate bodies and agencies which were representative of the energies of the age. Overcrowding and poverty resulted from rapid urban expansion and industrialization. New building forms, such as office blocks and warehouses, responded to a new generation of needs, technology and materials and gave a different interpretation to "organic" decoration.

The American architect, Louis Sullivan (1856-1924), searched for an architecture which honestly reflected the purpose, structure and spirit of the age. His motto was "form follows function", but the flamboyance of Sullivan's decoration never obscured the legibility of his structures and it invariably reinforced the shape or line.

The Twentieth Century

In reaction to the decadence of the Art Nouveau style, Adolf Loos believed that "ornamentation should be eliminated from all useful objects". The Bauhaus designers of the 1920s followed this notion to produce an aesthetic synonymous with the machine age. The handcrafts of ornamentation and decoration had no place in the processes of mass production. The pure white cubism of International Style architecture was intended to express an appropriate usage of modern technology and materials, breaking away from traditional forms. However, Modern Movement architecture did not satisfy more human needs, and it took no account of the basic urge of the individual to express his own identity. Mies van der Rohe, for example, was primarily concerned with the expression of efficiency, refinement and the sophistication of steel and glass construction, to the extent that in such cases as the Lake Shore Drive apartments (1949-51), the differences between corporate and domestic buildings are submerged. Other buildings spoke more of industrialized building and assembly processes, taking their form from Mies' credo, "less is more". These concerns were of little interest to most building users who, when left to their own devices, would decorate or ornament their homes with traditional symbols which give buildings a more directly recognizable form and meaning.

Building Materials and Architectural Q

Two thousand years ago, the Roman architect Vitruvius recognized three different requirements of architecture: *utilitas, firmitas, venustas.* These are best known in English in the words of Henry Wotton, Elizabeth I's remarkable ambassador to Venice: "Fine building hath three qualities; commodity, firmness and delight." When trying to define what makes a good building, it is difficult to better this formulation even today.

This book is not primarily concerned with "commodity" – the role of buildings in containing and ordering social activities, and thereby reflecting social organization. The emphasis has been on "firmness", the soundness of structures through the use of materials. "Delight" has only been discussed as it has arisen through the sensibility of designers in their choice and exploitation of these materials.

Each chapter has inevitably focussed on architecture which displays the use of its material in a particularly expressive, typical or developed way: for example, the stone vaulting of the high Gothic period. Taking this example from the story of stone, there are two points to be noted. First, there are other similar and important high Gothic buildings in brick, and also in timber. More importantly, the engineering achievement of the awesome Gothic nave of Chartres

Cathedral, for example, does not substantiate the conclusion that the meaning of great medieval architecture is contained in such technical feats. In fact, the Gothic cathedral, which has been called the most creative achievement in the history of Western architecture, can only be understood as the singularly sensitive response of artistic form to the theological vision of the twelfth century, such as the doctrinal meaning of light. The "modernist" view of the cathedral as simply a supremely rational structural achievement is a mechanistic fallacy which originated in nineteenth-century France.

Bearing in mind that the meaning of architecture is culturally much richer than a brief glance at history might suggest, it is useful nevertheless to trace the chronological development of Western architecture. Almost all this development comes within a tradition of masonry (brick, stone and, at times, mass concrete) assisted by timber (with iron beginning to supplant timber's role 200 years ago). Since the middle of last century, however, the list of possible ingredients has dramatically expanded. The traditional pattern of building has been radically altered, with frames of concrete and metal, tents and inflatable fabrics, rigid plastics and transparent sheets offering utterly new architectural possibilities.

Below and right *St Paul's Cathedral*, London (1675–1710, Sir Christopher Wren). This great cathedral was designed by a scientist with architectural genius. The high dome, surmounted by a masonry steeple, lantern and huge golden orb and cross, virtually seemed a structural impossibility in the late seventeenth century. Wren achieved his artistic ideal by using a clear and logical structure as the basis: the actual load-bearing dome is a conical brick structure (with oval holes to lessen its own weight) which transmits the weight of the lantern and outer dome downwards through flying buttresses round the base of the dome. The buttresses are hidden behind a Corinthinian collonade. The brick dome is also hidden; the awesome beauty of the dome's exterior and interior is created by deceptive shells. The outer dome is in fact a hemispherical veneer on timber framing, and the inner dome is saucer-shaped and much lower, supporting only itself.

Chronological Development

Western cultural tradition can be traced back to ancient Greece in an unbroken path, which scarcely touches more Eastern traditions until recent times. The sharply cut and precisely aligned pure forms of fifth-century B.C. Greek architecture were made of unmortared marble and dressed stone (with the assistance of timber). It was an architecture characterized by the trabeated form, that is, with horizontal members ("entablature") carried on columns which surrounded masonry interiors of lesser architectural importance. Highly stylized details and proportional systems for collonades were developed, the major ones being known as the Doric, Ionic and Corinthian Orders.

From this highpoint, Greek architecture eventually blended into that of the Romans, who took on the Greek motifs and the orders but developed a very different concept of architecture. They used freestone and marble to clad their buildings, but the main structural material was cast concrete, usually faced with bricks. The Roman architect probably also trained as an engineer; in this period and increasingly through the following centuries the architect moved away from the position of artist, which he had held in Greece, to that of technician.

While the Greeks, building with walls or post-and-beam systems, never bothered with arches, which they must have known about, the Romans developed this form on a collossal scale, and in brilliantly innovative ways. They produced huge bridges composed of arches on arches; more important were their great internal spaces, made of tunnel vaults and cross ("groin") vaults, and their domes, such as the magnificent covering of the Pantheon (A.D. 120-4).

Later Classical building, after the recognition of Christianity in A.D. 313, displayed a new lightness after the massive imperial structures. The mass concrete technology died away and the basilican churches, mostly of brick, with stone or marble cladding and timber roofs, had plain exteriors which made no reference to the Classical temple form. By the sixth century, however, centralized churches, under the influence of Byzantine style, developed the Graeco-Roman tradition rather differently. The great Cathedral of the Holy Ghost (Hagia Sofia) in Byzantium, with its saucer dome of corbelled hollow brick jars rising to 182 feet (55.6m) over an open space of 105 x 210 feet (32 x 64m), is in a sense the culmination of the art of imperial Rome.

After this period, European architecture – by now an architecture of religious establishments – made use of freestone walls with arches, but rarely used vaults. Columns were replaced by squat piers, buildings became agglomerations of parts, collections of spaces and mass enlivened by towers. By the eleventh century, powerful walls, both internal and external, were being articulated to a considerable degree with projections, blind arcades and niches. Vaulting was used again and experimented with; freestone remained the standard material, occasionally replaced by brick and marble in Italy.

The important innovation of the rib vault meant that bays of a vault could cover plan shapes that were not square. This resulted in the development of the pointed arch (segmental rather than semicircular). Through the centuries of Gothic architecture, the rib system was developed and refined, replacing load-bearing walls and solid cross vaults with a network of traceried structure built of small stones. The wall surfaces were increasingly reduced to pure supporting structures, and the space between was filled with windows. Previously, the mass of walling had been essential to resist the components of the load; now, buttresses and flying buttresses took the weight outside the columns. With this system of three-dimensional support, largely at right-angles to the window plane, the heights of vaults could be tremendously increased without widening the plan to unusable and unbuildable proportions. This resulted in buildings which seemed virtually "dematerialized", the huge vaults lying in a perpetual, mysterious greenish twilight, lit from the planes of stained glass. In such buildings, any mass of masonry was concentrated on the facade, which became covered with the most intricate and iconographic sculpture.

The Gothic tradition continued to develop over northern Europe, moving away from pure clarity to the high Gothic of Salisbury (1220-65) or Chartres Cathedrals (1194-1260). Still built with the same materials, walls became solid again, interiors more precise, proportions less exaggerated and surfaces richly decorated with stone filigree. In secular architecture, refinement was a late development, coming to Europe via Venice. (However Arabic models, such as the late fourteenth-century palace at Granada, the Alhambra, were built a century earlier.) Complex wooden structures, particularly in England, were being used not only for religious building (as at Ely and York Cathedrals) but also, with the new invention of the hammer-beam principle, for secular buildings requiring a wide span, such as the magnificent Westminster Hall (1394-1402).

At the same time, in the mid-fifteenth century, a renaissance began in Florence which was to remain a lively and developing force for the next 350 years. The

language of classical form was recalled: column and pilaster, entablature and temple front, together with the classical system of proportion. The buildings were mostly made of freestone (sometimes faced, sometimes stuccoed brick) and decoration was used sparingly. The ideal was to create a sense of order and harmony between the parts of a building, and the inside and outside.

Even before this date, the role of the architect had begun to change in northern Italy. We know the names of many Gothic master-masons, and we know how highly regarded they were as masters of their craft, but there was no notion of individual creativity in their culture. However, when Florence appointed the painter Giotto as its master-mason in 1334, a change in the concept of the designer began and, by the mid-fifteenth century, in northern Italy at least, the architect was established as an artist. After 1500, Renaissance ideas spread north, initially to France, and inspired the

design of secular buildings such as palaces and town halls, while sacred architecture continued in the Gothic tradition alongside.

By this time – the era of Inigo Jones (1573-1652) in London and England's early Renaissance in architecture – the Italians had moved on to the phase known as Baroque, a style which used the same language, Renaissance, but with greater profusion and in a more plastic and fluent manner. Baroque architecture, built mainly in stone, often with integral sculpture and painting on its flowing forms, increasingly took on an organic, sinuous character.

The cultural mixture was now rich and self-conscious. There were great public debates about what buildings should look like. A typical Renaissance issue was whether or not incomplete Gothic churches should be finished with "modern" facades. Two of the three greatest masters of the Baroque, Francestco Borromini (1599-1667) and Guarino Guarini (1624-83), were

Left and below There was an intense concern with the materials and means of construction in mid-nineteenth century England. The court of the University Museum of Oxford, by Deane and Woodward, *(left)* which was begun in 1855, illustrates a splendid exploitation of glass and iron, with the Gothic ribbing echoed by the smaller polychrome arches and even the skeletal exhibits. Ruskin was unusually inspired by this building, and sometimes stood on the scaffolding exhorting the stonemasons. By contrast, Ruskin dismissed the Crystal Palace (1851) *(below)* as "a greenhouse larger than ever a greenhouse was built before". It was noted at the time, however, that the interior appeared to be of almost boundless spaciousness, and the result was quite different from the space within the Museum court.

trained in the Gothic tradition; while the third and last, Balthasar Neumann, was a military engineer. Neumann's masterpiece, the mid-eighteenth century Pilgrimage Church, Vierzehnheiligen (1744-72) was completed in the same year as the Colebrookdale iron bridge in England, the first structure of the new industrial age.

At the end of the "age of reason", around the beginning of the nineteenth century, architecture was ossified in an abstract classical style of simple basic forms, with only minimal decoration. No longer flowing or "organic", this architecture was controlled and rational: its freestone and stucco outsides hid calculated metal chain reinforcing (as in the facade of Ste. Geneviève, Paris), as well as roofs and even columns of iron.

The Industrial Revolution brought utterly new building requirements, which could not be resolved by repeating traditional means, and while architects faltered, engineers came to the forefront. First, they exploited the new materials such as glass and iron, both of which, though known since antiquity, had now become available in new forms and shapes, quality and quantity, which allowed radically different building techniques. Secondly, they exploited the new possibilities of construction and management techniques to build huge, repetitive structures very quickly. Thirdly, they made use of new industrial techniques, such as machine sawing, and mass-produced nails.

Meanwhile architects, holding on to the remnants of their Renaissance status as artists, saw themselves as the purveyors of

sensibilty and culture, rather than offering skills which might either supplant or complement those of the engineers. With the rise of the nouveau-riche bourgeois class, architects had a ready market, and buildings based on mixtures of different styles proliferated. The notion of "style" in architecture is an early nineteenth-century invention, and a later nineteenth-century obsession.

After much heart-searching and various attempts at different approaches towards the end of the nineteenth century, including "free style" in England, "shingle style" in New England and art nouveau in Europe, twentieth-century architects went on to define their role by trying to identify with engineers. This was achieved by taking over what they assumed to be the engineers' criteria and, at its most extreme, it involved changing the Vitruvian trio of qualities into an equation: commodity plus firmness equals delight. In this way, delight was defined out of existence. "Modernism" suggested that reason together with abstraction, conditioned only by available materials and building techniques, should be the only factors which determined the character of architecture. As the dissatisfaction with so much postwar architecture, with the mass of dull housing and offices and the trend towards a banal international uniformity, has demonstrated, this was a simplistic and not very fruitful proposition.

We live at a time and in a culture, therefore, which is not at peace with its recent architecture. The *Architects' Journal* of January 10, 1935 published a chronological table which prophesied the development of architecture over the next hundred years. The anonymous authors, (the architect Serge Chermayeff and the critic Sir James Richards) foretold that in 1988: "The word 'modern' now denotes the style current in the 1930s (c.f. 'Gothic')." That statement was remarkably perceptive, remembering that "Gothic" had been introduced as a term of abuse against medieval building, and that in the mid-1930s, the word "style" was taboo.

"Modernism" today, however, denotes more than the style current in the 1930s. Its aesthetic origins were in the eighteenth century, it gained momentum as a set of ideas in the nineteenth century, but it achieved its expression in the 1930s.

Contemporary Themes in Architecture

A recurring criterion of architectural quality has always been to do with the use of materials. However, Modernism, the new architecture of the mid-twentieth century, also proposed others. The first notion was "form follows function". Architecture was seen as fitting around organized and separated activities, the form being determined by the nature of these zoned activities, neglecting, for example, the social or urban importance of the building, or the values of ambiguity or contradiction within their design. The second and related goal was to produce an architecture whose buildings were mechanisms, fitting together mechanically and using the minimum of material in innovative ways. Thirdly, architecture was seen as offering a new type of dynamic spatial experience. This aesthetic, built on Le Corbusier's *architecture promenade,* was linked to the fragmented imagery of Cubism. Its power produced some magnificent buildings, but its imagery, such as the notion of "transparency", has also been used to justify many exposed and alienated environments.

Honesty of Expression

Perhaps the strongest, and certainly the commanding criterion of Modernism was the notion of honesty of expression. This idea first arose in the eighteenth century with the writings of Abbé Laugier (1713-69), who gave the example that columns should be preferred to pilasters, as they were not only structural, but they appeared so. This is an aesthetic stance. But, confusingly, over the last century and a half, the Modernist attitude to an honesty of expression has been closely associated with morality. It was tied to such reform movements as Catholic revivalism in the 1840s, the early socialism of William Morris and his circle, the welfare-state architecture of the Bauhaus, and the Hertfordshire metal-frame school building programme in England in the 1950s.

Within honesty of expression is the notion of constructional clarity. In 1841, A.W.N. Pugin (1812-52) called for there to "be no features about a building that are not necessary for convenience, construction or propriety... the smallest detail should serve a purpose... construction should vary with the materials employed..." (*The True Principles of Pointed or Christian Architecture,* 1841). Less than a decade later, John Ruskin added, "Nobody wants ornaments in this world, but everyone wants integrity. All the fair devices that ever were fancied are not worth a lie. Leave your walls as bare as a planed board, or build them of baked mud

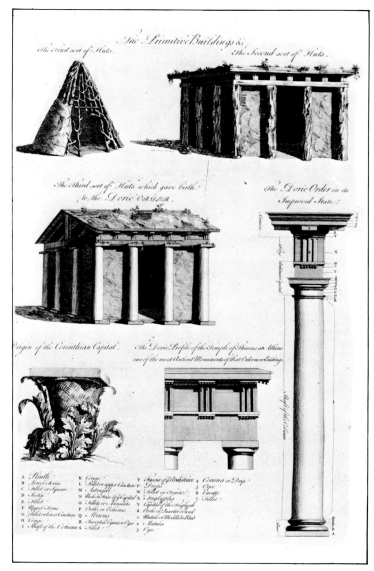

and chopped straw, if need be; but do not rough-cast them with falsehood." (*Seven Lamps of Architecture,* 1847).

As this aesthetic took hold, such features as the smoothness of a surface, the concealment of irregularities behind plaster, became as suspect as smoothness of character. In 1862, the leading English rationalist historian, James Fergusson, called for ceiling timbers to be "exposed, rudely squared, with the bolts and screws all shown." Exactly a century later, so-called "brutalists" made a virtue of crudely exposed materials and joints, exaggerating the wood-grain relief left on concrete surfaces by shuttering, or glorying in exposed structure, mechanical service ducts, shafts and coils.

This attitude can inform an architecture which is concerned with the process and production of building. Here, again, aesthetic ideals are linked with social ideals, sometimes leading to a romantic view of the role of builders and craftsmen – Ruskin used to stand on the scaffolding

reading edifying texts to the stone masons. William Morris stated that his aim was to design things which were pleasant to construct, and to construct things that were pleasant to use. When architecture is *not* concerned with an expression of either materials or the process of building, there will be less appreciation of the difficulties which may arise in construction, in human as well as organizational terms: some building trades are not just exhausting, but often unsatisfying and dangerous as well.

Perhaps the most attractive statement of the Modernist tradition of explicitness was made by the great twentieth-century architect Louis Kahn (1901-74), who argued that buildings should somehow retain the marks of their production – the process of their construction should remain explicit. This direct legibility gives a tough coherence to much of the great architecture of the past and remains a powerful influence on architects today. The English architect, Edward Cullinan, is typical of many who aim to clarify the use of various materials

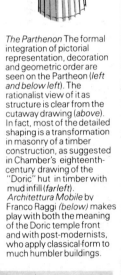

The Parthenon The formal integration of pictorial representation, decoration and geometric order are seen on the Partheon (*left and below left*). The rationalist view of it as structure is clear from the cutaway drawing (*above*). In fact, most of the detailed shaping is a transformation in masonry of a timber construction, as suggested in Chamber's eighteenth-century drawing of the "Doric" hut in timber with mud infill (*far left*).
Architettura Mobile by Franco Raggi *(below)* makes play with both the meaning of the Doric temple front and with post-modernists, who apply classical form to much humbler buildings.

and structural systems. His studio's trademarks, like hanging timber windows and roof frames from solid masonry are not only good examples of constructional clarity, but also show a concern with making buildings pleasant to build.

Commonsense

A commonsense approach to architecture has an aesthetic sensibility of its own, although it is primarily concerned with using materials and technology which are appropriate in the context of a particular social requirement. This is evident in the work of Walter Segal, for example, who has been developing a system of housing in England which can be built by its inexperienced occupants, without relying on the building industry. The system is based on precise calculation of structural loading on each member, direct and clear methods of jointing on site, the use of uncut factory-made board materials for the outer skin and high quality minimal section stress-graded timber for the skeleton. This approach, which depends so thoroughly on commonsense, and is therefore original, cannot help but produce its own charm.

Segal's work is in the tradition which includes the house Charles and Ray Eames built for themselves in 1951 and stretches back even further to the rigorous commonsense projects of the last century (rarely involving architects). These are typified by I. K. Brunel's (1806-59) remarkable hospital for the Crimean War, which was shipped in prefabricated units and erected with great speed and efficiency at Renkioi.

In these three buildings there is exhibited a very clear architecture, but one which is not bound by the materials. Segal uses timber, because it is most appropriate for self-builders who have no previous building experience and will be using only simple handtools. For some years, Segal has been waiting to use metal framing in the same simple and radical way. Brunel, on this occasion, also used wood, but not because of any beliefs he held about the material. The metal catalogue components used by the Eames gave their house a meccano quality, together with a hint of Japanese calm, space and flexibility. Each of these designers was interested in the possibilities offered by fabrication on site, the process of construction, control over the environment, and the use of manufactured components and factory materials.

When the aesthetic of "explicitness" dominates commonsense, the result is very different. This has led, in recent years, to the production of vast constructional "toys" that never quite become architecture. In the Centre Pompidou in Paris, a monument to this approach, the transparency of production forms a sort of bogus democratic veneer to that autocratic, magnificent and rather frightening castle of culture.

Left *Bayard Building*, New York City (Louis Sullivan). This detail is of a front elevation, showing the entrance to the Bayard Building. The idea "form follows function" originated with Sullivan, and the Modernists reduced the concept to its most vacuous level; here, however, is an example of his rational, magnificent architectural style. His metal-framed, commercial buildings always display a leanness of design with a concern for surface detail, often with the use of intricately patterned terracotta tiles as cladding.

Right A lithograph of a design by K.F. von Schinkel. The architect was aware of the simple yet powerful aesthetic appeal of the classical style, and in this drawing has placed the idealized image in a nineteenth-century, north European setting. He made the idea "realistic" by proposing the construction of an invisible wall between the columns. The proposal was made, however, long before such an idea was technically possible. Glass walls, constructed of large sheets joined by neoprene gaskets, are now familiar, and his idea does not seem so far-fetched.

However, other developments are possible, using the starting point of common-sense. The American architect Bruce Goff shows an outrageous, but exquisite, sensitivity to materials: his houses make exotic use of sequins, paper plates, tinsel, coal sprayed with lanolin, ropes coiled on ceilings, plywood finished with shoe polish, goosefeathers, string and the perspex domes from aeroplanes. Goff has even used brightly coloured synthetic carpeting as a roof covering. The Belgian architect Lucien Kroll also displays an explicit use of materials with equal gaiety and without recourse to the ordered minimalism of Modernism. With Atelier Kroll, there is also an added concern for social context, most obvious in their work at Louvain University, where the superficially random and anarchic appearance of the buildings reflects much discussion about the decision-making processes. The considerable skill and humanity of Kroll's buildings is quite different from the puritanical treatment of concrete by leaving the marks of shuttering exposed, even down to the bolt holes, or the arid exposure of gaudy service pipes. The problem with those types of buildings is they rely on the understanding of a private, architectural language, which inevitably ignores the more repelling messages being given out.

The Vernacular

Modernism, in its search for integrity, has always taken a particular interest in "vernacular" building, or traditional regional forms. The vernacular was admired and even envied for its natural "rightness" and studied by early Modernists in the hope that it might inspire their work.

Vernacular architecture, the product of a reasonably homogenous and slow-changing culture, consists of highly integrated constructions. While decoration is often complex, it is also full of meaning and not overwhelming; while forms are clearly based on techniques, materials, social organization, and climatic and cultural patterns, they are also highly stylized. All of these factors are subtly balanced: the architecture is a formal tradition determined by society, and is never based on theoretical attitudes, such as notions about materials and utility.

Another important aspect of vernacular traditions is the way materials are used. The Modernist notion that wood produces essentially "timberish" buildings and brick essentially "bricky" buildings has a lot to do with a simplistic view both of history and the vernacular. The Chinese timber roofs of the T'ang dynasty (such as Kuan-yin Hall) are highly stylized post-

Above and below Eric Mendelsohn turned one of his sketches of abstract forms (*below*), some of which had names such as *Bach Cantata*, into a genuine observatory: the Einstein Tower, Potsdam (1927) (*above*). It is a dramatic, expressionist sculpture, but instead of being moulded in its natural concrete, is built of rendered masonry.

Right A drawing by
Vaudoyer of his imaginary
"House of a
Cosmopolitan". Vaudoyer's
eighteenth-century image
is both surprising and
fantastic. Pure classical and
pure geometric designs are
juxtaposed (Doric columns
support a spherical shell) to
form the idealized
combination of a vertical
transversed by a circle.
Below The Summer Palace
in Peking is instantly
recognizable as Chinese,
and may in this sense be
considered to be
vernacular. The Chinese
created a style of building
which reflected their
society and their
philosophies, and which
hardly changed for
centuries. Vernacular does
not, however, necessarily
mean simple. The individual
style of the many roofs, for
example, which are
concave in section with
upturned eaves and heavily
decorated and
ornamented, is a result of a
great number of complex
intellectual considerations.

and-lintel constructions of great ingenuity,
but they are not "logical" in their use of
material. The complexity of the roofs is
purely formal and contains much "redundant" material. Neither is Greek Classical
architecture logical in material terms. The
post-and-lintel form of the Parthenon
(447-432 B.C.) is structurally inelegant in
stone: the detail is a clear, stylized version
of earlier timber construction. The building
material is only logical in that it provides a
base for integrated sculptural decoration.

Vernacular traditions, in the sense of
popular culture, can also illuminate a
whole range of responses to materials. The
home-improvement market displays many
of our beliefs about the symbolic use of
different materials. "Natural stone" is
available to clad Victorian terrace houses
built in brick; Doric porticos or Georgian
bow windows come in plaster and fibreglass. Double-glazed picture windows with
aluminium frames come with diamond
leaded panes applied to the inner layer.

Some of our everyday myths are new. In a
culture conditioned to expect fake objects
we think of plastic merely as a substitute
material. Some myths are deep-seated, and
are most obvious in the ancient story of the
three little pigs and their houses. These
attitudes can have serious and far-reaching
effects. Building societies have been unwil-
ling to finance timber-framed houses, and
fire regulations penalize timber over metal,
even though timber as a structural material
behaves both more predictable and less
disastrously in a fire. Stone, on the other
hand, is seen as "everlasting", although
stone buildings which have been wrongly
bedded deteriorate beyond repair at great
speed, and the oldest inhabited buildings
in Britain are timber-framed.

There are also more general myths to do
with the scarcity of a material and feelings
about the quality and quantity of craftsmanship which may go into its preparation.
We appreciate the glitter of precious metals
and stones, but also marvel at the mirror-
image laminations of marble facings in
Hagia Sophia, the meticulous accuracy of
the unmortared masonry of the Egyptian
pyramids, at the temples of ancient Greece,
or the interlocked walls of Machu Picchu (c.
1500). It is no surprise to find conscious
attempts to duplicate an admired material—
for example, the marbelling of plastered
columns, or the painting of texture and
stain on stuccoed brick terraces in early
nineteenth-century England to imitate
Bath stone.

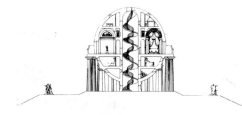

Left The city of Machu Picchu is situated above the Urubamba gorge, high in the Peruvian Andes. The geometric regularity of the city plan, which was designed around a central plaza with a sun temple surrounded by palaces, reflects the strength of the centralized governmental control of the Inca people. It is interesting to note that despite their magnificent architectural achievements, including a mountain road that stretched over 3,250 miles (5,230 km) with bridges spanning rivers and deep valleys, the Incas had no wheels and did not discover the principle of the true arch. The ruined walls, seen here, are of solid granite.
Inset The walls were built of great blocks of stone which were interlocked with the angles fitting exactly – polygonal masonry. This picture of the entrance gate to Sacsahuamán, a mountain fortress defending the Inca capital Cuzco, illustrates their great building skill. The unbroken north wall, erected between A.D. 1438 and 1500, is 1,500 feet (457 m) long. Some of the blocks are 27 feet (8 m) high.

Criticisms of Modernism

Modern architecture has been criticized on
many counts, not least of which are the
many unacceptable buildings and harsh
environments which its proponents have
produced. However, criticisms can also be
made on a more theoretical level. The
seemingly straightforward tenets of the
movement have, in practice, given rise to a
number of paradoxes.

The first paradox concerns the Modernist
approach to materials and construction.
The obsession for honest and direct expression, the desire to achieve quality through
detailing, can have an almost religious
significance. This is appropriate in the
exquisite timber Ise Shrine in Japan, so
admired by modern designers. However,
when this same fastidiousness is applied
irrespective of a building's social use or
importance, then it becomes very difficult
to read where the building fits in the social
world.

Charles Jencks, in *The Language of Post
Modern Architecture*, shows up this confusion by referring to the IIT campus
designed by Mies van der Rohe
(1885-1969). The cathedral, a building with
tall nave and side aisles, with clearstory
windows and a slender campanile turns out
to be "the boiler house, a solecism of such
stunning wit that it cannot be truly appreciated until we see the actual chapel, which
looks like a boiler house." However, the
confusion which this attitude produces is
not just an issue of styling – making
buildings comprehensible should not be a
matter of putting clearer stylistic signs on
them. It is important to realize, as Mies at
IIT did not, that a boiler house is not as
important as a chapel, however essential its
purpose, and that is the reason their
designs should not be confusing.

The second paradox of Modernism is
that, underneath the rhetoric, very little
modern architecture is actually truthful to
materials; instead, what is displayed is a
certain taste concerning the apparent materials. In the 1930s, Le Corbusier
(1887-1965) covered blockwork with stucco
to make it look like concrete, just as the late
Georgians had done to make their terrace
houses look as if they were built of Bath
stone. Erich Mendelsohn (1887-1953) built
his Einstein Tower (1921), its flowing form a
response to the fluid poured nature of
concrete, not out of concrete itself, but
again of masonry walls covered to appear
like concrete. In the United States in the
1960s, architects then known as the "New
York Five" built neo-Corbusier houses,
using wood and white paint to resemble
concrete. This was in exactly the same
tradition as their ancestors, who not only
had white neo-classical wooden mansions,
simulating the architecture of Renaissance

Italy, but even substituted Ionic columns for Corinthian on occasions when the slave labour was not dextrous enough to carve the Corinthian capitals.

The most celebrated example concerns the tall buildings of Mies van der Rohe in the United States. Mies had developed his immaculate, pristine steel aesthetic in his designs for single-storey buildings. These objects were drained of social meaning, almost to the point where people seemed intruders. Although it could be argued that this produces a hermetic, even boring architecture, it has a clear integrity. However, when Mies was building higher than a single storey, he was forced by fire safety regulations to build in reinforced concrete. After that, he stuck a secondary steel frame on the outside of the buildings to make them look steel-framed. Within the the architectural profession, this was seen as a betrayal; but more than anything else, this "betrayal" showed the fragility of erecting an approach to architecture on such a poverty-stricken theoretical basis.

Another Modernist misapprehension is the assumption that the best designers must be in the forefront of technical innovation. It is true that some inquisitive architects have always tried to develop new technical possibilities; others have been technically innovative almost by chance. Leopold von Klenze's (1784-1864) "Valhalla", a copy of the Parthenon, built 150 years ago on a hill outside Regensburg, had an innovative metal roof, but the intention was not to display technical ingenuity. In the same spirit is K.F. Schinkel's (1781-1841) drawing of glass running between Ionic columns, demanding what looks like a neoprene gasket and glass sheet sizes which were quite impossible at the time. It was another 50 years before this detail could actually be built. When Alexander Thomson (1817-75) did build it, and, in the same building, ran glazing as a separate screen behind the structural columns, he was later called "proto-modern" by the Modernists, who completely misunderstood the aesthetic intentions of great nineteenth-century designers like Schinkel and Thomson. (Modernists tended to transfer their attitudes to history and believe that any decent architecture from the past must have shared their values).

However, despite wishful thinking, architects are not often among the technical innovators. Some do have visionary ideas; some are inventive by creatively borrowing from other disciplines, like Buckminster Fuller, or Eero Saarinen (1910-61) and his use of Cor-Ten steel on a large building. Some work on the edge of possibility, like Frei Otto or Jean Prouvé, but they are very rare. By and large, new technologies have not come up with the magic ingredients or possibilities that architects have hoped for and have been conditioned to expect by Modernism.

Commonsense in architecture The "kit of parts" approach, adopted both by Walter Segal in his self-build housing (*left*) and by the Eames brothers for their house in Santa Monica (*right, far right and above*) can produce a very clear architecture of its own. Both of these examples have a Japanese flavour – the building supplies a plain, undecorated background, in which setting more elaborate objects can be displayed.

Decoration and Facades

Other criteria are also involved in the search for architectural quality. It is to some extent an effect of recent architectural taste that we sometimes find the simplicity of Victorian industrial structures easier to understand and appreciate than the richly ornamented civic buildings of the same period, with their profusion of colour and decoration. Modernism went out of its way to produce buildings without recognizable fronts, sides and backs, but which were objects in space, all of whose aspects were of equal importance. Traditionally, much of the meaning of a building was read in its decorated facade; without either a recognizable front or any form of decoration, buildings can be responsible for creating appalling confusion.

For Ruskin, the building was a frame for ornament; not just decorated construction, but constructed decoration. A taste for decoration, however, is different from an understanding of the value of the facade. The Georgians showed this in a way which is very akin to Modernism. They spent much effort covering up the exposed structures of timber-frame buildings (which did not help the preservation of the oak) and, to achieve clean lines and planes, they replaced the traditional casement window (which to this day remains the standard form in Europe) with the sash. The casement was simple, sensible and highly usable; the sash was much more complex to manufacture and keep in good working order, but it made the facades look cleaner and purer – as close as possible to the black holes drawn for windows in the elevations reproduced in Colen Campbell's *Vitruvius*

Britannicus, the primer of Georgian taste.

In the Renaissance, Andrea Palladio (1508-80) used all types of materials, with no attempt at structural ingenuity, but in an entirely new kind of architectural expression. His architecture did not depend on the intrinsic qualities of brick, stucco or stone, but on space, proportion and harmony. He used plain plaster and exposed rafters in a farm villa, severe clean grandeur for the church of the Redentore and gay and colourful *trompe l'oeil* frescoes by Vernonese in the salon of Barbaro's villa at Maser.

Today, in a reaction to the exclusiveness of recent architectural taste, facades and decoration are again being considered. "Post-modern" architecture, as it is known, is a style whose most cohesive force is an obsession with language and symbols. Robert Venturi, a leading theorist, describes buildings as "decorated sheds", their meaning enriched by the complexity and contradiction of the language used. Occasionally this approach is ironic and fresh, as in the work of Hans Hollein, which displays an elegant handling and appreciation of materials. However, in this type of architecture, both materials and the process and form of construction are often just means to other ends. This type of architecture can be seen as a witty, but elitist game, which also in its attempts at a populist image, tends to be patronising. Although a sense of humour in buildings is refreshing after the solemnity of much Modernism, it is not an enduring strength.

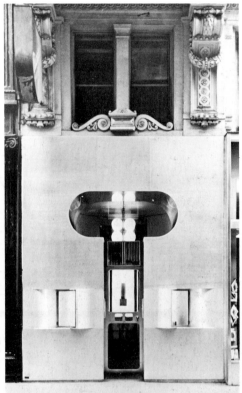

Below and left The work of the Austrian architect Hans Hollein shows a use of materials which emphasizes their particular qualities. In the jewellery shop in Vienna (1975) metal tubes explode through a shattered facade (*below*). The gold layers are folded through the fissure in the smooth marble, giving an ironic sensuality. The exterior of the candle shop, also in Vienna, (*left*) is plain, flat, shiny metal, applied over the typically Viennese facade and making a shocking juxtaposition.

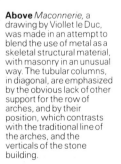

Above *Maçonnerie*, a drawing by Viollet le Duc, was made in an attempt to blend the use of metal as a skeletal structural material, with masonry in an unusual way. The tubular columns, in diagonal, are emphasized by the obvious lack of other support for the row of arches, and by their position, which contrasts with the traditional line of the arches, and the verticals of the stone building.

An Attitude to Materials

After Modernism, architects have begun to realize that "delight" depends on more than "commodity" and "firmness". A building is not the same as an efficient mechanism, nor is it a tool like a spoon or a hammer. Architects can only envy the directness with which craftsmen are able to produce these natural, elegant forms. Architecture is much more complex: a difficult social art of a different order.

At the same time, it is not possible to look to the past for a definition of architectural quality. One of the problems of post-modern architecture, tied to its lack of concern with direct and sensible uses of materials, is that it is reduced to concentrating all the meaning of buildings on their surfaces. This is usually achieved by reworking traditional gestures and does not provide a fresh response to current social attitudes and requirements.

Architecture is a synthetic process, and one which is considerably dependent on the technical characteristics of raw and manufactured materials, their specific historical precedents and their future potential. The qualities of each separate material can be displayed enthusiastically, even with partisan vigour. However, although great architecture has always displayed a wholehearted acceptance of the chosen materials and their possibilities, the process of design is not determined merely by the choice of ingredients. Even when the result seems obvious, other implicit choices are being made, to do with cultural rules and function.

Architectural quality is to do with integrity. Goethe, arguing for the qualities of German Gothic architecture against the neo-classical style of that time, said: "If it makes its impression from its own, unique, inner, independent sensibility, untroubled by, ignorant even, of everything foreign to it, then whether it is born of rough savagery or educated sensitivity, it is integral and alive." This perception is just as appropriate to architecture today.

Glossary

APSE
The semicircular end of a church sanctuary, first applied to a Roman basilica.

ARCADE
A roofed and colonnaded route.

ARCHITRAVE
The lowest of the three main parts of an entablature. The term is also applied to the moulded frame around a door or window.

AXONOMETRIC PROJECTION
A geometrical drawing showing a building in three dimensions.

BALUSTER
A pillar or column supporting a handrail or coping, in a series forming a balustrade.

BAROQUE
A late Renaissance seventeenth-century style of architecture, primarily found in Italy and Germany, characterized by flowing forms, exuberant decoration and complex spatial compositions.

BASILICA
An oblong building with double colonnades internally and a semicircular apse at the end. Mainly applied to Roman or early Christian architecture.

BETON BRUT
Concrete left in its natural state once the casting formwork has been removed.

CANTILEVER
An unsupported structural projection, eg a cantilever beam or balcony.

CAPITAL
The head of a column.

CENTERING
A temporary wooden framework used to support an arch or dome during construction.

CLADDING
A non-load-bearing external envelope or covering to a building.

CLAPBOARD
A term used in the United States for weatherboarding – overlapping horizontal boards covering a frame.

CLASSICAL
The architecture originating in ancient Greece or Rome, the rules and forms of which were revived to establish the Renaissance in Europe in the fifteenth and sixteenth centuries.

CLEARSTOREY
The upper wall of a building pierced by a row of windows.

COFFER
A sunken panel, usually decorative, formed in a ceiling.

COLLAR
A horizontal tie-beam in a timber roof linking the principal rafters to form an A-shaped truss.

CONVERSION (of timber)
Sawing logs parallel to their length to reduce them to rectangular cross-sections.

COPING
A capping or covering to the top of a wall to provide weather protection.

CORBEL
A block projecting from a wall face, usually in brick or stone, often to support a beam.

CORNICE
A projecting moulding running along the top of a building.

CROSS– or GROIN–VAULT
Vaults characterized by arched diagonal groins, which are formed by the intersection of two barrel vaults.

CROWN POST
A short post standing upright on the tie-beam of a timber roof, linked by other braces to the rafters to provide support.

CRUCKS
Pairs of large curved timbers used as the principal framing of a house, commonly in use in England until the sixteenth century.

DE STIJL
A Dutch geometric abstract movement in the arts between 1917 and 1931 which had a lasting effect on the development of modern architecture and industrial design.

DENTILS
Small square blocks used in series in Ionic and Corinthian cornices in classical architecture.

DETAIL
A part of a building drawn to a large scale in order to illustrate its construction.

DRY JOINT
A joint without mortar between the stones of a wall.

ELEVATION
A drawing showing one face of a building in the vertical plane.

ENTABLATURE
The upper part of the classical orders of architecture, consisting of architrave, frieze and cornice.

ENTASIS
A very slight convex curve on a column designed to correct the optical illusion of the column appearing to curve inwards if the sides were built straight.

FACADE
The face of a building.

FAIENCE
Glazed earthenware, often used as decoration in buildings. Faience was originally made in Faenza in Italy.

FASCIA
A plain horizontal band usually found in the architrave of an order. Also, a board or plate covering the ends of roof rafters.

FENESTRATION
The arrangement of windows in a building.

FLYING BUTTRESS
An arch or half-arch transmitting the thrust of a vault or roof from the upper part of a wall to an outer support.

FORMWORK
The temporary casing, usually made from timber or metal, into which "wet" concrete is poured. When the concrete is set, the formwork is removed or "struck".

FREESTONE
Any stone that cuts well in all directions, especially fine-grained limestone or sandstone.

FRIEZE
The middle division of an entablature, between the architrave and the cornice in classical architecture. Also the decorated band along the upper part of an internal wall, immediately below the cornice.

FROG
Indentation on the bed face of a brick to reduce its weight.

GAUGED BRICKWORK
Brickwork constructed with soft bricks sawn or rubbed to shape and laid with very fine joints.

GEODESIC DOME
A spherical dome construction in which all the structural members are interconnected to give stability in all directions. The geodesic dome was primarily developed in the United States by Buckminster Fuller.

GOTHIC/NEO-GOTHIC
Gothic is the name generally given to the pointed style of medieval architecture prevalent in western Europe between the thirteenth and fifteenth centuries. The term neo-Gothic refers to the Gothic revival mainly prevalent in western Europe, and to an extent in the United States, during the nineteenth century.

HAMMERBEAM
A hammerbeam roof is a late Gothic form of roof without a direct tie. Hammerbeams lessen the span and thus allow shorter timbers.

HYPOSTYLE HALL
A pillared hall in which the roof rests on columns in the central space, rather than spanning unsupported from side to side.

I-SECTION
A section of I-shaped rolled steel used in structural steelwork.

INFILL
A term mainly applied to the insertion of a new building between two existing ones.

INFLATABLE
The term refers to modern lightweight enclosures which are held up by air. There are two main types – those that are held up by inflated ribs and those where the internal air pressure is kept slightly above atmospheric air-pressure in order to support the structure itself. The latter requires an air-lock at entrances.

INTERNATIONAL STYLE
A term coined in the United States to refer to the equivalent of the Modern Movement in Europe (see Modern Movement).

JOINERY
The making and fixing of wood finishes to a building, as opposed to carpentry (heavy carcassing work) on the one hand and cabinet-making (specialist fine work) on the other.

LOAD-BEARING
Usually refers to a wall which is supporting other elements in a building (roof, floors etc.).

LOGGIA
A gallery behind an open arcade or colonnade.

MACHICOLATION
A projecting wall or parapet, built on the outside of castles, with openings in the floor behind, through which molten lead or missiles could be dropped.

MASONRY CONSTRUCTION
The craft of stone wall building including the preparation and fixing of the stones. Also loosely applied to any form of construction involving the layout of bricks or blocks.

METOPE
The square space between two triglyphs in the frieze of a Doric order in classical architecture.

MODERN MOVEMENT
A term referring to the new European architectural style of the early twentieth century. It was characterized by undecorated cubic forms, white render and large windows providing a horizontal emphasis.

MORTICE AND TENON
A joint between two sections of timber, usually at right-angles to each other, in which the projecting tenon is glued or pinned into the cut-out mortice.

MOTTE AND BAILEY
A defence system consisting of an earthen mound (motte) placed within an enclosure (bailey).

MULLION
A vertical member dividing a window or other opening into separate sections.

MUSHROOM COLUMN
A column used in reinforced concrete construction which is flared at the top in order to support the floor slab directly instead of via beams.

NAVE
The central aisle of a church.

NEOPRENE GASKET
A section of extruded neoprene (synthetic rubber) into which window glazing is set to give a weatherproof joint.

ORDERS
An order in classical architecture consists of a column shaft and capital supporting an entablature. The Greeks recognized three orders:
The DORIC order is unique in that a column has no base. The shaft is fluted and the capital plain.
The IONIC order is lighter and more elegant, with slim fluted columns and a capital decorated with volutes.
The CORINTHIAN order has a bell-shaped capital from which eight acanthus stalks emerge to support modest volutes. The shaft is generally fluted.

ORGANIC
Refers to an architectural expression loosely based on natural organic forms, and related to fundamental physical structures.

ORIEL WINDOW
An upper storey overhanging window, normally carried on corbels.

PEDIMENT
The low-pitched gable above the entablature in classical architecture. In Renaissance architecture and later, it refers to any roof end, whether triangular, semicircular or broken.

PENDENTIVE
The triangular curved overhanging surface by means of which a circular dome is supported over a square or polygonal plane.

PIANO MOBILE
The main floor of a house containing the principal reception rooms, raised one floor above ground level, with a higher ceiling height than the other floors.

PILASTER
A shallow pier or rectangular column projecting only slightly from a wall face.

PILOTIS
Pillars on an unenclosed ground floor carrying a building.

PISE DE TERRE
Walling made of cob – an unburnt brick.

PITCHED ROOF
A roof consisting of two planes sloping up to a central ridge.

PLAN
The layout of a building drawn in a horizontal plane.

PLASTIC
In the sense of form, plastic refers to the way in which a building is expressed in curved and flowing lines, unrelated to a grid or a composition of straight lines.

PODIUM
A continuous raised base or pedestal supporting columns.

POINTED ARCH
An arch consisting of two curves, each with a radius equal to the span and meeting in a central point at the top. The common form of arch in Gothic architecture.

PORTICO
A colonnaded space forming an entrance and centrepiece of the facade, with a roof supported on at least one side by columns.

POST-AND-BEAM
A post-and-beam structure consists of a horizontal beam supported on vertical posts.

QUOIN
A term generally applied to the dressed stones laid at the corners of a building.

REGULA
The short band between the tenia and guttae on a Doric entablature in classical architecture.

RENDER
The application of stucco or cement mortar to the face of a wall to give a continuous and smooth finish.

RENAISSANCE
Refers directly to the restoration of ancient Roman standards and motifs in Italy during the fifteenth and sixteenth centuries. In architecture, the term describes the revival of classical forms and their reinterpretation which spread throughout western Europe and beyond in subsequent centuries.

RIB
A projecting band on a ceiling or vault.

ROMAN ARCH
A semicircular arch construction developed by the Romans and mainly used in utility structures such as aqueducts, and in the Colosseum.

ROMANESQUE
The style of architecture current between the eighth and twelfth centuries, before the advent of Gothic. Romanesque was characterized by clear plans and use of the round arch.

ROOF LIGHT
A fixed or opening window in a roof.

SARSEN
A sandstone boulder found on chalk downs.

SCOTIA
A concave moulding on the base of a column which casts a strong shadow.

SECTION
A drawing showing a vertical "cut" through a building along a particular plane.

SERVICES
A term referring to the distribution of all services – electrical wiring, heating and hot water pipes, air conditioning ducts, telephone cables, and so on – throughout a building.

SET-BACK
The withdrawal of a building line, usually on upper floor, forming a stepped configuration to the building.

SHINGLE STYLE
A style of domestic architecture which developed in the United States in the late nineteenth century, characterized by external walls being clad in shingles (wooden tiles) over timber frames.

SHUTTERING
A commonly used term for formwork.

SKIN
A term referring to the outer "clothing" or membrane of a building – the brick walls, the glass and steel cladding and so on.

SPACE FRAME
A three-dimensional framework in which all the members are interconnected to act as a single entity. Space frames are used for covering large spaces uninterrupted by supporting columns.

SPAN
The horizontal distance between vertical supports – in other words, the length of a beam between two columns.

STRING COURSE
A moulding or projecting course of stone or brick running horizontally along the face of a building.

STUDWORK
A frame construction of intermediate horizontal and vertical members, over which wallboards are laid and nailed to the studs.

STYLOBATE
The upper step or platform on which stands a colonnade.

SUSPENDED STRUCTURE
A structure whereby the floors are hung from a support above, rather than being propped from below.

TRABEATED
"Trabeated" describes buildings constructed on the post-and-beam principle, as in Greek architecture.

TRANSEPT
The transverse arms of a cross-shaped church, usually between the nave and the chancel.

TRANSOM
A horizontal bar across a window or panel.

TRIGLYPHS
Blocks with vertical grooves separating the metopes in a Doric frieze in classical architecture.

TRUSS
A number of members framed together to bridge a space.

TUFA
A building stone of rough or cellular texture. The commonest form of Roman building stone was tufa, formed from volcanic dust.

VERNACULAR
A term, when applied to architecture, referring to traditional and indigenous styles of the past.

VOLUMETRIC
A term referring to the three-dimensional spatial qualities of a space.

VOUSSOIR
The truncated wedge-shaped blocks used to form an arch.

Index

Page numbers in *italic* refer to the captions and illustrations.

Acknowledgements

The illustrations are reproduced by kind permission of the following: **2-3** Richard Bryant; **5** Martin Charles; **6** Sonia Halliday; **7** Foster Associates; **8** Richard Bryant, Peter Mackertich (i); **9** Alsop, Finch and Lyall (al), Architectural Press (ar), Picturepoint (l); **10** Ronald Sheridan's Photo Library (a and br), Richard Bryant (b), Bastian Valkenburg (cr); **11** Peter Mackertich (a), Michael Freeman (bl), Picturepoint (br); **12** Sonia Halliday; **13** Gollins, Melvin and Ward; **14** Ronald Sheridan's Photo Library; **15** German National Tourist Office (l), Ronald Sheridan's Photo Library (r); **16** Peter Mackertich (al), Foster Associates (c), Architectural Association (b); **17** A.F. Kersting; **18** Roy White (Terry Farrell Partnership) (a), Martin Lazenby (Terry Farrell Partnership) (b); **19** The Tooley Foster Partnership (a), Simon Hudspith (c, b); **20** Elizabeth Whiting (l), Richard Bryant (r); **21** Architectural Press; **22** Sonia Halliday (a), Mary-Ann Kennedy (b); **23** Architectural Press (a), Michael Freeman (b); **24, 25** John Maine; **26** Sonia Halliday; **27** Michael Freeman (al), Sonia Halliday (ar), Michael Freeman (cl), Ronald Sheridan's Photo Library (cr and bl), Sonia Halliday (br); **29** Ronald Sheridan's Photo Library (al), Sonia Halliday (bl and br); **30** Ronald Sheridan's Photo Library, Sonia Halliday (il and b), Werner Forman Archive (ic and ir); **32** Werner Forman Archive; **33** Sonia Halliday (a), Ronald Sheridan's Photo Library (br); **35** Werner Forman Archive, Sonia Halliday (i); **36, 37** Ronald Sheridan's Photo Library; **38, 39** Werner Forman Archive, Sonia Halliday (il and ir); **40** Sonia Halliday (l), Ronald Sheridan's Photo Library (a and r); **42, 43** Ronald Sheridan's Photo Library; **44, 45, 46, 47** A.F. Kersting; **48, 49** Architectural Press; **50, 51** Picturepoint; **52** Cement and Concrete Association; **53** Archives d'Architecture Moderne, Brussels; **54** British Tourist Authority; **55, 56** Michael Freeman; **57, 58, 59, 60, 61** Werner Forman Archive; **62** Alan Hutchinson Library; **63** Ronald Sheridan's Photo Library; **64, 65, 66** Douglas Dickins; **67** Ronald Sheridan's Photo Library (a), Edwin Smith (l); **68, 69** Edwin Smith; **70** Edwin Smith (a), Richard Bryant (b); **71** Richard Bryant (al), Edwin Smith (ar and l); **72** Mary-Ann Kennedy; **73** Ronald Sheridan's Photo Library; **74** Norman McGrath; **75** Peter Mackertich (al and ar), Norman McGrath (b); **76** Sune Sundahi; **77** Architectural Press; **78, 79** Architectural Press; **80, 81** Basildon Development Corporation; **82** Richard Bryant (a), Sonia Halliday (b); **83** Richard Bryant; **85** Werner Forman Archive (al), Brick Development Association (r); **86, 87, 89** Ronald Sheridan's Photo Library; **90** Sonia Halliday; **91** Ronald Sheridan's Photo Library; **92** Picturepoint; **93** England Scene; **94** Brick Development Association (a), Ronald Sheridan's Photo Library (b); **95** Brick Development Association (al and ar), Ronald Sheridan's Photo Library (b); **96. 97, 98** Brick Development Association; **99** J. Allen Cash Ltd; **100** Design Aspect; **101** Mary-Ann Kennedy (al and ar), Brick Development Association (l); **102** Architectural Association (al), Mary-Ann Kennedy (ar), Architectural Press (b); **103** Johnson/Burgee Architects; **104, 105** Jeremy Dixon; **106** Mary Evans Picture Library (a, bl), Bruce Coleman (br); **107** Peter Mackertich; **108, 109** Ironbridge Gorge Museum; **110** Shropshire County Council; **111** Bulloz; **112** A.F. Kersting; **113** Mary Evans Picture Library; **114** Mary-Ann Kennedy (al and ar), Ronald Sheridan's Photo Library (b); **115** Peter Mackertich; **116** Chrysler (a and i), AEG (b); **117** Mary-Ann Kennedy (a), Ronald Sheridan's Photo Library (b); **118** Architectural Press; **119** Design Aspect (l), French Tourist Office (r); **120** Cummins Engine Co.; **121** Peter Mackertich; **122, 123** Foster Associates; **124** Richard Bryant (a), Tim Street-Porter (b); **125** Richard Bryant; **126** Bastian Valkenburg; **127** Bastian Valkenburg (b), Cement and Concrete Association (a); **128, 130** Cement and Concrete Association; **131** Mark Dartford (al and ar), Cement and Concrete Association (l); **132, 133** Cement and Concrete Association; **134** Sport and General (al), Cement and Concrete Association (ar and b); **135, 136** Cement and Concrete Association; **137** Mark Dartford (a), Bastian Valkenburg (b); **138** Bastian Valkenburg; **139** Cement and Concrete Association (al), Bastian Valkenburg (ar and b); **140, 141, 142, 143** Cement and Concrete Association; **144** Alan Hutchinson Library (a), Cement and Concrete Association (b); **145** Cement and Concrete Association; **146** Peter Mackertich (a, b), Richard Bryant (c); **147** Richard Bryant (l), Sonia Halliday (r); **148** Tony Gidley Productions, Pilkington Glass Museum; **149** Sonia Halliday; **150** Werner Forman Archive; **151** Sonia Halliday (a), Bruce Coleman (b); **152** British Tourist Authority; **153** Douglas Dickins; **154** Michael Freeman; **155** Peter Mackertich (a), Richard Bryant (bl), Design Aspect (br); **156** A.F. Kersting; **157** Bryan Avery (l), A.F. Kersting (r); **158** Architectural Press; **159** Architectural Press (l), Werner Forman Archive (r); **160, 161** John Donat, Foster Associates; **162** Michael Freeman (a, c, b), Johnson/Burgee Architects (r); **163** Mary-Ann Kennedy; **164** Architectural Press (a), Bryan Avery (b); **165** Alan Hutchinson Library; **166** Laura Cohn (a), Bryan Avery (b); **167, 168** Bryan Avery; **169, 171** Architectural Press; **172** Picturepoint; **173, 174** Architectural Press; **175** Zefa (a), Bryan Avery (b); **176** Architectural Press; **177** Architectural Association (a), Architectural Press (c, b); **178** Picturepoint (a), Derek Stow and Partners (b); **179** Richard Bryant; **180** courtesy Phaidon Press; **181** Ullstein (l), courtesy Phaidon Press (r); **182** Picturepoint (a), British Tourist Authority (b); **183** Picturepoint (l), Ronald Sheridan's Photo Library (r); **184, 185** A.F. Kersting; **186** Peter Mackertich; **187** A.F. Kersting (l), Sonia Halliday (a); **188** Ronald Sheridan's Photo Library; **189** Sunday Times; **190** Peter Mackertich (al and l), Ronald Sheridan's Photo Library (r); **191, 192, 193** Ronald Sheridan's Photo Library; **194** Sonia Halliday (a, l), Ronald Sheridan's Photo Library (r); **195** Design Aspect (a), Architectural Press (b); **196** Heidrich Blessing; **197** Architectural Press; **198, 199** Ronald Sheridan's Photo Library; **200** Bryan Avery; **201** Mary Evans Picture Library; **202** John McKean; **203** Ronald Sheridan's Photo Library (a), Werner Forman Archive (l), John McKean (r); **204** John McKean; **205** Ullstein (a), Mark Dartford (b); **206** John McKean (a), Ronald Sheridan's Photo Library (b); **207** Ronald Sheridan's Photo Library; **208, 209** Architectural Press; **210** John McKean; **211** Architectural Press.

Key **(a)** above, **(b)** below, **(l)** left, **(r)** right, **(c)** centre, **(i)** inset.